The Odyssey

HOMER

PRESTWICK HOUSE
LITERARY TOUCHSTONE CLASSICS
P.O. BOX 658 • CLAYTON, DELAWARE 19938

SENIOR EDITOR: Paul Moliken

EDITORS: Lisa M. Miller and Pete Boysen

COVER DESIGN: Kelly Valentine Vasami

PRODUCTION: Jerry Clark

PRESTWICK HOUSE
LITERARY TOUCHSTONE CLASSICS

P.O. BOX 658 • CLAYTON, DELAWARE 19938
TEL: 1.800.932.4593
FAX: 1.888.718.9333
WEB: www.prestwickhouse.com

Prestwick House Teaching Units™, Activity Packs™, and Response Journals™ are the perfect complement for these editions. To purchase teaching resources for this book, visit www.prestwickhouse.com/material

ISBN-10   1-58049-389-0
ISBN-13 978-1-58049-389-5

CONTENTS

NOTES

What is a literary classic and why are these classic works important to the world?

A literary classic is a work of the highest excellence that has something important to say about life and/or the human condition and says it with great artistry. A classic, through its enduring presence, has withstood the test of time and is not bound by time, place, or customs. It speaks to us today as forcefully as it spoke to people one hundred or more years ago, and as forcefully as it will speak to people of future generations. For this reason, a classic is said to have universality.

What is known about the life of Homer is based primarily on scholarly speculation, not hard facts. His birth has been dated as far back as 1200 B.C., but based on the style evident in his two major poems, the *Iliad* and the *Odyssey*, some historians think he lived much later. In fact, a few ancient Greek writers who investigated his life believe that the works attributed to him were actually written by a woman. Some modern critics and others come to a different conclusion: a group of Homer's students or followers, who adapted and lengthened popular ballads of the time, composed both epic poems.

Seven different Greek cities claim that Homer was born within their boundaries, but since scholars cannot even agree whether Homer was an actual person, there is much doubt about these claims.

In the sixth century B.C., the stories of the Trojan War and Odysseus' long journey home were gathered and arranged in the order they are in at present so they could be recited at an Athenian festival. The *Odyssey* and the *Iliad*, as we know them, both date from these oral presentations.

Reading Pointers for Sharper Insights

Homer's two poems, the *Odyssey* and the *Iliad*, are among the first epics ever written. To better appreciate the *Odyssey*, it is essential to understand the nature of the genre. Epics generally contain the following elements:

- a hero on a quest
- legends of the past
- long speeches and elevated, flowery language
- epithets, epic similes, and other literary devices
- continuing battles between good and evil
- supernatural elements

As you read the *Odyssey*, take note of the following thematic concepts:

- **Hospitality as a serious and important obligation in the Greek culture**. Openness and offers of friendship to strangers will become pivotal to the action of the story. In Greek society, however, it was also necessary to be a polite and considerate guest. Both types of obligations will play a role in Odysseus' attempts to return home.

- **The dangers of *hubris*.** This Greek word translates loosely as excessive pride that leads to destruction. Odysseus would certainly have fallen victim to the gods because of his *hubris*, had not Athena intervened a few times on his behalf. When Odysseus brazenly taunts the Cyclops, the one-eyed monster almost destroys Odysseus' ships.

- **The importance of moderation.** Giving in to excess or temptation, whether food, drink, or other sensory pleasures, will cause a person harm. The Sirens' song leads to destruction, and the suitors' desire for Penelope and the home of Odysseus causes their death.

- **The expected roles for men and women in Greek society**. Notice the demanding and superior manner that the suitors use with Penelope. Telemachus' relationship with his mother and with the suitors changes, both as he grows older and as Odysseus' return seems less certain.

- **The role of Fate in the *Odyssey*.** Many characters, including Odysseus, receive hints as to what their fate will be. Whether they choose to heed or ignore this foreshadowing is up to them, however. The suitors are given enough warning of their coming destruction, which they ignore. Their motivations for wanting Penelope and her riches make them blind to the obvious dangers they face. Consequently, and as part of their destiny, Odysseus kills them.

- **The similarities between Greek gods and mortals.** The gods are portrayed anthropomorphically; they are jealous, fickle, capricious, and highly susceptible to sensual temptations. Sometimes they choose favorites; Athena chooses Odysseus, for example, because he is clever, and the goddess of wisdom appreciates this trait. Gods and goddesses help people for no logical reason and with no concern for the number of other mortals who die as a result. While the gods are given credit for all that is good, they are not blamed for bringing destruction to mortals.

Greek Gods and Goddesses

* = *appears in the Odyssey*

*Aphrodite – goddess of beauty and love (Roman: Venus)
*Apollo – god of music, healing, and light (Roman: Apollo)
*Ares – god of war (Roman: Mars)
*Artemis – goddess of the moon, hunting, and the protector of women
    (Roman: Diana)
Asclepius – god of medicine
*Athena – goddess of wisdom, justice, art, invention, and industry (Roman:
    Minerva)
*Circe – a goddess well versed in sorcery, drugs, and herbs
*Demeter – goddess of the harvest and fertility (Roman: Ceres)
*Dionysus – god of wine and fertility (Roman: Bacchus)
Eileithyia – goddess of childbirth
Eirene – goddess of Peace
Enyo – goddess of war (Roman: Bellona)
Erida – goddess of hatred
*Eos – goddess of the wind, and the dawn (Roman: Aurora)
Eris – goddess of strife (Roman: Discordia)
Eros – god of love and lust (Roman: Cupid)
*Gaia – earth; mother earth; primary goddess of fertility
*Hades – god of the underworld (Roman: Pluto)
*Hebe – goddess of youth
Hectate – goddess of the moon, witchcraft, night, and the underworld
*Hephaestus – god of fire (Roman: Vulcan)
*Hera – Queen of the gods; goddess of marriage and childbirth (Roman:
    Juno)
*Hermes – the messenger for the gods; god of wealth, luck, and travelers
    (Roman: Mercury)
Hestia – goddess of the hearth and domestic joy (Roman: Vesta)
Hygeia – goddess of health
Hymen – god of weddings
Hypnos – god of sleep (Roman: Somnus)
Iris – goddess of the rainbow and messenger for the gods
Mnemosyne – goddess of memory; mother of the muses
Morpheus – god of dreams
Nemesis – goddess of moderation
Nyx – ancient goddess of night (Roman: Nox)
*Oceanus – god of the ocean
Pan – god of pastures, flocks, and shepherds (Roman: Faunus)
*Persephone – Queen of the underworld; goddess of vegetation (Roman:
    Proserpine)
Pontus – ancient sea god
*Poseidon – god of the sea (Roman: Neptune)

Prometheus – rebel god who gave fire to mortals in defiance of Zeus
Selene – goddess of the moon (Roman: Luna)
Thanatos – god of death
*__Themis__ – goddess of laws, justice, and order
Uranus – ancient god of the sky
*__Zeus__ – King of the gods; god of light and the sky (Roman: Jupiter/Jove)

B O O K   I

The gods in council
Athena's visit to Ithaca
The challenge from Telemachus to the suitors

TELL ME, O MUSE,[†] of that ingenious hero who traveled far and wide after he had sacked the famous town of Troy. Many cities did he visit, and many were the nations with whose manners and customs he was acquainted; moreover he suffered much by sea while trying to save his own life and bring his men safely home; but do what he might he could not save his men, for they perished through their own sheer folly in eating the cattle of the Sun-god Apollo; so the god prevented them from ever reaching home.[†] Tell me, too, about all these things, oh daughter of Zeus, from whatsoever source you may know them.

So now all who escaped death in battle or by shipwreck had got safely home except Odysseus, and he, though he was longing to return to his wife and country, was detained by the goddess Calypso, who had got him into a large cave and wanted to marry him. But as years went by, there came a time when the gods settled that he should go back to Ithaca; even then, however, when he was among his own people, his troubles were not yet over; nevertheless all the gods had now begun to pity him except Poseidon, who still persecuted him without ceasing and would not let him get home.

Now Poseidon had gone off to the Ethiopians,[†] who are at the world's end,

---

[†]Terms marked in the text with (†) can be looked up in the Glossary for additional information.

and lie in two halves, the one looking West and the other East. He had gone there to accept a hecatomb of sheep and oxen, and was enjoying himself at his festival; but the other gods met in the house of Olympian Zeus, and the sire of gods and men spoke first. At that moment he was thinking of Aegisthus, who had been killed by Agamemnon's son Orestes;† so he said to the other gods:

"See now, how men lay blame upon us gods for what is after all nothing but their own folly. Look at Aegisthus; he must needs make love to Agamemnon's wife unrighteously and then kill Agamemnon, though he knew it would be the death of him; for I sent Hermes to warn him† not to do either of these things, inasmuch as Orestes would be sure to take his revenge when he grew up and wanted to return home. Hermes told him this in all good will but he would not listen, and now he has paid for everything in full."

Then Athena said, "Father, son of Cronus, King of kings, it served Aegisthus right, and so it would anyone else who does as he did; but Aegisthus is neither here nor there; it is for Odysseus that my heart bleeds, when I think of his sufferings in that lonely sea-girt island, far away, poor man, from all his friends.† It is an island covered with forest, in the very middle of the sea, and a goddess lives there, daughter of the magician Atlas, who looks after the bottom of the ocean, and carries the great columns that keep heaven and earth asunder. This daughter of Atlas has got hold of poor unhappy Odysseus, and keeps trying by every kind of blandishment to make him forget his home, so that he is tired of life, and thinks of nothing but how he may once more see the smoke of his own chimneys. You, sir, take no heed of this, and yet when Odysseus was before Troy did he not propitiate you with many a burnt sacrifice? Why then should you keep on being so angry with him?"

And Zeus said, "My child, what are you talking about? How can I forget Odysseus than whom there is no more capable man on earth, nor more liberal in his offerings to the immortal gods that live in heaven? Bear in mind, however, that Poseidon is still furious with Odysseus for having blinded an eye of Polyphemus king of the Cyclopes. Polyphemus is son to Poseidon by the nymph Thoosa, daughter to the sea-king Phorcys; therefore though he will not kill Odysseus outright, he torments him by preventing him from getting home. Still, let us lay our heads together and see how we can help him to return; Poseidon will then be pacified, for if we are all of a mind he can hardly stand out against us."

And Athena said, "Father, son of Cronus, King of kings, if, then, the gods now mean that Odysseus should get home, we should first send Hermes to the Ogygian island to tell Calypso that we have made up our minds and that he is to return. In the meantime I will go to Ithaca, to put heart into Odysseus' son Telemachus; I will embolden him to call the Achaeans in assembly, and speak out to the suitors of his mother Penelope, who persist in eating up any number of his sheep and oxen; I will also conduct him to Sparta and to Pylos,† to see if he can hear anything about the return of his dear father—for this will make people speak well of him."

So saying she bound on her glittering golden sandals, imperishable, with which she can fly like the wind over land or sea; she grasped the redoubtable bronze-shod spear, so stout and sturdy and strong,[†] wherewith she quells the ranks of heroes who have displeased her, and down she darted from the topmost summits of Olympus, whereon forthwith she was in Ithaca, at the gateway of Odysseus' house, disguised as a visitor, Mentes, chief of the Taphians, and she held a bronze spear in her hand. There she found the lordly suitors seated on hides of the oxen which they had killed and eaten, and gambling in front of the house. Men-servants and pages were bustling about to wait upon them, some mixing wine with water in the mixing-bowls, some cleaning down the tables with wet sponges and laying them out again, and some cutting up great quantities of meat.

Telemachus saw her long before anyone else did. He was sitting moodily among the suitors thinking about his brave father, and how he would send them flying out of the house, if he were to come to his own again and be honored as in days gone by. Thus brooding as he sat among them, he caught sight of Athena and went straight to the gate, for he was vexed that a stranger should be kept waiting for admittance.[†] He took her right hand in his own, and bade her give him her spear. "Welcome," said he, "to our house, and when you have partaken of food you shall tell us what you have come for."

He led the way as he spoke, and Athena followed him. When they were within he took her spear and set it in the spear-stand against a strong bearing-post along with the many other spears of his unhappy father, and he conducted her to a richly decorated seat under which he threw a cloth of damask. There was a footstool also for her feet, and he set another seat near her for himself, away from the suitors, that she might not be annoyed while eating by their noise and insolence, and that he might ask her more freely about his father.

A maid servant then brought them water in a beautiful golden ewer and poured it into a silver basin for them to wash their hands, and she drew a clean table beside them. An upper servant brought them bread, and offered them many good things of what there was in the house, the carver fetched them plates of all manner of meats and set cups of gold by their side, and a manservant brought them wine and poured it out for them.

Then the suitors came in and took their places on the benches and seats. Forthwith men servants poured water over their hands, maids went round with the bread-baskets, pages filled the mixing-bowls with wine and water, and they laid their hands upon the good things that were before them. As soon as they had had enough to eat and drink they wanted music and dancing, which are the crowning embellishments of a banquet, so a servant brought a lyre to Phemius, whom they compelled perforce to sing to them. As soon as he touched his lyre and began to sing Telemachus spoke low to Athena, with his head close to hers that no man might hear.

"I hope, sir," said he, "that you will not be offended with what I am going to say. Singing comes cheap to those who do not pay for it, and all this is done at the cost of one whose bones lie rotting in some wilderness or grinding to powder in the surf. If these men were to see my father come back to Ithaca they would pray for longer legs rather than a longer purse, for money would not serve them; but he, alas, has fallen on an ill fate, and even when people do sometimes say that he is coming, we no longer heed them; we shall never see him again. And now, sir, tell me and tell me true, who you are and where you come from. Tell me of your town and parents, what manner of ship you came in, how your crew brought you to Ithaca, and of what nation they declared themselves to be—for you cannot have come by land. Tell me also truly, for I want to know, are you a stranger to this house, or have you been here in my father's time? In the old days we had many visitors for my father went about much himself."

And Athena answered, "I will tell you truly and particularly all about it. I am Mentes, son of Anchialus, and I am King of the Taphians.† I have come here with my ship and crew, on a voyage to men of a foreign tongue being bound for Temesa† with a cargo of iron, and I shall bring back copper. As for my ship, it lies over yonder off the open country away from the town, in the haror Rheithron under the wooded mountain Neritum. Our fathers were friends before us, as old Laertes will tell you, if you will go and ask him. They say, however, that he never comes to town now, and lives by himself in the country, faring hardly, with an old woman to look after him and get his dinner for him, when he comes in tired from pottering about his vineyard. They told me your father was at home again, and that was why I came, but it seems the gods are still keeping him back, for he is not dead yet not on the mainland. It is more likely he is on some sea-girt island in mid ocean, or a prisoner among savages who are detaining him against his will. I am no prophet, and know very little about omens, but I speak as it is borne in upon me from heaven, and assure you that he will not be away much longer; for he is a man of such resource that even though he were in chains of iron he would find some means of getting home again. But tell me, and tell me true, can Odysseus really have such a fine looking fellow for a son? You are indeed wonderfully like him about the head and eyes, for we were close friends before he set sail for Troy where the flower of all the Argives† went also. Since that time we have never either of us seen the other."

"My mother," answered Telemachus, "tells me I am son to Odysseus, but it is a wise child that knows his own father. Would that I were son to one who had grown old upon his own estates, for, since you ask me, there is no more ill-starred man under heaven than he who they tell me is my father."†

And Athena said, "There is no fear of your race dying out yet, while Penelope has such a fine son as you are. But tell me, and tell me true, what is the meaning of all this feasting, and who are these people? What is it all about? Have you some banquet, or is there a wedding in the family—for no one seems to be bringing any provisions of his own? And the guests—how atrociously they are behaving; what riot they make over the whole house; it is enough to disgust any respectable person who comes near them."

"Sir," said Telemachus, "as regards your question, so long as my father was here it was well with us and with the house, but the gods in their displeasure have willed it otherwise, and have hidden him away more closely than mortal man was ever yet hidden. I could have borne it better even though he were dead, if he had fallen with his men before Troy, or had died with friends around him when the days of his fighting were done; for then the Achaeans would have built a mound over his ashes,† and I should myself have been heir to his renown; but now the storm-winds have spirited him away we know not whither; he is gone without leaving so much as a trace behind him, and I inherit nothing but dismay. Nor does the matter end simply with grief for the loss of my father; heaven has laid sorrows upon me of yet another kind; for the chiefs from all our islands, Dulichium, Same, and the woodland island of Zacynthus, as also all the principal men of Ithaca itself, are eating up my house under the pretext of paying their court to my mother, who will neither explicitly say that she will not marry,† nor yet bring matters to an end; so they are making havoc of my estate, and before long will do so also with myself."

"Is that so?" exclaimed Athena, "then you do indeed want Odysseus home again. Give him his helmet, shield, and a couple of lances, and if he is the man he was when I first knew him in our house, drinking and making merry, he would soon lay his hands about these rascally suitors, were he to stand once more upon his own threshold. He was then coming from Ephyra, where he had been to beg poison for his arrows from Ilus, son of Mermerus. Ilus feared the ever-living gods and would not give him any, but my father let him have some, for he was very fond of him. If Odysseus is the man he then was these suitors will have a short shrift and a sorry wedding.

"But there! It rests with heaven to determine whether he is to return,† and take his revenge in his own house or no; I would, however, urge you to set about trying to get rid of these suitors at once. Take my advice, call the Achaean heroes in assembly to-morrow morning—lay your case before them, and call heaven to bear you witness. Bid the suitors take themselves off, each to his own place, and if your mother's mind is set on marrying again, let her go back to her father, who will find her a husband and provide her with all the marriage gifts that so dear a daughter may expect. As for yourself, let me prevail upon you to take the best ship you can get, with a crew of twenty men, and go in quest of your father who has so long been missing. Someone may tell you something, or (and people often hear things in this way) some heaven-sent message may direct you. First go to Pylos and ask Nestor; thence go on to Sparta and visit Menelaus, for he got home last of all the Achaeans; if you hear that your father is alive and on his way home, you can put up with the waste these suitors will make for yet another twelve months. If on the other hand you hear of his death, come home at once, celebrate his funeral rites with all due pomp, build a barrow to his memory, and make your mother marry again. Then, having done all this, think it well over in your mind how, by fair means or foul, you may kill these suitors in your own house. You are too old to plead infancy any longer; have you not heard how people are sing-ing Orestes' praises for having killed his father's murderer Aegisthus? You are a fine, smart looking fellow; show your mettle, then, and make yourself a name in story. Now, however, I must go back to my ship and to my crew, who will be impatient if I keep them waiting longer; think the matter over for yourself, and remember what I have said to you."

"Sir," answered Telemachus, "it has been very kind of you to talk to me in this way, as though I were your own son, and I will do all you tell me; I know you want to be getting on with your voyage, but stay a little longer till you have taken a bath and refreshed yourself. I will then give you a present, and you shall go on your way rejoicing; I will give you one of great beauty and value—a keepsake such as only dear friends give to one another."

Athena answered, "Do not try to keep me, for I would be on my way at once. As for any present you may be disposed to make me, keep it till I come again, and I will take it home with me. You shall give me a very good one, and I will give you one of no less value in return."

With these words she flew away like a bird into the air,[†] but she had given Telemachus courage, and had made him think more than ever about his father. He felt the change, wondered at it, and knew that the stranger had been a god,[†] so he went straight to where the suitors were sitting.

Phemius was still singing, and his hearers sat rapt in silence as he told the sad tale of the return from Troy, and the ills Athena had laid upon the Achaeans. Penelope, daughter of Icarius, heard his song from her room upstairs, and came down by the great staircase, not alone, but attended by two of her handmaids. When she reached the suitors she stood by one of the bearing posts that supported the roof of the cloisters with a staid maiden on either side of her. She held a veil, moreover, before her face, and was weeping bitterly.

"Phemius," she cried, "you know many another feat of gods and heroes, such as poets love to celebrate. Sing the suitors some one of these, and let them drink their wine in silence, but cease this sad tale, for it breaks my sorrowful heart, and reminds me of my lost husband whom I mourn ever without ceasing, and whose name was great over all Hellas and middle Argos."†

"Mother," answered Telemachus, "let the bard sing what he has a mind to; bards do not make the ills they sing of; it is Zeus, not they, who makes them, and who sends weal or woe upon mankind according to his own good pleasure. This fellow means no harm by singing the ill-fated return of the Danaans, for people always applaud the latest songs most warmly. Make up your mind to it and bear it; Odysseus is not the only man who never came back from Troy, but many another went down as well as he. Go, then, within the house and busy yourself with your daily duties, your loom, your distaff, and the ordering of your servants; for speech is man's matter, and mine above all others—for it is I who am master here."

She went wondering back into the house, and laid her son's saying in her heart. Then, going upstairs with her handmaids into her room, she mourned her dear husband till Athena shed sweet sleep over her eyes. But the suitors were clamorous throughout the covered cloisters, and prayed each one that he might be her bed fellow.

Then Telemachus spoke, "Shameless," he cried, "and insolent suitors, let us feast at our pleasure now, and let there be no brawling, for it is a rare thing to hear a man with such a divine voice as Phemius has; but in the morning meet me in full assembly that I may give you formal notice to depart, and feast at one another's houses, turn and turn about, at your own cost. If on the other hand you choose to persist in spunging upon one man, heaven help me, but Zeus shall reckon with you in full, and when you fall in my father's house there shall be no man to avenge you."

The suitors bit their lips as they heard him, and marveled at the boldness of his speech. Then, Antinous, son of Eupeithes, said, "The gods seem to have given you lessons in bluster and tall talking; may Zeus never grant you to be chief in Ithaca as your father was before you."

Telemachus answered, "Antinous, do not chide with me, but, god willing, I will be chief too if I can. Is this the worst fate you can think of for me? It is no bad thing to be a chief, for it brings both riches and honor. Still, now that Odysseus is dead there are many great men in Ithaca both old and young, and some other may take the lead among them; nevertheless I will be chief in my own house, and will rule those whom Odysseus has won for me."

Then Eurymachus, son of Polybus, answered, "It rests with heaven to decide who shall be chief among us, but you shall be master in your own house and over your own possessions; no one while there is a man in Ithaca shall do you violence nor rob you. And now, my good fellow, I want to know about this stranger. What country does he come from? Of what family is he, and where is his estate? Has he brought you news about the return of your father, or was he on business of his own? He seemed a well to do man, but he hurried off so suddenly that he was gone in a moment before we could get to know him."

"My father is dead and gone," answered Telemachus, "and even if some rumour reaches me I put no more faith in it now. My mother does indeed sometimes send for a soothsayer and question him, but I give his prophecy-ings no heed. As for the stranger, he was Mentes, son of Anchialus, chief of the Taphians, an old friend of my father's." But in his heart he knew that it had been the goddess.†

The suitors then returned to their singing and dancing until the evening; but when night fell upon their pleasuring they went home to bed each in his own abode. Telemachus' room was high up in a tower that looked on to the outer court; hither, then, he hied, brooding and full of thought. A good old woman, Euryclea, daughter of Ops, the son of Pisenor, went before him with a couple of blazing torches. Laertes had bought her with his own money when she was quite young; he gave the worth of twenty oxen for her, and showed as much respect to her in his household as he did to his own wedded wife, but he did not take her to his bed for he feared his wife's resentment. She it was who now lighted Telemachus to his room, and she loved him better than any of the other women in the house did, for she had nursed him when he was a baby. He opened the door of his bed room and sat down upon the bed; as he took off his shirt he gave it to the good old woman, who folded it tidily up, and hung it for him over a peg by his bed side, after which she went out, pulled the door to by a silver catch, and drew the bolt home by means of the strap. But Telemachus as he lay covered with a woollen fleece kept thinking all night through of his intended voyage and of the counsel that Athena had given him.

B O O K I I

Assembly of the people of Ithaca
Speeches of Telemachus and of the suitors
Telemachus makes his preparations for Pylos with Athena disguised as Mentor.

NOW WHEN THE child of morning, rosy-fingered Dawn,[†] appeared Telemachus rose and dressed himself. He bound his sandals on to his comely feet, girded his sword about his shoulder, and left his room looking like an immortal god. He at once sent the criers round to call the people in assembly, so they called them and the people gathered thereon; then, when they were got together, he went to the place of assembly spear in hand—not alone, for his two hounds went with him. Athena endowed him with a presence of such divine comeliness[†] that all marveled at him as he went by, and when he took his place in his father's seat even the oldest councillors made way for him.

Aegyptius, a man bent double with age, and of infinite experience, was the first to speak. His son Antiphus had gone with Odysseus to Ilius,[†] land of noble steeds, but the savage Cyclops had killed him when they were all shut up in the cave, and had cooked his last dinner for him. He had three sons left, of whom two still worked on their father's land, while the third, Eurynomus, was one of the suitors; nevertheless their father could not get over the loss of Antiphus, and was still weeping for him when he began his speech.

"Men of Ithaca," he said, "hear my words. From the day Odysseus left us there has been no meeting of our councillors until now; who then can it be, whether old or young, that finds it so necessary to convene us? Has he got wind of some host approaching, and does he wish to warn us, or would he speak upon some other matter of public moment? I am sure he is an excellent person, and I hope Zeus will grant him his heart's desire."

Telemachus took this speech as of good omen and rose at once, for he was bursting with what he had to say. He stood in the middle of the assembly and the good herald Pisenor brought him his staff. Then, turning to Aegyptius, "Sir," said he, "it is I, as you will shortly learn, who have convened you, for it is I who am the most aggrieved. I have not got wind of any host approaching about which I would warn you, nor is there any matter of public moment on which I would speak. My grievance is purely personal, and turns on two great misfortunes which have fallen upon my house. The first of these is the loss of my excellent father, who was chief among all you here present, and was like a father to every one of you; the second is much more serious, and ere long will be the utter ruin of my estate. The sons of all the chief men among you are pestering my mother to marry them against her will. They are afraid to go to her father Icarius, asking him to choose the one he likes best, and to provide marriage gifts for his daughter, but day by day they keep hanging about my father's house, sacrificing our oxen, sheep, and fat goats for their banquets, and never giving so much as a thought to the quantity of wine they drink. No estate can stand such recklessness; we have now no Odysseus to ward off harm from our doors, and I cannot hold my own against them. I shall never all my days be as good a man as he was, still I would indeed defend myself if I had power to do so, for I cannot stand such treatment any longer; my house is being disgraced and ruined. Have respect, therefore, to your own consciences and to public opinion. Fear, too, the wrath of heaven, lest the gods should be displeased and turn upon you.† I pray you by Zeus and Themis, who is the beginning and the end of councils, do not hold back, my friends, and leave me singlehanded—unless it be that my brave father Odysseus did some wrong to the Achaeans which you would now avenge on me, by aiding and abetting these suitors. Moreover, if I am to be eaten out of house and home at all, I had rather you did the eating yourselves, for I could then take action against you to some purpose, and serve you with notices from house to house till I got paid in full, whereas now I have no remedy."

With this Telemachus dashed his staff to the ground and burst into tears.† Everyone was very sorry for him, but they all sat still and no one ventured to make him an angry answer, save only Antinous, who spoke thus:

"Telemachus, insolent braggart that you are, how dare you try to throw the blame upon us suitors? It is your mother's fault not ours, for she is a very artful woman. This three years past, and close on four, she had been driving us out of our minds, by encouraging each one of us, and sending him messages without meaning one word of what she says. And then there was that other trick she played us. She set up a great tambour frame in her room, and began to work on an enormous piece of fine needlework. 'Sweet hearts,' said she,

'Odysseus is indeed dead, still do not press me to marry again immediately, wait—for I would not have skill in needlework perish unrecorded—till I have completed a pall for the hero Laertes, to be in readiness against the time when death shall take him. He is very rich, and the women of the place will talk if he is laid out without a pall.'

"This was what she said, and we assented; whereon we could see her working on her great web all day long, but at night she would unpick the stitches again by torchlight. She fooled us in this way for three years and we never found her out, but as time wore on and she was now in her fourth year, one of her maids who knew what she was doing told us, and we caught her in the act of undoing her work, so she had to finish it whether she would or no. The suitors, therefore, make you this answer, that both you and the Achaeans may understand—'Send your mother away, and bid her marry the man of her own and of her father's choice;' for I do not know what will happen if she goes on plaguing us much longer with the airs she gives herself on the score of the accomplishments Athena has taught her, and because she is so clever. We never yet heard of such a woman; we know all about Tyro, Alcmena, Mycene, and the famous women of old, but they were nothing to your mother, any one of them.† It was not fair of her to treat us in that way, and as long as she continues in the mind with which heaven has now endowed her, so long shall we go on eating up your estate; and I do not see why she should change, for she gets all the honor and glory, and it is you who pay for it, not she. Understand, then, that we will not go back to our lands, neither here nor elsewhere, till she has made her choice and married some one or other of us."

Telemachus answered, "Antinous, how can I drive the mother who bore me from my father's house? My father is abroad and we do not know whether he is alive or dead. It will be hard on me if I have to pay Icarius the large sum which I must give him if I insist on sending his daughter back to him.† Not only will he deal rigorously with me, but heaven will also punish me; for my mother when she leaves the house will call on the Erinyes† to avenge her; besides, it would not be a creditable thing to do, and I will have nothing to say to it. If you choose to take offense at this, leave the house and feast elsewhere at one another's houses at your own cost turn and turn about. If, on the other hand, you elect to persist in spunging upon one man, heaven help me, but Zeus shall reckon with you in full, and when you fall in my father's house there shall be no man to avenge you."

As he spoke Zeus sent two eagles† from the top of the mountain, and they flew on and on with the wind, sailing side by side in their own lordly flight. When they were right over the middle of the assembly they wheeled and circled about, beating the air with their wings and glaring death into the eyes of them that were below; then, fighting fiercely and tearing at one another, they flew off towards the right over the town. The people wondered as they saw them, and asked each other what all this might be; whereon Halitherses, who was the best prophet and reader of omens among them, spoke to them plainly and in all honesty, saying:

"Hear me, men of Ithaca, and I speak more particularly to the suitors, for I see mischief brewing for them. Odysseus is not going to be away much longer; indeed he is close at hand to deal out death and destruction, not on them alone, but on many another of us who live in Ithaca. Let us then be wise in time, and put a stop to this wickedness before he comes. Let the suitors do so of their own accord; it will be better for them, for I am not prophesying without due knowledge; everything has happened to Odysseus as I foretold when the Argives set out for Troy, and he with them. I said that after going through much hardship and losing all his men he should come home again in the twentieth year and that no one would know him; and now all this is coming true."[†]

Eurymachus son of Polybus then said, "Go home, old man, and prophesy to your own children, or it may be worse for them. I can read these omens myself much better than you can; birds are always flying about in the sunshine somewhere or other, but they seldom mean anything. Odysseus has died in a far country, and it is a pity you are not dead along with him, instead of prating here about omens and adding fuel to the anger of Telemachus which is fierce enough as it is. I suppose you think he will give you something for your family, but I tell you—and it shall surely be—when an old man like you, who should know better, talks a young one over till he becomes troublesome, in the first place his young friend will only fare so much the worse—he will take nothing by it, for the suitors will prevent this—and in the next, we will lay a heavier fine, sir, upon yourself than you will at all like paying, for it will bear hardly upon you. As for Telemachus, I warn him in the presence of you all to send his mother back to her father, who will find her a husband and provide her with all the marriage gifts so dear a daughter may expect. Till then we shall go on harassing him with our suit; for we fear no man, and care neither for him, with all his fine speeches, nor for any fortune-telling of yours. You may preach as much as you please, but we shall only hate you the more. We shall go back and continue to eat up Telemachus' estate without paying him, till such time as his mother leaves off tormenting us by keeping us day after day on the tiptoe of expectation, each vying with the other in his suit for a prize of such rare perfection.[†] Besides we cannot go after the other women whom we should marry in due course, but for the way in which she treats us."

Then Telemachus said, "Eurymachus, and you other suitors, I shall say no more, and entreat you no further, for the gods and the people of Ithaca now know my story. Give me, then, a ship and a crew of twenty men to take me hither and thither, and I will go to Sparta and to Pylos in quest of my father who has so long been missing. Someone may tell me something, or (and people often hear things in this way) some heaven-sent message may direct me. If I can hear of him as alive and on his way home I will put up with the waste you suitors will make for yet another twelve months. If on the other hand I hear of his death, I will return at once, celebrate his funeral rites with all due pomp, build a barrow to his memory, and make my mother marry again."

With these words he sat down, and Mentor who had been a friend of Odysseus, and had been left in charge of everything with full authority over the servants, rose to speak. He, then, plainly and in all honesty addressed them thus:

"Hear me, men of Ithaca, I hope that you may never have a kind and well-disposed ruler any more, nor one who will govern you equitably; I hope that all your chiefs henceforward may be cruel and unjust, for there is not one of you but has forgotten Odysseus, who ruled you as though he were your father. I am not half so angry with the suitors, for if they choose to do violence in the naughtiness of their hearts, and wager their heads that Odysseus will not return, they can take the high hand and eat up his estate, but as for you others I am shocked at the way in which you all sit still without even trying to stop such scandalous goings on—which you could do if you chose, for you are many and they are few."

Leiocritus, son of Evenor, answered him saying, "Mentor, what folly is all this, that you should set the people to stay us? It is a hard thing for one man to fight with many about his victuals. Even though Odysseus himself were to set upon us while we are feasting in his house, and do his best to oust us, his wife, who wants him back so very badly, would have small cause for rejoicing, and his blood would be upon his own head if he fought against such great odds. There is no sense in what you have been saying. Now, therefore, do you people go about your business, and let his father's old friends, Mentor and Halitherses, speed this boy on his journey, if he goes at all—which I do not think he will, for he is more likely to stay where he is till someone comes and tells him something."†

On this he broke up the assembly, and every man went back to his own abode, while the suitors returned to the house of Odysseus.

Then Telemachus went all alone by the sea side, washed his hands in the grey waves, and prayed to Athena.

"Hear me," he cried, "you god who visited me yesterday, and bade me sail the seas in search of my father who has so long been missing. I would obey you, but the Achaeans, and more particularly the wicked suitors, are hindering me that I cannot do so."

As he thus prayed, Athena came close up to him in the likeness and with the voice of Mentor. "Telemachus," said she, "if you are made of the same stuff as your father you will be neither fool nor coward henceforward, for Odysseus never broke his word nor left his work half done. If, then, you take after him, your voyage will not be fruitless, but unless you have the blood of Odysseus and of Penelope in your veins I see no likelihood of your succeeding. Sons are seldom as good men as their fathers; they are generally worse, not better; still, as you are not going to be either fool or coward henceforward, and are not entirely without some share of your father's wise discernment, I look with hope upon your undertaking. But mind you never make common cause with any of those foolish suitors, for they have neither sense nor virtue, and give no thought to death and to the doom that will shortly fall on one and all of them, so that they shall perish on the same day. As for your voyage, it shall not be long delayed; your father was such an old friend of mine that I will find you a ship, and will come with you myself. Now, however, return home, and go about among the suitors; begin getting provisions ready for your voyage; see everything well stowed, the wine in jars, and the barley meal, which is the staff of life, in leathern bags, while I go round the town and beat up volunteers at once. There are many ships in Ithaca both old and new; I will run my eye over them for you and will choose the best; we will get her ready and will put out to sea without delay."

Thus spoke Athena daughter of Zeus, and Telemachus lost no time in doing as the goddess told him. He went moodily home, and found the suitors flaying goats and singeing pigs in the outer court. Antinous came up to him at once and laughed as he took his hand in his own, saying, "Telemachus, my fine fire-eater, bear no more ill blood neither in word nor deed, but eat and drink with us as you used to do. The Achaeans will find you in everything—a ship and a picked crew to boot—so that you can set sail for Pylos at once and get news of your noble father."

"Antinous," answered Telemachus, "I cannot eat in peace, nor take pleasure of any kind with such men as you are. Was it not enough that you should waste so much good property of mine while I was yet a boy? Now that I am older and know more about it, I am also stronger, and whether here among this people, or by going to Pylos, I will do you all the harm I can. I shall go, and my going will not be in vain—though, thanks to you suitors, I have neither ship nor crew of my own, and must be passenger not captain."

As he spoke he snatched his hand from that of Antinous. Meanwhile the others went on getting dinner ready about the buildings,† jeering at him tauntingly as they did so.†

"Telemachus," said one youngster, "means to be the death of us; I suppose he thinks he can bring friends to help him from Pylos, or again from Sparta, where he seems bent on going. Or will he go to Ephyra as well, for poison to put in our wine and kill us?"†

Another said, "Perhaps if Telemachus goes on board ship, he will be like his father and perish far from his friends. In this case we should have much to do, for we could then divide up his property amongst us: as for the house we can let his mother and the man who marries her have that."

This was how they talked. But Telemachus went down into the lofty and spacious store-room where his father's treasure of gold and bronze lay heaped up upon the floor, and where the linen and spare clothes were kept in open chests. Here, too, there was a store of fragrant olive oil, while casks of old, well-ripened wine, unblended† and fit for a god to drink, were ranged against the wall in case Odysseus should come home again after all. The room was closed with well-made doors opening in the middle; moreover the faithful old house-keeper Euryclea, daughter of Ops the son of Pisenor, was in charge of everything both night and day. Telemachus called her to the store-room and said:

"Nurse, draw me off some of the best wine you have, after what you are keeping for my father's own drinking, in case, poor man, he should escape death, and find his way home again after all. Let me have twelve jars, and see that they all have lids; also fill me some well-sewn leathern bags with barley meal—about twenty measures in all. Get these things put together at once, and say nothing about it. I will take everything away this evening as soon as my mother has gone upstairs for the night. I am going to Sparta and to Pylos to see if I can hear anything about the return of my dear father."

When Euryclea heard this she began to cry, and spoke fondly to him, saying, "My dear child, what ever can have put such notion as that into your head? Where in the world do you want to go to—you, who are the one hope of the house? Your poor father is dead and gone in some foreign country nobody knows where, and as soon as your back is turned these wicked ones here will be scheming to get you put out of the way, and will share all your possessions among themselves; stay where you are among your own people, and do not go wandering and worrying your life out on the barren ocean."

"Fear not, nurse," answered Telemachus, "my scheme is not without heaven's sanction; but swear that you will say nothing about all this to my mother, till I have been away some ten or twelve days, unless she hears of my having gone, and asks you; for I do not want her to spoil her beauty by crying."

The old woman swore most solemnly that she would not, and when she had completed her oath, she began drawing off the wine into jars, and getting the barley meal into the bags, while Telemachus went back to the suitors.

Then Athena thought of another matter. She took his shape, and went round the town to each one of the crew, telling them to meet at the ship by sundown. She went also to Noemon son of Phronius, and asked him to let her have a ship—which he was very ready to do. When the sun had set and darkness was over all the land, she got the ship into the water, put all the tackle on board her that ships generally carry, and stationed her at the end of the harbor. Presently the crew came up, and the goddess spoke encouragingly to each of them.

Furthermore she went to the house of Odysseus, and threw the suitors into a deep slumber. She caused their drink to fuddle them, and made them drop their cups from their hands, so that instead of sitting over their wine, they went back into the town to sleep, with their eyes heavy and full of drowsiness.[†] Then she took the form and voice of Mentor, and called Telemachus to come outside.

"Telemachus," said she, "the men are on board and at their oars, waiting for you to give your orders, so make haste and let us be off."

On this she led the way, while Telemachus followed in her steps. When they got to the ship they found the crew waiting by the waterside, and Telemachus said, "Now my men, help me to get the stores on board; they are all put together in the cloister, and my mother does not know anything about it, nor any of the maid servants except one."

With these words he led the way and the others followed after. When they had brought the things as he told them, Telemachus went on board, Athena going before him and taking her seat in the stern of the vessel, while Telemachus sat beside her. Then the men loosed the hawsers and took their places on the benches. Athena sent them a fair wind from the West, that whistled over the deep blue waves whereon Telemachus told them to catch hold of the ropes and hoist sail, and they did as he told them. They set the mast in its socket in the cross plank, raised it, and made it fast with the forestays; then they hoisted their white sails aloft with ropes of twisted oxhide. As the sail bellied out with the wind, the ship flew through the deep blue water, and the foam hissed against her bows as she sped onward. Then they made all fast throughout the ship, filled the mixing bowls to the brim, and made drink offerings to the immortal gods that are from everlasting, but more particularly to the grey-eyed daughter of Zeus.[†]

Thus, then, the ship sped on her way through the watches of the night from dark till dawn,

B O O K 3 I I I

Telemachus visits Nestor at Pylos.

B UT AS THE sun was rising from the fair sea into the firmament of heaven to shed light on mortals and immortals, they reached Pylos the city of Neleus. Now the people of Pylos were gathered on the sea shore to offer sacrifice of black bulls to Poseidon, lord of the Earthquake. There were nine guilds with five hundred men in each, and there were nine bulls to each guild. As they were eating the inward meats and burning the thigh bones† on the embers in the name of Poseidon, Telemachus and his crew arrived, furled their sails, brought their ship to anchor, and went ashore.

Athena led the way and Telemachus followed her. Presently she said, "Telemachus, you must not be in the least shy or nervous; you have taken this voyage to try and find out where your father is buried and how he came by his end; so go straight up to Nestor that we may see what he has got to tell us. Beg of him to speak the truth, and he will tell no lies, for he is an excellent person."

"But how, Mentor," replied Telemachus, "dare I go up to Nestor, and how am I to address him? I have never yet been used to holding long conversations with people, and am ashamed to begin questioning one who is so much older than myself."

"Some things, Telemachus," answered Athena, "will be suggested to you by your own instinct, and heaven will prompt you further; for I am assured that the gods have been with you from the time of your birth until now."

She then went quickly on, and Telemachus followed in her steps till they reached the place where the guilds of the Pylian people were assembled. There they found Nestor sitting with his sons, while his company round him were busy getting dinner ready, and putting pieces of meat on to the spits while other pieces were cooking. When they saw the strangers they crowded round them, took them by the hand and bade them take their places. Nestor's son Pisistratus at once offered his hand to each of them, and seated them on some soft sheepskins that were lying on the sands near his father and his brother Thrasymedes. Then he gave them their portions of the inward meats and poured wine for them into a golden cup, handing it to Athena first, and saluting her at the same time.

"Offer a prayer, sir," said he, "to King Poseidon, for it is his feast that you are joining;† when you have duly prayed and made your drink offering, pass the cup to your friend that he may do so also. I doubt not that he too lifts his hands in prayer, for man cannot live without God in the world. Still he is younger than you are, and is much of an age with myself, so I will give you the precedence."

As he spoke he handed her the cup. Athena thought it very right and proper of him to have given it to herself first; she accordingly began praying heartily to Poseidon. "O thou," she cried, "that encirclest the earth, vouchsafe to grant the prayers of thy servants that call upon thee. More especially we pray thee send down thy grace on Nestor and on his sons; thereafter also make the rest of the Pylian people some handsome return for the goodly hecatomb they are offering you. Lastly, grant Telemachus and myself a happy issue, in respect of the matter that has brought us in our ship to Pylos."

When she had thus made an end of praying, she handed the cup to Telemachus and he prayed likewise. By and by, when the outer meats were roasted and had been taken off the spits, the carvers gave every man his portion and they all made an excellent dinner. As soon as they had had enough to eat and drink, Nestor, knight of Gerene, began to speak.

"Now," said he, "that our guests have done their dinner, it will be best to ask them who they are. Who, then, sir strangers, are you, and from what port have you sailed? Are you traders? or do you sail the seas as rovers with your hand against every man, and every man's hand against you?"

Telemachus answered boldly, for Athena had given him courage to ask about his father and get himself a good name.

"Nestor," said he, "son of Neleus, honor to the Achaean name, you ask whence we come, and I will tell you. We come from Ithaca under Neritum, and the matter about which I would speak is of private not public import. I seek news of my unhappy father Odysseus, who is said to have sacked the town of Troy in company with yourself. We know what fate befell each one of the other heroes who fought at Troy, but as regards Odysseus heaven has hidden from us the knowledge even that he is dead at all, for no one can certify us in what place he perished, nor say whether he fell in battle on the mainland, or was lost at sea amid the waves of Amphitrite. Therefore I am suppliant at your knees, if haply you may be pleased to tell me of his melancholy end, whether you saw it with your own eyes, or heard it from some other traveler, for he was a man born to trouble. Do not soften things out of any pity for me, but tell me in all plainness exactly what you saw. If my brave father Odysseus ever did you loyal service, either by word or deed, when you Achaeans were harassed among the Trojans, bear it in mind now as in my favor and tell me truly all."

"My friend," answered Nestor, "you recall a time of much sorrow to my mind, for the brave Achaeans suffered much both at sea, while privateering under Achilles, and when fighting before the great city of king Priam. Our best men all of them fell there—Ajax, Achilles, Patroclus peer of gods in counsel, and my own dear son Antilochus, a man singularly fleet of foot and in fight valiant. But we suffered much more than this; what mortal tongue indeed could tell the whole story? Though you were to stay here and question me for five years, or even six, I could not tell you all that the Achaeans suffered, and you would turn homeward weary of my tale before it ended. Nine long years did we try every kind of stratagem, but the hand of heaven was against us; during all this time there was no one who could compare with your father in subtlety—if indeed you are his son—I can hardly believe my eyes—and you talk just like him too—no one would say that people of such different ages could speak so much alike. He and I never had any kind of difference from first to last neither in camp nor council, but in singleness of heart and purpose we advised the Argives how all might be ordered for the best.

"When, however, we had sacked the city of Priam, and were setting sail in our ships as heaven had dispersed us, then Zeus saw fit to vex the Argives on their homeward voyage; for they had not all been either wise or understanding, and hence many came to a bad end through the displeasure of Zeus' daughter Athena,† who brought about a quarrel between the two sons of Atreus.†

"The sons of Atreus called a meeting which was not as it should be, for it was sunset and the Achaeans were heavy with wine. When they explained why they had called the people together, it seemed that Menelaus was for sailing homeward at once, and this displeased Agamemnon, who thought that we should wait till we had offered hecatombs to appease the anger of Athena. Fool that he was, he might have known that he would not prevail with her, for when the gods have made up their minds they do not change them lightly. So the two stood bandying hard words, whereon the Achaeans sprang to their feet with a cry that rent the air, and were of two minds as to what they should do.

"That night we rested and nursed our anger, for Zeus was hatching mischief against us. But in the morning some of us drew our ships into the water and put our goods with our women on board, while the rest, about half in number, stayed behind with Agamemnon. We—the other half—embarked and sailed; and the ships went well, for heaven had smoothed the sea. When we reached Tenedos we offered sacrifices to the gods, for we were longing to get home; cruel Zeus, however, did not yet mean that we should do so, and raised a second quarrel in the course of which some among us turned their ships back again, and sailed away under Odysseus to make their peace with Agamemnon; but I, and all the ships that were with me pressed forward, for I saw that mischief was brewing. The son of Tydeus went on also with me, and his crews with him. Later on Menelaus joined us at Lesbos, and found us making up our minds about our course—for we did not know whether to go outside Chios by the island of Psyra, keeping this to our left, or inside Chios, over against the stormy headland of Mimas. So we asked heaven for a sign, and were shown one to the effect that we should be soonest out of danger if we headed our ships across the open sea to Euboea. This we therefore did, and a fair wind sprang up which gave us a quick passage during the night to Geraestus, where we offered many sacrifices to Poseidon for having helped us so far on our way. Four days later Diomed and his men stationed their ships in Argos, but I held on for Pylos, and the wind never fell light from the day when heaven first made it fair for me.

"Therefore, my dear young friend, I returned without hearing anything about the others. I know neither who got home safely nor who were lost but, as in duty bound, I will give you without reserve the reports that have reached me since I have been here in my own house. They say the Myrmidons returned home safely under Achilles' son Neoptolemus; so also did the valiant son of Poias, Philoctetes. Idomeneus, again, lost no men at sea, and all his followers who escaped death in the field got safe home with him to Crete. No matter how far out of the world you live, you will have heard of Agamemnon and the bad end he came to at the hands of Aegisthus—and a fearful reckoning did Aegisthus presently pay. See what a good thing it is for a man to leave a son behind him to do as Orestes did, who killed false Aegisthus the murderer of his noble father. You too, then—for you are a tall smart-looking fellow—show your mettle and make yourself a name in story."

"Nestor son of Neleus," answered Telemachus, "honor to the Achaean name, the Achaeans applaud Orestes and his name will live through all time for he has avenged his father nobly. Would that heaven might grant me to do like vengeance on the insolence of the wicked suitors, who are ill treating me and plotting my ruin; but the gods have no such happiness in store for me and for my father, so we must bear it as best we may."

"My friend," said Nestor, "now that you remind me, I remember to have heard that your mother has many suitors, who are ill disposed towards you and are making havoc of your estate. Do you submit to this tamely, or are public feeling and the voice of heaven against you? Who knows but what

Odysseus may come back after all, and pay these scoundrels in full, either single-handed or with a force of Achaeans behind him?† If Athena were to take as great a liking to you as she did to Odysseus when we were fighting before Troy (for I never yet saw the gods so openly fond of anyone as Athena then was of your father), if she would take as good care of you as she did of him, these wooers would soon some of them forget their wooing."

Telemachus answered, "I can expect nothing of the kind; it would be far too much to hope for. I dare not let myself think of it. Even though the gods themselves willed it no such good fortune could befall me."

On this Athena said, "Telemachus, what are you talking about? Heaven has a long arm if it is minded to save a man; and if it were me, I should not care how much I suffered before getting home, provided I could be safe when I was once there. I would rather this, than get home quickly, and then be killed in my own house as Agamemnon was by the treachery of Aegisthus and his wife. Still, death is certain, and when a man's hour is come, not even the gods can save him, no matter how fond they are of him."†

"Mentor," answered Telemachus, "do not let us talk about it any more. There is no chance of my father's ever coming back; the gods have long since counselled his destruction. There is something else, however, about which I should like to ask Nestor, for he knows much more than anyone else does. They say he has reigned for three generations so that it is like talking to an immortal. Tell me, therefore, Nestor, and tell me true; how did Agamemnon come to die in that way? What was Menelaus doing? And how came false Aegisthus to kill so far better a man than himself? Was Menelaus away from Achaean Argos, voyaging elsewhither among mankind, that Aegisthus took heart and killed Agamemnon?"

"I will tell you truly," answered Nestor, "and indeed you have yourself divined how it all happened. If Menelaus when he got back from Troy had found Aegisthus still alive in his house, there would have been no barrow heaped up for him, not even when he was dead, but he would have been thrown outside the city to dogs and vultures, and not a woman would have mourned him, for he had done a deed of great wickedness;† but we were over there, fighting hard at Troy, and Aegisthus, who was taking his ease quietly in the heart of Argos, cajoled Agamemnon's wife Clytemnestra with incessant flattery.

"At first she would have nothing to do with his wicked scheme, for she was of a good natural disposition; moreover there was a bard with her, to whom Agamemnon had given strict orders on setting out for Troy, that he was to keep guard over his wife; but when heaven had counselled her destruction, Aegisthus carried this bard off to a desert island and left him there for crows and seagulls to batten upon—after which she went willingly enough to the house of Aegisthus. Then he offered many burnt sacrifices to the gods, and decorated many temples with tapestries and gilding, for he had succeeded far beyond his expectations.

"Meanwhile Menelaus and I were on our way home from Troy, on good terms with one another. When we got to Sunium, which is the point of Athens, Apollo with his painless shafts killed Phrontis the steersman of Menelaus' ship (and never man knew better how to handle a vessel in rough weather) so that he died then and there with the helm in his hand, and Menelaus, though very anxious to press forward, had to wait in order to bury his comrade and give him his due funeral rites. Presently, when he too could put to sea again, and had sailed on as far as the Malean heads, Zeus counselled evil against him and made it blow hard till the waves ran mountains high. Here he divided his fleet and took the one half towards Crete where the Cydonians dwell round about the waters of the river Iardanus. There is a high headland hereabouts stretching out into the sea from a place called Gortyn, and all along this part of the coast as far as Phaestus the sea runs high when there is a south wind blowing, but after Phaestus the coast is more protected, for a small headland can make a great shelter. Here this part of the fleet was driven on to the rocks and wrecked; but the crews just managed to save themselves. As for the other five ships, they were taken by winds and seas to Egypt, where Menelaus gathered much gold and substance among people of an alien speech. Meanwhile Aegisthus here at home plotted his evil deed. For seven years after he had killed Agamemnon he ruled in Mycene, and the people were obedient under him, but in the eighth year Orestes came back from Athens to be his bane, and killed the murderer of his father. Then he celebrated the funeral rites of his mother and of false Aegisthus by a banquet to the people of Argos, and on that very day Menelaus came home, with as much treasure as his ships could carry.

"Take my advice then, and do not go traveling about for long so far from home, nor leave your property with such dangerous people in your house; they will eat up everything you have among them, and you will have been on a fool's errand. Still, I should advise you by all means to go and visit Menelaus, who has lately come off a voyage among such distant peoples as no man could ever hope to get back from, when the winds had once carried him so far out of his reckoning; even birds cannot fly the distance in a twelve-month, so vast and terrible are the seas that they must cross. Go to him, therefore, by sea, and take your own men with you; or if you would rather travel by land you can have a chariot, you can have horses, and here are my sons who can escort you to Lacedaemon where Menelaus lives. Beg of him to speak the truth, and he will tell you no lies, for he is an excellent person."

As he spoke the sun set and it came on dark, whereon Athena said, "Sir, all that you have said is well; now, however, order the tongues of the victims to be cut, and mix wine that we may make drink-offerings to Poseidon, and the other immortals, and then go to bed, for it is bed time. People should go away early and not keep late hours at a religious festival."†

Thus spoke the daughter of Zeus, and they obeyed her saying. Men servants poured water over the hands of the guests, while pages filled the mixing-bowls with wine and water, and handed it round after giving every man his drink offering; then they threw the tongues of the victims into the fire, and stood up to make their drink offerings. When they had made their offerings and had drunk each as much as he was minded, Athena and Telemachus were for going on board their ship, but Nestor caught them up at once and stayed them.

"Heaven and the immortal gods," he exclaimed, "forbid that you should leave my house to go on board of a ship. Do you think I am so poor and short of clothes, or that I have so few cloaks and as to be unable to find comfortable beds both for myself and for my guests? Let me tell you I have store both of rugs and cloaks, and shall not permit the son of my old friend Odysseus to camp down on the deck of a ship—not while I live—nor yet will my sons after me, but they will keep open house as I have done."

Then Athena answered, "Sir, you have spoken well, and it will be much better that Telemachus should do as you have said; he, therefore, shall return with you and sleep at your house, but I must go back to give orders to my crew,† and keep them in good heart. I am the only older person among them; the rest are all young men of Telemachus' own age, who have taken this voyage out of friendship; so I must return to the ship and sleep there. Moreover to-morrow I must go to the Cauconians where I have a large sum of money long owing to me. As for Telemachus, now that he is your guest, send him to Lacedaemon in a chariot, and let one of your sons go with him. Be pleased to also provide him with your best and fleetest horses."

When she had thus spoken, she flew away in the form of an eagle, and all marveled as they beheld it. Nestor was astonished, and took Telemachus by the hand. "My friend," said he, "I see that you are going to be a great hero some day, since the gods wait upon you thus while you are still so young. This can have been none other of those who dwell in heaven than Zeus' redoubtable daughter, the Trito-born, who showed such favor towards your brave father among the Argives. Holy queen," he continued, "vouchsafe to send down thy grace upon myself, my good wife, and my children. In return, I will offer you in sacrifice a broad-browed heifer of a year old, unbroken, and never yet brought by man under the yoke. I will gild her horns, and will offer her up to you in sacrifice."

Thus did he pray, and Athena heard his prayer. He then led the way to his own house, followed by his sons and sons in law. When they had got there and had taken their places on the benches and seats, he mixed them a bowl of sweet wine that was eleven years old when the housekeeper took the lid off the jar that held it. As he mixed the wine, he prayed much and made drink offerings to Athena, daughter of Aegis-bearing Zeus. Then, when they had made their drink offerings and had drunk each as much as he was minded, the others went home to bed each in his own abode; but Nestor put Telemachus to sleep in the room that was over the gateway along with Pisistratus, who was the only unmarried son now left him. As for himself, he slept in an inner room of the house, with the queen his wife by his side.

Now when the child of morning rosy-fingered Dawn appeared, Nestor left his couch and took his seat on the benches of white and polished marble that stood in front of his house. Here aforetime sat Neleus, peer of gods in counsel, but he was now dead, and had gone to the house of Hades; so Nestor sat in his seat sceptre in hand, as guardian of the public weal. His sons as they left their rooms gathered round him, Echephron, Stratius, Perseus, Aretus, and Thrasymedes; the sixth son was Pisistratus, and when Telemachus joined them they made him sit with them. Nestor then addressed them.

"My sons," said he, "make haste to do as I shall bid you. I wish first and foremost to propitiate the great goddess Athena, who manifested herself visibly to me during yesterday's festivities. Go, then, one or other of you to the plain, tell the stockman to look me out a heifer, and come on here with it at once. Another must go to Telemachus' ship, and invite all the crew, leaving two men only in charge of the vessel. Someone else will run and fetch Laerceus the goldsmith to gild the horns of the heifer. The rest, stay all of you where you are; tell the maids in the house to prepare an excellent dinner, and to fetch seats, and logs of wood for a burnt offering. Tell them also to bring me some clear spring water."

On this they hurried off on their several errands. The heifer was brought in from the plain, and Telemachus' crew came from the ship; the goldsmith brought the anvil, hammer, and tongs, with which he worked his gold, and Athena herself came to accept the sacrifice. Nestor gave out the gold, and the smith gilded the horns of the heifer that the goddess might have pleasure in their beauty. Then Stratius and Echephron brought her in by the horns; Aretus fetched water from the house in a ewer that had a flower pattern on it, and in his other hand he held a basket of barley meal; sturdy Thrasymedes stood by with a sharp axe, ready to strike the heifer, while Perseus held a bucket. Then Nestor began with washing his hands and sprinkling the barley meal, and he offered many a prayer to Athena as he threw a lock from the heifer's head upon the fire.

When they had done praying and sprinkling the barley meal Thrasymedes dealt his blow, and brought the heifer down with a stroke that cut through the tendons at the base of her neck, whereon the daughters and daughters in law of Nestor, and his venerable wife Eurydice (she was eldest daughter to

Clymenus) screamed with delight.[†] Then they lifted the heifer's head from off the ground, and Pisistratus cut her throat. When she had done bleeding and was quite dead, they cut her up. They cut out the thigh bones all in due course, wrapped them round in two layers of fat, and set some pieces of raw meat on the top of them; then Nestor laid them upon the wood fire and poured wine over them, while the young men stood near him with five-pronged spits in their hands. When the thighs were burned and they had tasted the inward meats, they cut the rest of the meat up small, put the pieces on the spits and toasted them over the fire.

Meanwhile lovely Polycaste, Nestor's youngest daughter, washed Telemachus. When she had washed him and anointed him with oil, she brought him a fair mantle and shirt, and he looked like a god as he came from the bath and took his seat by the side of Nestor. When the outer meats were done they drew them off the spits and sat down to dinner where they were waited upon by some worthy henchmen, who kept pouring them out their wine in cups of gold. As soon as they had had enough to eat and drink Nestor said, "Sons, put Telemachus' horses to the chariot that he may start at once."

Thus did he speak, and they did even as he had said, and yoked the fleet horses to the chariot. The housekeeper packed them up a provision of bread, wine, and sweet meats fit for the sons of princes. Then Telemachus got into the chariot, while Pisistratus gathered up the reins and took his seat beside him. He lashed the horses on and they flew forward nothing loth into the open country, leaving the high citadel of Pylos behind them. All that day did they travel, swaying the yoke upon their necks till the sun went down and darkness was over all the land. Then they reached Pherae where Diocles lived, who was son to Ortilochus and grandson to Alpheus. Here they passed the night and Diocles entertained them hospitably. When the child of morning, rosy-fingered Dawn, appeared, they again yoked their horses and drove out through the gateway under the echoing gatehouse. Pisistratus lashed the horses on and they flew forward; presently they came to the corn lands of the open country, and in the course of time completed their journey, so well did their steeds take them.

B O O K   I V

*The visit to King Menelaus, who tells his story
Meanwhile, the suitors in Ithaca plot against Telemachus.*

NOW WHEN THE sun had set and darkness was over the land, they reached the low lying city of Lacedaemon, where they drove straight to the abode of Menelaus and found him in his own house, feasting with his many clansmen in honor of the wedding of his son, and also of his daughter, whom he was marrying to the son of that valiant warrior Achilles. He had given his consent and promised her to him while he was still at Troy, and now the gods were bringing the marriage about; so he was sending her with chariots and horses to the city of the Myrmidons over whom Achilles' son was reigning. For his only son he had found a bride from Sparta, the daughter of Alector. This son, Megapenthes, was born to him of a bond-woman, for heaven vouchsafed Helen no more children after she had borne Hermione, who was fair as golden Aphrodite herself.

So the neighbors and kinsmen of Menelaus were feasting and making merry in his house. There was a bard also to sing to them and play his lyre, while two tumblers went about performing in the midst of them when the man struck up with his tune.

Telemachus and the son of Nestor stayed their horses at the gate, whereon Eteoneus servant to Menelaus came out, and as soon as he saw them ran hurrying back into the house to tell his Master. He went close up to him and said, "Menelaus, there are some strangers come here, two men, who look like sons of Zeus. What are we to do? Shall we take their horses out, or tell them to find friends elsewhere as they best can?"

Menelaus was very angry and said, "Eteoneus, son of Boethous, you never used to be a fool, but now you talk like a simpleton. Take their horses out, of course, and show the strangers in that they may have supper; you and I have stayed often enough at other people's houses before we got back here, where heaven grant that we may rest in peace henceforward."[†]

So Eteoneus bustled back and bade the other servants come with him. They took their sweating steeds from under the yoke, made them fast to the mangers, and gave them a feed of oats and barley mixed. Then they leaned the chariot against the end wall of the courtyard, and led the way into the house. Telemachus and Pisistratus were astonished when they saw it, for its splendor was as that of the sun and moon; then, when they had admired everything to their heart's content, they went into the bath room and washed themselves.

When the servants had washed them and anointed them with oil, they brought them woollen cloaks and shirts, and the two took their seats by the side of Menelaus. A maid-servant brought them water in a beautiful golden ewer, and poured it into a silver basin for them to wash their hands; and she drew a clean table beside them. An upper servant brought them bread, and offered them many good things of what there was in the house, while the carver fetched them plates of all manner of meats and set cups of gold by their side.

Menelaus then greeted them saying, "Fall to, and welcome; when you have done supper I shall ask who you are, for the lineage of such men as you cannot have been lost. You must be descended from a line of sceptre-bearing kings, for poor people do not have such sons as you are."

On this he handed them a piece of fat roast loin, which had been set near him as being a prime part, and they laid their hands on the good things that were before them; as soon as they had had enough to eat and drink, Telemachus said to the son of Nestor, with his head so close that no one might hear, "Look, Pisistratus, man after my own heart, see the gleam of bronze and gold—of amber, ivory, and silver. Everything is so splendid that it is like seeing the palace of Olympian Zeus. I am lost in admiration."

Menelaus overheard him and said, "No one, my sons, can hold his own with Zeus, for his house and everything about him is immortal; but among mortal men—well, there may be another who has as much wealth as I have, or there may not; but at all events I have traveled much and have undergone much hardship, for it was nearly eight years before I could get home with my fleet. I went to Cyprus, Phoenicia and the Egyptians; I went also to the Ethiopians, the Sidonians, and the Erembians, and to Libya where the lambs have horns as soon as they are born, and the sheep lamb down three times a year. Everyone in that country, whether master or man, has a great deal of cheese, meat, and good milk, for the ewes yield all the year round. But while I was traveling and getting great riches among these people, my brother was secretly and shockingly murdered through the perfidy of his wicked wife, so that I have no pleasure in being lord of all this wealth. Whoever your parents may be they must have told you about all this, and of my heavy loss in the ruin of a stately mansion fully and magnificently furnished. Would that I had only a third of what I now have so that I had stayed at home, and all those were living who perished on the plain of Troy, far from Argos. I often grieve, as I sit here in my house, for one and all of them. At times I cry aloud for sorrow, but presently I leave off again, for crying is cold comfort and one soon tires of it. Yet grieve for these as I may, I do so for one man more than for them all. I cannot even think of him without loathing both food and sleep, so miserable does he make me, for no one of all the Achaeans worked so hard or risked so much as he did. He took nothing by it, and has left a legacy of sorrow to myself, for he has been gone a long time, and we know not whether he is alive or dead. His old father, his long-suffering wife Penelope, and his son Telemachus, whom he left behind him an infant in arms, are plunged in grief on his account."

Thus spoke Menelaus, and the heart of Telemachus yearned as he thought of his father. Tears fell from his eyes as he heard him thus mentioned, so that he held his cloak before his face with both hands. When Menelaus saw this he doubted whether to let him choose his own time for speaking, or to ask him at once and find what it was all about.

While he was thus in two minds Helen came down from her high vaulted and perfumed room, looking as lovely as Artemis herself. Adraste brought her a seat, Alcippe a soft woollen rug while Phylo fetched her the silver workbox which Alcandra wife of Polybus had given her. Polybus lived in Egyptian Thebes, which is the richest city in the whole world; he gave Menelaus two baths, both of pure silver, two tripods, and ten talents of gold; besides all this, his wife gave Helen some beautiful presents, to wit, a golden distaff, and a silver work box that ran on wheels, with a gold band round the top of it. Phylo now placed this by her side, full of fine spun yarn, and a distaff charged with violet colored wool was laid upon the top of it.† Then Helen took her seat, put her feet upon the footstool, and began to question her husband.

"Do we know, Menelaus," said she, "the names of these strangers who have come to visit us? Shall I guess right or wrong?—but I cannot help saying what I think. Never yet have I seen either man or woman so like somebody else (indeed when I look at him I hardly know what to think) as this young man is like Telemachus, whom Odysseus left as a baby behind him, when you Achaeans went to Troy with battle in your hearts, on account of my most shameless self."

"My dear wife," replied Menelaus, "I see the likeness just as you do. His hands and feet are just like Odysseus; so is his hair, with the shape of his head and the expression of his eyes. Moreover, when I was talking about Odysseus, and saying how much he had suffered on my account, tears fell from his eyes, and he hid his face in his mantle."

Then Pisistratus said, "Menelaus, son of Atreus, you are right in thinking that this young man is Telemachus, but he is very modest, and is ashamed to come here and begin opening up discourse with one whose conversation is so divinely interesting as your own.[†] My father, Nestor, sent me to escort him hither, for he wanted to know whether you could give him any counsel or suggestion. A son has always trouble at home when his father has gone away leaving him without supporters; and this is how Telemachus is now placed, for his father is absent, and there is no one among his own people to stand by him."

"Bless my heart," replied Menelaus, "then I am receiving a visit from the son of a very dear friend, who suffered much hardship for my sake. I had always hoped to entertain him with most marked distinction when heaven had granted us a safe return from beyond the seas. I should have founded a city for him in Argos, and built him a house. I should have made him leave Ithaca with his goods, his son, and all his people, and should have sacked for them some one of the neighboring cities that are subject to me. We should thus have seen one another continually, and nothing but death could have interrupted so close and happy an intercourse. I suppose, however, that heaven grudged us such great good fortune, for it has prevented the poor fellow from ever getting home at all."

Thus did he speak, and his words set them all a weeping. Helen wept, Telemachus wept, and so did Menelaus, nor could Pisistratus keep his eyes from filling, when he remembered his dear brother Antilochus whom the son of bright Dawn had killed. Thereon he said to Menelaus,

"Sir, my father Nestor, when we used to talk about you at home, told me you were a person of rare and excellent understanding. If, then, it be possible, do as I would urge you. I am not fond of crying while I am getting my supper. Morning will come in due course, and in the forenoon I care not how much I cry for those that are dead and gone. This is all we can do for the poor things. We can only shave our heads for them and wring the tears from our cheeks. I had a brother who died at Troy; he was by no means the worst man there; you are sure to have known him—his name was Antilochus; I never set eyes upon him myself, but they say that he was singularly fleet of foot and in fight valiant."

"Your discretion, my friend," answered Menelaus, "is beyond your years. It is plain you take after your father. One can soon see when a man is son to one whom heaven has blessed both as regards wife and offspring—and it has blessed Nestor from first to last all his days, giving him a green old age in his own house, with sons about him who are both well disposed and valiant. We will put an end therefore to all this weeping, and attend to our supper again.

Let water be poured over our hands. Telemachus and I can talk with one another fully in the morning."

On this Asphalion, one of the servants, poured water over their hands and they laid their hands on the good things that were before them.

Then Zeus' daughter Helen thought of another matter. She drugged the wine with an herb that banishes all care, sorrow, and ill humor. Whoever drinks wine thus drugged cannot shed a single tear all the rest of the day, not even though his father and mother both of them drop down dead, or he sees a brother or a son hewn in pieces before his very eyes. This drug, of such sovereign power and virtue, had been given to Helen by Polydamna wife of Thon, a woman of Egypt, where there grow all sorts of herbs, some good to put into the mixing bowl and others poisonous. Moreover, everyone in the whole country is a skilled physician, for they are of the race of Paeeon. When Helen had put this drug in the bowl, and had told the servants to serve the wine round, she said:

"Menelaus, son of Atreus, and you my good friends, sons of honorable men (which is as Zeus wills, for he is the giver both of good and evil, and can do what he chooses), feast here as you will, and listen while I tell you a tale in season. I cannot indeed name every single one of the exploits of Odysseus, but I can say what he did when he was before Troy, and you Achaeans were in all sorts of difficulties. He covered himself with wounds and bruises, dressed himself all in rags, and entered the enemy's city looking like a menial or a beggar, and quite different from what he did when he was among his own people. In this disguise he entered the city of Troy, and no one said anything to him. I alone recognized him and began to question him, but he was too cunning for me.† When, however, I had washed and anointed him and had given him clothes, and after I had sworn a solemn oath not to betray him to the Trojans till he had got safely back to his own camp and to the ships, he told me all that the Achaeans meant to do. He killed many Trojans and got much information before he reached the Argive camp, for all which things the Trojan women made lamentation, but for my own part I was glad, for my heart was beginning to yearn after my home, and I was unhappy about the wrong that Aphrodite had done me in taking me over there, away from my country, my girl, and my lawful wedded husband, who is indeed by no means deficient either in person or understanding."

Then Menelaus said, "All that you have been saying, my dear wife, is true. I have traveled much, and have had much to do with heroes, but I have never seen such another man as Odysseus. What endurance too, and what courage he displayed within the wooden horse, wherein all the bravest of the Argives were lying in wait to bring death and destruction upon the Trojans. At that moment you came up to us; some god who wished well to the Trojans must have set you on to it and you had Deiphobus with you. Three times did you go all round our hiding place and pat it; you called our chiefs each by his own name, and mimicked all our wives—Diomed, Odysseus, and I from our seats inside heard what a noise you made. Diomed and I could not make up our minds whether to spring out then and there, or to answer you from inside, but Odysseus held us all in check, so we sat quite still, all except Anticlus, who was beginning to answer you, when Odysseus clapped his two brawny hands over his mouth, and kept them there. It was this that saved us all, for he muzzled Anticlus till Athena took you away again."[†]

"How sad," exclaimed Telemachus, "that all this was of no avail to save him, nor yet his own iron courage. But now, sir, be pleased to send us all to bed, that we may lie down and enjoy the blessed boon of sleep."

On this Helen told the maid servants to set beds in the room that was in the gatehouse, and to make them with good red rugs, and spread coverlets on the top of them with woollen cloaks for the guests to wear. So the maids went out, carrying a torch, and made the beds, to which a man-servant presently conducted the strangers. Thus, then, did Telemachus and Pisistratus sleep there in the forecourt, while the son of Atreus lay in an inner room with lovely Helen by his side.

When the child of morning, rosy-fingered Dawn appeared, Menelaus rose and dressed himself. He bound his sandals on to his comely feet, girded his sword about his shoulders, and left his room looking like an immortal god.[†] Then, taking a seat near Telemachus he said:

"And what, Telemachus, has led you to take this long sea voyage to Lacedaemon? Are you on public, or private business? Tell me all about it."

"I have come, sir," replied Telemachus, "to see if you can tell me anything about my father. I am being eaten out of house and home; my fair estate is being wasted, and my house is full of miscreants who keep killing great numbers of my sheep and oxen, on the pretense of paying their addresses to my mother. Therefore, I am suppliant at your knees if haply you may tell me about my father's melancholy end, whether you saw it with your own eyes, or heard it from some other traveler; for he was a man born to trouble. Do not soften things out of any pity for myself, but tell me in all plainness exactly what you saw. If my brave father Odysseus ever did you loyal service either by word or deed, when you Achaeans were harassed by the Trojans, bear it in mind now as in my favor and tell me truly all."

Menelaus on hearing this was very much shocked. "So," he exclaimed, "these cowards would usurp a brave man's bed? A hind might as well lay her new born young in the lair of a lion, and then go off to feed in the forest or in some grassy dell: the lion when he comes back to his lair will make short work with the pair of them—and so will Odysseus with these suitors. By father Zeus, Athena, and Apollo, if Odysseus is still the man that he was when

he wrestled with Philomeleides in Lesbos, and threw him so heavily that all
the Achaeans cheered him—if he is still such and were to come near these
suitors, they would have a short shrift and a sorry wedding. As regards your
questions, however, I will not prevaricate nor deceive you, but will tell you
without concealment all that the old man of the sea told me.

"I was trying to come on here, but the gods detained me in Egypt, for my
hecatombs had not given them full satisfaction, and the gods are very strict
about having their dues.[†] Now off Egypt, about as far as a ship can sail in a
day with a good stiff breeze behind her, there is an island called Pharos—it
has a good harbor from which vessels can get out into open sea when they
have taken in water—and here the gods becalmed me twenty days without so
much as a breath of fair wind to help me forward. We should have run clean
out of provisions and my men would have starved, if a goddess had not taken
pity upon me and saved me in the person of Idothea, daughter to Proteus, the
old man of the sea, for she had taken a great fancy to me.

"She came to me one day when I was by myself, as I often was, for the men
used to go with their barbed hooks, all over the island in the hope of catching
a fish or two to save them from the pangs of hunger. 'Stranger,' said she, 'it
seems to me that you like starving in this way—at any rate it does not greatly
trouble you, for you stick here day after day, without even trying to get away
though your men are dying by inches.'

"'Let me tell you,' said I, 'whichever of the goddesses you may happen to
be, that I am not staying here of my own accord, but must have offended the
gods that live in heaven. Tell me, therefore, for the gods know everything,
which of the immortals it is that is hindering me in this way, and tell me also
how I may sail the sea so as to reach my home.'

"'Stranger,' replied she, 'I will make it all quite clear to you. There is an old
immortal who lives under the sea hereabouts and whose name is Proteus. He
is an Egyptian, and people say he is my father; he is Poseidon's head man and
knows every inch of ground all over the bottom of the sea. If you can snare
him and hold him tight, he will tell you about your voyage, what courses you
are to take, and how you are to sail the sea so as to reach your home. He will
also tell you, if you so will, all that has been going on at your house both good
and bad, while you have been away on your long and dangerous journey.'

"'Can you show me,' said I, 'some stratagem by means of which I may
catch this old god without his suspecting it and finding me out? For a god is
not easily caught—not by a mortal man.'

"'Stranger,' said she, 'I will make it all quite clear to you. About the time
when the sun shall have reached mid heaven, the old man of the sea comes
up from under the waves, heralded by the West wind that furs the water over
his head. As soon as he has come up he lies down, and goes to sleep in a great
sea cave, where the seals—Halosydne's chickens as they call them—come up

also from the grey sea, and go to sleep in shoals all round him; and a very strong and fish-like smell do they bring with them. Early to-morrow morning I will take you to this place and will lay you in ambush. Pick out, therefore, the three best men you have in your fleet, and I will tell you all the tricks that the old man will play you.

"'First he will look over all his seals, and count them; then, when he has seen them and tallied them on his five fingers, he will go to sleep among them, as a shepherd among his sheep. The moment you see that he is asleep seize him; put forth all your strength and hold him fast, for he will do his very utmost to get away from you. He will turn himself into every kind of creature that goes upon the earth, and will become also both fire and water; but you must hold him fast and grip him tighter and tighter, till he begins to talk to you and comes back to what he was when you saw him go to sleep; then you may slacken your hold and let him go; and you can ask him which of the gods it is that is angry with you, and what you must do to reach your home over the seas.'†

"Having so said she dived under the waves, whereon I turned back to the place where my ships were ranged upon the shore; and my heart was clouded with care as I went along. When I reached my ship we got supper ready, for night was falling, and camped down upon the beach.

"When the child of morning rosy-fingered Dawn appeared, I took the three men on whose prowess of all kinds I could most rely, and went along by the sea-side, praying heartily to heaven. Meanwhile the goddess fetched me up four seal skins from the bottom of the sea, all of them just skinned, for she meant playing a trick upon her father. Then she dug four pits for us to lie in, and sat down to wait till we should come up. When we were close to her, she made us lie down in the pits one after the other, and threw a seal skin over each of us. Our ambuscade would have been intolerable, for the stench of the fishy seals was most distressing—who would go to bed with a sea monster if he could help it?—but here, too, the goddess helped us, and thought of something that gave us great relief, for she put some ambrosia under each man's nostrils, which was so fragrant that it killed the smell of the seals.

"We waited the whole morning and made the best of it, watching the seals come up in hundreds to bask upon the sea shore, till at noon the old man of the sea came up too, and when he had found his fat seals he went over them and counted them. We were among the first he counted, and he never suspected any guile, but laid himself down to sleep as soon as he had done counting.† Then we rushed upon him with a shout and seized him; on which he began at once with his old tricks, and changed himself first into a lion with a great mane; then all of a sudden he became a dragon, a leopard, a wild boar; the next moment he was running water, and then again directly he was a tree, but we stuck to him and never lost hold, till at last the cunning old creature became distressed, and said, 'Which of the gods was it, Son of Atreus, that hatched this plot with you for snaring me and seizing me against my will? What do you want?'

" 'You know that yourself, old man,' I answered, 'you will gain nothing by trying to put me off. It is because I have been kept so long in this island, and see no sign of my being able to get away. I am losing all heart; tell me, then, for you gods know everything, which of the immortals it is that is hindering me, and tell me also how I may sail the sea so as to reach my home?'

"Then,' he said, 'if you would finish your voyage and get home quickly, you must offer sacrifices to Zeus and to the rest of the gods before embarking; for it is decreed that you shall not get back to your friends, and to your own house, till you have returned to the heaven-fed stream of Egypt, and offered holy hecatombs to the immortal gods that reign in heaven. When you have done this they will let you finish your voyage.'

"I was broken hearted when I heard that I must go back all that long and terrible voyage to Egypt; nevertheless, I answered, 'I will do all, old man, that you have laid upon me; but now tell me, and tell me true, whether all the Achaeans whom Nestor and I left behind us when we set sail from Troy have got home safely, or whether any one of them came to a bad end either on board his own ship or among his friends when the days of his fighting were done.'

"'Son of Atreus,' he answered, 'why ask me? You had better not know what I can tell you, for your eyes will surely fill when you have heard my story. Many of those about whom you ask are dead and gone, but many still remain, and only two of the chief men among the Achaeans perished during their return home. As for what happened on the field of battle—you were there yourself. A third Achaean leader is still at sea, alive, but hindered from return-ing. Ajax was wrecked, for Poseidon drove him on to the great rocks of Gyrae; nevertheless, he let him get safe out of the water, and in spite of all Athena's hatred[†] he would have escaped death, if he had not ruined himself by boast-ing.[†] He said the gods could not drown him even though they had tried to do so, and when Poseidon heard this large talk, he seized his trident in his two brawny hands, and split the rock of Gyrae in two pieces. The base remained where it was, but the part on which Ajax was sitting fell headlong into the sea and carried Ajax with it; so he drank salt water and was drowned.

"'Your brother and his ships escaped, for Hera protected him, but when he was just about to reach the high promontory of Malea, he was caught by a heavy gale which carried him out to sea again sorely against his will, and drove him to the foreland where Thyestes used to dwell, but where Aegisthus was then living. By and by, however, it seemed as though he was to return safely after all, for the gods backed the wind into its old quarter and they reached home; whereon Agamemnon kissed his native soil, and shed tears of joy at finding himself in his own country.

"'Now there was a watchman whom Aegisthus kept always on the watch, and to whom he had promised two talents of gold. This man had been looking out for a whole year to make sure that Agamemnon did not give him the slip and prepare war; when, therefore, this man saw Agamemnon go by, he went and told Aegisthus, who at once began to lay a plot for him. He picked twenty of his bravest warriors and placed them in ambuscade on one side the cloister, while on the opposite side he prepared a banquet. Then he sent his chariots and horsemen to Agamemnon, and invited him to the feast, but he meant foul play. He got him there, all unsuspicious of the doom that was awaiting him, and killed him when the banquet was over as though he were butchering an ox in the shambles; not one of Agamemnon's followers was left alive, nor yet one of Aegisthus', but they were all killed there in the cloisters.'

"Thus spoke Proteus, and I was broken hearted as I heard him. I sat down upon the sands and wept; I felt as though I could no longer bear to live nor look upon the light of the sun. Presently, when I had had my fill of weeping and writhing upon the ground, the old man of the sea said, 'Son of Atreus, do not waste any more time in crying so bitterly; it can do no manner of good; find your way home as fast as ever you can, for Aegisthus may be still alive, and even though Orestes has been beforehand with you in killing him, you may yet come in for his funeral.'

"On this I took comfort in spite of all my sorrow, and said, 'I know, then, about these two; tell me, therefore, about the third man of whom you spoke; is he still alive, but at sea, and unable to get home? or is he dead? Tell me, no matter how much it may grieve me.'

"'The third man,' he answered, 'is Odysseus who dwells in Ithaca. I can see him in an island sorrowing bitterly in the house of the nymph Calypso, who is keeping him prisoner, and he cannot reach his home for he has no ships nor sailors to take him over the sea. As for your own end, Menelaus, you shall not die in Argos, but the gods will take you to the Elysian plain, which is at the ends of the world. There fair-haired Rhadamanthus reigns, and men lead an easier life than anywhere else in the world, for in Elysium there falls not rain, nor hail, nor snow, but Oceanus breathes ever with a West wind that sings softly from the sea, and gives fresh life to all men. This will happen to you because you have married Helen, and are Zeus' son-in-law.'†

"As he spoke he dived under the waves, whereon I turned back to the ships with my companions, and my heart was clouded with care as I went along. When we reached the ships we got supper ready, for night was falling, and camped down upon the beach. When the child of morning, rosy-fingered Dawn appeared, we drew our ships into the water, and put our masts and sails within them; then we went on board ourselves, took our seats on the benches, and smote the grey sea with our oars. I again stationed my ships in the heaven-fed stream of Egypt, and offered hecatombs that were full and sufficient. When I had thus appeased heaven's anger, I raised a barrow to the memory of Agamemnon that his name might live for ever, after which I had a quick passage home, for the gods sent me a fair wind.

"And now for yourself—stay here some ten or twelve days longer, and I will then speed you on your way. I will make you a noble present of a chariot and three horses. I will also give you a beautiful chalice that so long as you live you may think of me whenever you make a drink-offering to the immortal gods."[†]

"Son of Atreus," replied Telemachus, "do not press me to stay longer; I should be contented to remain with you for another twelve months; I find your conversation so delightful that I should never once wish myself at home with my parents; but my crew whom I have left at Pylos are already impatient, and you are detaining me from them. As for any present you may be disposed to make me, I had rather that it should be a piece of plate. I will take no horses back with me to Ithaca, but will leave them to adorn your own stables, for you have much flat ground in your kingdom where lotus thrives, as also meadow-sweet and wheat and barley, and oats with their white and spreading ears; whereas in Ithaca we have neither open fields nor racecourses, and the country is more fit for goats than horses, and I like it the better for that. None of our islands have much level ground, suitable for horses, and Ithaca least of all."

Menelaus smiled and took Telemachus' hand within his own. "What you say," said he, "shows that you come of good family. I both can, and will, make this exchange for you, by giving you the finest and most precious piece of plate in all my house. It is a mixing bowl by Hephaestus' own hand, of pure silver, except the rim, which is inlaid with gold. Phaedimus, king of the Sidonians, gave it me in the course of a visit which I paid him when I returned thither on my homeward journey. I will make you a present of it."

Thus did they converse and guests kept coming to the king's house. They brought sheep and wine, while their wives had put up bread for them to take with them; so they were busy cooking their dinners in the courts.

Meanwhile the suitors were throwing discs or aiming with spears at a mark on the levelled ground in front of Odysseus' house, and were behaving with all their old insolence. Antinous and Eurymachus, who were their ringleaders and much the foremost among them all, were sitting together when Noemon son of Phronius came up and said to Antinous,

"Have we any idea, Antinous, on what day Telemachus returns from Pylos? He has a ship of mine, and I want it, to cross over to Elis: I have twelve brood mares there with yearling mule foals by their side not yet broken in, and I want to bring one of them over here and break him."

They were astounded when they heard this, for they had made sure that Telemachus had not gone to the city of Neleus. They thought he was only away somewhere on the farms, and was with the sheep, or with the swineherd; so Antinous said, "When did he go? Tell me truly, and what young men did he take with him? Were they freemen or his own bondsmen—for he might manage that too? Tell me also, did you let him have the ship of your own free will because he asked you, or did he take it without your leave?"

"I lent it him," answered Noemon, "what else could I do when a man of his position said he was in a difficulty, and asked me to oblige him? I could not possibly refuse. As for those who went with him they were the best young men we have, and I saw Mentor go on board as captain—or some god who was exactly like him.† I cannot understand it, for I saw Mentor here myself yesterday morning, and yet he was then setting out for Pylos."

Noemon then went back to his father's house, but Antinous and Eurymachus were very angry. They told the others to leave off playing, and to come and sit down along with themselves. When they came, Antinous son of Eupeithes spoke in anger. His heart was black with rage, and his eyes flashed fire as he said:

"Good heavens, this voyage of Telemachus is a very serious matter; we had made sure that it would come to nothing, but the young fellow has got away in spite of us, and with a picked crew too. He will be giving us trouble presently; may Zeus take him before he is full grown. Find me a ship, therefore, with a crew of twenty men, and I will lie in wait for him in the straits between Ithaca and Samos; he will then rue the day that he set out to try and get news of his father."

Thus did he speak, and the others applauded his saying; they then all of them went inside the buildings.

It was not long ere Penelope came to know what the suitors were plotting; for a man servant, Medon, overheard them from outside the outer court as they were laying their schemes within, and went to tell his mistress. As he crossed the threshold of her room Penelope said: "Medon, what have the suitors sent you here for? Is it to tell the maids to leave their master's business and cook dinner for them? I wish they may neither woo nor dine henceforward, neither here nor anywhere else, but let this be the very last time, for the waste you all make of my son's estate. Did not your fathers tell you when you were children, how good Odysseus had been to them—never doing anything high-handed, nor speaking harshly to anybody? Kings may say things sometimes, and they may take a fancy to one man and dislike another, but Odysseus never did an unjust thing by anybody—which shows what bad hearts you have, and that there is no such thing as gratitude left in this world."

Then Medon said, "I wish, Madam, that this were all; but they are plotting something much more dreadful now—may heaven frustrate their design. They are going to try and murder Telemachus as he is coming home from Pylos and Lacedaemon, where he has been to get news of his father."

Then Penelope's heart sank within her, and for a long time she was speechless; her eyes filled with tears, and she could find no utterance. At last, however, she said, "Why did my son leave me? What business had he to go sailing off in ships that make long voyages over the ocean like sea-horses? Does he want to die without leaving anyone behind him to keep up his name?"

"I do not know," answered Medon, "whether some god set him on to it, or whether he went on his own impulse to see if he could find out if his father was dead, or alive and on his way home."

Then he went downstairs again, leaving Penelope in an agony of grief. There were many seats in the house, but she had no heart for sitting on any one of them; she could only fling herself on the floor of her own room and cry; whereon all the maids in the house, both old and young, gathered round her and began to cry too, till at last in a transport of sorrow she exclaimed,

"My dears, heaven has been pleased to try me with more affliction than any other woman of my age and country. First I lost my brave and lion-hearted husband, who had every good quality under heaven, and whose name was great over all Hellas and middle Argos, and now my darling son is at the mercy of the winds and waves, without my having heard one word about his leaving home. You hussies, there was not one of you would so much as think of giving me a call out of my bed, though you all of you very well knew when he was starting. If I had known he meant taking this voyage, he would have had to give it up, no matter how much he was bent upon it, or leave me a corpse behind him—one or other. Now, however, go some of you and call old Dolius, who was given me by my father on my marriage, and who is my gardener. Bid him go at once and tell everything to Laertes, who may be able to hit on some plan for enlisting public sympathy on our side, as against those who are trying to exterminate his own race and that of Odysseus."

Then the dear old nurse Euryclea said, "You may kill me, Madam, or let me live on in your house, whichever you please, but I will tell you the real truth. I knew all about it, and gave him everything he wanted in the way of bread and wine, but he made me take my solemn oath that I would not tell you anything for some ten or twelve days, unless you asked or happened to hear of his having gone, for he did not want you to spoil your beauty by crying. And now, Madam, wash your face, change your dress, and go upstairs with your maids to offer prayers to Athena, daughter of Aegis-bearing Zeus, for she can save him even though he be in the jaws of death. Do not trouble Laertes: he has trouble enough already. Besides, I cannot think that the gods hate the race of the son of Arceisius so much, but there will be a son left to come up after him, and inherit both the house and the fair fields that lie far all round it."

With these words she made her mistress leave off crying, and dried the tears from her eyes. Penelope washed her face, changed her dress, and went upstairs with her maids. She then put some bruised barley into a basket and began praying to Athena.

"Hear me," she cried, "Daughter of Aegis-bearing Zeus, unweariable. If ever Odysseus while he was here burned you fat thigh bones of sheep or heifer, bear it in mind now as in my favor, and save my darling son from the villainy of the suitors."

She cried aloud as she spoke, and the goddess heard her prayer; meanwhile the suitors were clamorous throughout the covered cloister, and one of them said:

"The queen is preparing for her marriage with one or other of us. Little does she dream that her son has now been doomed to die."

This was what they said, but they did not know what was going to happen. Then Antinous said, "Comrades, let there be no loud talking, lest some of it get carried inside. Let us be up and do that in silence, about which we are all of a mind."

He then chose twenty men, and they went down to their ship and to the sea side; they drew the vessel into the water and got her mast and sails inside her; they bound the oars to the thole-pins with twisted thongs of leather, all in due course, and spread the white sails aloft, while their fine servants brought them their armor. Then they made the ship fast a little way out, came on shore again, got their suppers, and waited till night should fall.

But Penelope lay in her own room upstairs unable to eat or drink, and wondering whether her brave son would escape, or be overpowered by the wicked suitors. Like a lioness caught in the toils with huntsmen hemming her in on every side she thought and thought till she sank into a slumber, and lay on her bed bereft of thought and motion.

Then Athena bethought her of another matter, and made a vision in the likeness of Penelope's sister Iphthime daughter of Icarius who had married Eumelus and lived in Pherae. She told the vision to go to the house of Odysseus, and to make Penelope leave off crying, so it came into her room by the hole through which the thong went for pulling the door to, and hovered over her head saying,

"You are asleep, Penelope: the gods who live at ease will not suffer you to weep and be so sad. Your son has done them no wrong, so he will yet come back to you."

Penelope, who was sleeping sweetly at the gates of dreamland, answered, "Sister, why have you come here? You do not come very often, but I suppose that is because you live such a long way off. Am I, then, to leave off crying and refrain from all the sad thoughts that torture me? I, who have lost my brave and lion-hearted husband, who had every good quality under heaven, and whose name was great over all Hellas and middle Argos; and now my darling son has gone off on board of a ship—a foolish fellow who has never been used to roughing it, nor to going about among gatherings of men. I am even more anxious about him than about my husband; I am all in a tremble when I think of him, lest something should happen to him, either from the people among whom he has gone, or by sea, for he has many enemies who are plotting against him, and are bent on killing him before he can return home."

Then the vision said, "Take heart, and be not so much dismayed. There is one gone with him whom many a man would be glad enough to have stand by his side, I mean Athena; it is she who has compassion upon you, and who has sent me to bear you this message."

"Then," said Penelope, "if you are a god or have been sent here by divine commission, tell me also about that other unhappy one—is he still alive, or is he already dead and in the house of Hades?"

And the vision said, "I shall not tell you for certain whether he is alive or dead, and there is no use in idle conversation."†

Then it vanished through the thong-hole of the door and was dissipated into thin air; but Penelope rose from her sleep refreshed and comforted, so vivid had been her dream.

Meantime the suitors went on board and sailed their ways over the sea, intent on murdering Telemachus. Now there is a rocky islet called Asteris, of no great size, in mid channel between Ithaca and Samos, and there is a harbor on either side of it where a ship can lie. Here then the Achaeans placed themselves in ambush.

BOOK V

Calypso
Odysseus reaches Scheria on a raft.

AND NOW, AS Dawn rose from her couch beside Tithonus—harbinger of light alike to mortals and immortals—the gods met in council and with them, Zeus the lord of thunder, who is their king. Thereon Athena began to tell them of the many sufferings of Odysseus, for she pitied him away there in the house of the nymph Calypso.

"Father Zeus," said she, "and all you other gods that live in everlasting bliss, I hope there may never be such a thing as a kind and well-disposed ruler any more, nor one who will govern equitably. I hope they will be all henceforth cruel and unjust, for there is not one of his subjects but has forgotten Odysseus, who ruled them as though he were their father. There he is, lying in great pain in an island where dwells the nymph Calypso, who will not let him go; and he cannot get back to his own country, for he can find neither ships nor sailors to take him over the sea. Furthermore, wicked people are now trying to murder his only son Telemachus, who is coming home from Pylos and Lacedaemon, where he has been to see if he can get news of his father."†

"What, my dear, are you talking about?" replied her father, "did you not send him there yourself, because you thought it would help Odysseus to get home and punish the suitors? Besides, you are perfectly able to protect Telemachus, and to see him safely home again, while the suitors have to come hurry-skurrying back without having killed him."

When he had thus spoken, he said to his son Hermes, "Hermes, you are our messenger, go therefore and tell Calypso we have decreed that poor

Odysseus is to return home. He is to be convoyed neither by gods nor men, but after a perilous voyage of twenty days upon a raft he is to reach fertile Scheria, the land of the Phaeacians, who are near of kin to the gods, and will honor him as though he were one of ourselves. They will send him in a ship to his own country, and will give him more bronze and gold and raiment than he would have brought back from Troy, if he had had all his prize money and had got home without disaster. This is how we have settled that he shall return to his country and his friends."

Thus he spoke, and Hermes, guide and guardian, slayer of Argus, did as he was told. Forthwith he bound on his glittering golden sandals with which he could fly like the wind over land and sea. He took the wand with which he seals men's eyes in sleep or wakes them just as he pleases, and flew holding it in his hand over Pieria; then he swooped down through the firmament till he reached the level of the sea, whose waves he skimmed like a cormorant that flies fishing every hole and corner of the ocean, and drenching its thick plumage in the spray. He flew and flew over many a weary wave, but when at last he got to the island which was his journey's end, he left the sea and went on by land till he came to the cave where the nymph Calypso lived.[†]

He found her at home. There was a large fire burning on the hearth, and one could smell from far the fragrant reek of burning cedar and sandal wood. As for herself, she was busy at her loom, shooting her golden shuttle through the warp and singing beautifully. Round her cave there was a thick wood of alder, poplar, and sweet smelling cypress trees, wherein all kinds of great birds had built their nests—owls, hawks, and chattering sea-crows that occupy their business in the waters. A vine loaded with grapes was trained and grew luxuriantly about the mouth of the cave; there were also four running rills of water in channels cut pretty close together, and turned here and there so as to irrigate the beds of violets and luscious herbage over which they flowed. Even a god could not help being charmed with such a lovely spot, so Hermes stood still and looked at it; but when he had admired it sufficiently he went inside the cave.

Calypso knew him at once—for the gods all know each other, no matter how far they live from one another—but Odysseus was not within; he was on the sea-shore as usual, looking out upon the barren ocean with tears in his eyes, groaning and breaking his heart for sorrow. Calypso gave Hermes a seat and said: "Why have you come to see me, Hermes—honored, and ever welcome—for you do not visit me often? Say what you want; I will do it for you at once if I can, and if it can be done at all; but come inside, and let me set refreshment before you."

As she spoke she drew a table loaded with ambrosia beside him and mixed him some red nectar, so Hermes ate and drank till he had had enough, and then said:

"We are speaking god and goddess to one another, and you ask me why I have come here, and I will tell you truly as you would have me do. Zeus sent me; it was no doing of mine; who could possibly want to come all this way over the sea where there are no cities full of people to offer me sacrifices or choice hecatombs? Nevertheless I had to come, for none of us other gods can cross Zeus, nor transgress his orders. He says that you have here the most ill-starred of all those who fought nine years before the city of King Priam and sailed home in the tenth year after having sacked it. On their way home they sinned against Athena, who raised both wind and waves against them, so that all his brave companions perished, and he alone was carried here by wind and tide. Zeus says that you are to let this man go at once, for it is decreed that he shall not perish here, far from his own people, but shall return to his house and country and see his friends again."

Calypso trembled with rage when she heard this, "You gods," she exclaimed, "ought to be ashamed of yourselves. You are always jealous and hate seeing a goddess take a fancy to a mortal man, and live with him in open matrimony. So when rosy-fingered Dawn made love to Orion, you precious gods were all of you furious till Artemis went and killed him in Ortygia. So again when Ceres fell in love with Iasion, and yielded to him in a thrice-ploughed fallow field, Zeus came to hear of it before so very long and killed Iasion with his thunderbolts. And now you are angry with me too because I have a man here.† I found the poor creature sitting all alone astride of a keel, for Zeus had struck his ship with lightning and sunk it in mid ocean, so that all his crew were drowned, while he himself was driven by wind and waves on to my island. I got fond of him and cherished him, and had set my heart on making him immortal, so that he should never grow old all his days; still I cannot cross Zeus, nor bring his counsels to nothing; therefore, if he insists upon it, let the man go beyond the seas again; but I cannot send him anywhere myself for I have neither ships nor men who can take him. Nevertheless I will readily give him such advice, in all good faith, as will be likely to bring him safely to his own country."

"Then send him away," said Hermes, "or Zeus will be angry with you and punish you".

On this he took his leave, and Calypso went out to look for Odysseus, for she had heard Zeus' message. She found him sitting upon the beach with his eyes ever filled with tears, and dying of sheer home sickness; for he had got tired of Calypso, and though he was forced to sleep with her in the cave by night, it was she, not he, that would have it so. As for the day time, he spent it on the rocks and on the sea shore, weeping, crying aloud for his despair, and always looking out upon the sea. Calypso then went close up to him said:

"My poor fellow, you shall not stay here grieving and fretting your life out any longer. I am going to send you away of my own free will; so go, cut some beams of wood, and make yourself a large raft with an upper deck that it may carry you safely over the sea. I will put bread, wine, and water on board to save you from starving. I will also give you clothes, and will send you a fair wind to take you home, if the gods in heaven so will it—for they know more about these things, and can settle them better than I can."

Odysseus shuddered as he heard her. "Now goddess," he answered, "there is something behind all this; you cannot be really meaning to help me home when you bid me do such a dreadful thing as put to sea on a raft. Not even a well found ship with a fair wind could venture on such a distant voyage: nothing that you can say or do shall make me go on board a raft unless you first solemnly swear that you mean me no mischief."

Calypso smiled at this and caressed him with her hand: "You know a great deal," said she, "but you are quite wrong here. May heaven above and earth below be my witnesses, with the waters of the river Styx—and this is the most solemn oath which a blessed god can take—that I mean you no sort of harm, and am only advising you to do exactly what I should do myself in your place. I am dealing with you quite straightforwardly; my heart is not made of iron, and I am very sorry for you."

When she had thus spoken she led the way rapidly before him, and Odysseus followed in her steps; so the pair, goddess and man, went on and on till they came to Calypso's cave, where Odysseus took the seat that Hermes had just left. Calypso set meat and drink before him of the food that mortals eat; but her maids brought ambrosia and nectar for herself, and they laid their hands on the good things that were before them.† When they had satisfied themselves with meat and drink, Calypso spoke, saying:

"Odysseus, noble son of Laertes, so you would start home to your own land at once? Good luck go with you, but if you could only know how much suffering is in store for you before you get back to your own country, you would stay where you are, keep house along with me, and let me make you immortal, no matter how anxious you may be to see this wife of yours, of whom you are thinking all the time day after day; yet I flatter myself that I am no whit less tall or well-looking than she is, for it is not to be expected that a mortal woman should compare in beauty with an immortal."†

"Goddess," replied Odysseus, "do not be angry with me about this. I am quite aware that my wife Penelope is nothing like so tall or so beautiful as yourself. She is only a woman, whereas you are an immortal. Nevertheless, I want to get home, and can think of nothing else. If some god wrecks me when I am on the sea, I will bear it and make the best of it. I have had infinite trouble both by land and sea already, so let this go with the rest."

Presently the sun set and it became dark, whereon the pair retired into the inner part of the cave and went to bed.

When the child of morning rosy-fingered Dawn appeared, Odysseus put on his shirt and cloak, while the goddess wore a dress of a light gossamer fabric, very fine and graceful, with a beautiful golden girdle about her waist and a veil to cover her head. She at once set herself to think how she could speed Odysseus on his way. So she gave him a great bronze axe that suited his hands; it was sharpened on both sides, and had a beautiful olive-wood handle fitted firmly on to it. She also gave him a sharp adze, and then led the way to the far end of the island where the largest trees grew—alder, poplar and pine, that reached the sky—very dry and well seasoned, so as to sail light for him in the water. Then, when she had shown him where the best trees grew, Calypso went home, leaving him to cut them, which he soon finished doing. He cut down twenty trees in all and adzed them smooth, squaring them by rule in good workmanlike fashion. Meanwhile Calypso came back with some augers, so he bored holes with them and fitted the timbers together with bolts and rivets. He made the raft as broad as a skilled shipwright makes the beam of a large vessel, and he fixed a deck on top of the ribs, and ran a gunwale all round it. He also made a mast with a yard arm, and a rudder to steer with. He fenced the raft all round with wicker hurdles as a protection against the waves, and then he threw on a quantity of wood. By and by Calypso brought him some linen to make the sails, and he made these too, excellently, making them fast with braces and sheets. Last of all, with the help of levers, he drew the raft down into the water.

In four days he had completed the whole work, and on the fifth Calypso sent him from the island after washing him and giving him some clean clothes. She gave him a goat skin full of black wine, and another larger one of water; she also gave him a wallet full of provisions, and gave him much good meat. Moreover, she made the wind fair and warm for him, and gladly did Odysseus spread his sail before it, while he sat and guided the raft skilfully by means of the rudder. He never closed his eyes, but kept them fixed on the Pleiads, on late-setting Bootes, and on the Bear—which men also call the wain, and which turns round and round where it is, facing Orion, and alone never dipping into the stream of Oceanus—for Calypso had told him to keep this to his left. Days seven and ten did he sail over the sea, and on the eighteenth the dim outlines of the mountains on the nearest part of the Phaeacian coast appeared, rising like a shield on the horizon.

But King Poseidon, who was returning from the Ethiopians, caught sight of Odysseus a long way off, from the mountains of the Solymi. He could see him sailing upon the sea, and it made him very angry, so he wagged his head and muttered to himself, saying, "Good heavens, so the gods have been changing their minds about Odysseus while I was away in Ethiopia, and now he is close to the land of the Phaeacians, where it is decreed that he shall escape from the calamities that have befallen him. Still, he shall have much hardship yet before he has done with it."

Thereon he gathered his clouds together, grasped his trident, stirred it round in the sea, and roused the rage of every wind that blows till earth, sea, and sky were hidden in cloud, and night sprang forth out of the heavens. Winds from East, South, North, and West fell upon him all at the same time, and a tremendous sea got up, so that Odysseus' heart began to fail him. "Alas," he said to himself in his dismay, "what ever will become of me? I am afraid Calypso was right when she said I should have trouble by sea before I got back home. It is all coming true.† How black is Zeus making heaven with his clouds, and what a sea the winds are raising from every quarter at once. I am now safe to perish. Blest and thrice blest were those Danaans who fell before Troy in the cause of the sons of Atreus. Would that I had been killed on the day when the Trojans were pressing me so sorely about the dead body of Achilles, for then I should have had due burial and the Achaeans would have honored my name; but now it seems that I shall come to a most pitiable end."

As he spoke a sea broke over him with such terrific fury that the raft reeled again, and he was carried overboard a long way off. He let go the helm, and the force of the hurricane was so great that it broke the mast half way up, and both sail and yard went over into the sea. For a long time Odysseus was under water, and it was all he could do to rise to the surface again, for the clothes Calypso had given him weighed him down; but at last he got his head above water and spat out the bitter brine that was running down his face in streams. In spite of all this, however, he did not lose sight of his raft, but swam as fast as he could towards it, got hold of it, and climbed on board again so as to escape drowning. The sea took the raft and tossed it about as Autumn winds whirl tumbleweeds round and round upon a road.

When he was in this plight, Ino daughter of Cadmus, also called Leucothea, saw him. She had formerly been a mere mortal, but had been since raised to the rank of a marine goddess. Seeing in what great distress Odysseus now was, she had compassion upon him, and, rising like a sea-gull from the waves, took her seat upon the raft.

"My poor good man," said she, "why is Poseidon so furiously angry with you? He is giving you a great deal of trouble, but for all his bluster he will not kill you. You seem to be a sensible person, do then as I bid you; strip, leave your raft to drive before the wind, and swim to the Phaeacian coast where better luck awaits you. And here, take my veil and put it round your chest; it is enchanted, and you can come to no harm so long as you wear it. As soon as you touch land take it off, throw it back as far as you can into the sea, and then go away again." With these words she took off her veil and gave it him. Then she dived down again like a sea-gull and vanished beneath the dark blue waters.

But Odysseus did not know what to think. "Alas," he said to himself in his dismay, "this is only some one or other of the gods who is luring me to ruin by advising me to quit my raft.† At any rate I will not do so at present, for the land where she said I should be quit of all troubles seemed to be still a good way off. I know what I will do—I am sure it will be best—no matter what happens I will stick to the raft as long as her timbers hold together, but when the sea breaks her up I will swim for it; I do not see how I can do any better than this."†

While he was thus in two minds, Poseidon sent a terrible great wave that seemed to rear itself above his head till it broke right over the raft, which then went to pieces as though it were a heap of dry chaff tossed about by a whirlwind. Odysseus got astride of one plank and rode upon it as if he were on horseback; he then took off the clothes Calypso had given him, bound Ino's veil under his arms, and plunged into the sea—meaning to swim on shore. King Poseidon watched him as he did so, and wagged his head, muttering to himself and saying, "There now, swim up and down as you best can till you fall in with well-to-do people. I do not think you will be able to say that I have let you off too lightly." On this he lashed his horses and drove to Aegae where his palace is.

But Athena resolved to help Odysseus, so she bound the ways of all the winds except one, and made them lie quite still; but she roused a good stiff breeze from the North that should lay the waters till Odysseus reached the land of the Phaeacians where he would be safe.

Thereon he floated about for two nights and two days in the water, with a heavy swell on the sea and death staring him in the face; but when the third day broke, the wind fell and there was a dead calm without so much as a breath of air stirring. As he rose on the swell he looked eagerly ahead, and could see land quite near. Then, as children rejoice when their dear father begins to get better after having for a long time borne sore affliction sent him by some angry spirit, but the gods deliver him from evil, so was Odysseus thankful when he again saw land and trees, and swam on with all his strength that he might once more set foot upon dry ground. When, however, he got within earshot, he began to hear the surf thundering up against the rocks, for the swell still broke against them with a terrific roar. Everything was enveloped in spray; there were no harbors where a ship might ride, nor shelter of any kind, but only headlands, low-lying rocks, and mountain tops.

Odysseus' heart now began to fail him, and he said despairingly to himself, "Alas, Zeus has let me see land after swimming so far that I had given up all hope, but I can find no landing place, for the coast is rocky and surf-beaten, the rocks are smooth and rise sheer from the sea, with deep water close under them so that I cannot climb out for want of foot hold. I am afraid some great wave will lift me off my legs and dash me against the rocks as I leave the water—which would give me a sorry landing. If, on the other hand, I swim further in search of some shelving beach or harbor, a hurricane may carry me out to sea again sorely against my will, or heaven may send some great monster of the deep to attack me; for Amphitrite breeds many such, and I know that Poseidon is very angry with me."

While he was thus in two minds a wave caught him and took him with such force against the rocks that he would have been smashed and torn to pieces if Athena had not shown him what to do.† He caught hold of the rock with both hands and clung to it groaning with pain till the wave retired, so he was saved that time; but presently the wave came on again and carried him back with it far into the sea—tearing his hands as the suckers of a polypus are torn when someone plucks it from its bed, and the stones come up along with it—even so did the rocks tear the skin from his strong hands, and then the wave drew him deep down under the water.

Here poor Odysseus would have certainly perished even in spite of his own destiny, if Athena had not helped him to keep his wits about him.† He swam seaward again, beyond reach of the surf that was beating against the land, and at the same time he kept looking towards the shore to see if he could find some haven, or a spit that should take the waves aslant. By and by, as he swam on, he came to the mouth of a river, and here he thought would be the best place, for there were no rocks, and it afforded shelter from the wind. He felt that there was a current, so he prayed inwardly and said:

"Hear me, O King, whoever you may be, and save me from the anger of the sea-god Poseidon, for I approach you prayerfully. Anyone who has lost his way has at all times a claim even upon the gods, wherefore in my distress I draw near to your stream, and cling to the knees of your riverhood. Have mercy upon me, O king, for I declare myself your suppliant."

Then the god stopped his stream and stilled the waves, making all calm before him, and bringing him safely into the mouth of the river. Here at last Odysseus' knees and strong hands failed him, for the sea had completely broken him. His body was all swollen, and his mouth and nostrils ran down like a river with sea-water, so that he could neither breathe nor speak, and lay swooning from sheer exhaustion;† presently, when he had got his breath and came to himself again, he took off the scarf that Ino had given him and threw it back into the salt stream of the river, whereon Ino received it into her hands from the wave that bore it towards her. Then he left the river, laid himself down among the rushes, and kissed the bounteous earth.

"Alas," he cried to himself in his dismay, "what ever will become of me, and how is it all to end? If I stay here upon the river bed through the long watches of the night, I am so exhausted that the bitter cold and damp may make an end of me—for towards sunrise there will be a keen wind blowing from off the river. If, on the other hand, I climb the hill side, find shelter in the woods, and sleep in some thicket, I may escape the cold and have a good night's rest, but some savage beast may take advantage of me and devour me."

In the end he deemed it best to take to the woods, and he found one upon some high ground not far from the water. There he crept beneath two shoots of olive that grew from a single stock—the one an ungrafted sucker, while the other had been grafted.† No wind, however squally, could break through the cover they afforded, nor could the sun's rays pierce them, nor the rain get through them, so closely did they grow into one another. Odysseus crept under these and began to make himself a bed to lie on, for there was a great litter of dead leaves lying about—enough to make a covering for two or three men even in hard winter weather. He was glad enough to see this, so he laid himself down and heaped the leaves all round him. Then, as one who lives alone in the country, far from any neighbor, hides a brand as fire-seed in the ashes to save himself from having to get a light elsewhere,† even so did Odysseus cover himself up with leaves; and Athena shed a sweet sleep upon his eyes, closed his eyelids, and made him lose all memories of his sorrows.

B O O K V I

The meeting between Nausicaa and Odysseus.

S O HERE ODYSSEUS slept, overcome by sleep and toil; but Athena went off to the country and city of the Phaeacians—a people who used to live in the fair town of Hypereia, near the lawless Cyclopes. Now the Cyclopes were stronger than they and plundered them, so their king Nausithous moved them thence and settled them in Scheria, far from all other people. He surrounded the city with a wall, built houses and temples, and divided the lands among his people; but he was dead and gone to the house of Hades, and King Alcinous, whose counsels were inspired of heaven, was now reigning. To his house, then, did Athena go in to gain the return of Odysseus.

She went straight to the beautifully decorated bedroom in which there slept a girl who was as lovely as a goddess, Nausicaa, daughter to King Alcinous. Two maid servants were sleeping near her, both very pretty, one on either side of the doorway, which was closed with well made folding doors. Athena took the form of the famous sea captain Dymas' daughter, who was a bosom friend of Nausicaa and just her own age; then, coming up to the girl's bedside like a breath of wind, she hovered over her head and said:[†]

"Nausicaa, what can your mother have been about, to have such a lazy daughter? Here are your clothes all lying in disorder, yet you are going to be married almost immediately, and should not only be well dressed yourself, but should find good clothes for those who attend you. This is the way to get yourself a good name, and to make your father and mother proud of you. Suppose, then, that we make tomorrow a washing day, and start at daybreak. I will come and help you so that you may have everything ready as soon as possible, for all the best young men among your own people are courting you, and you are not going to remain a maid much longer. Ask your father, therefore, to have a wagon and mules ready for us at daybreak, to take the rugs, robes, and girdles, and you can ride, too, which will be much pleasanter for you than walking, for the washing-cisterns are some way from the town."

When she had said this Athena went away to Olympus, which they say is the everlasting home of the gods. Here no wind beats roughly, and neither rain nor snow can fall; but it abides in everlasting sunshine and in a great peacefulness of light, wherein the blessed gods are illumined for ever and ever.[†] This was the place to which the goddess went when she had given instructions to the girl.

By and by morning came and woke Nausicaa, who began wondering about her dream; she therefore went to the other end of the house to tell her father and mother all about it, and found them in their own room. Her mother was sitting by the fireside spinning her purple yarn with her maids around her, and she happened to catch her father just as he was going out to attend a meeting of the town council, which the Phaeacian aldermen had convened. She stopped him and said:

"Papa dear, could you manage to let me have a good big wagon? I want to take all our dirty clothes to the river and wash them. You are the chief man here, so it is only right that you should have a clean shirt when you attend meetings of the council. Moreover, you have five sons at home, two of them married, while the other three are good looking bachelors; you know they always like to have clean linen when they go to a dance, and I have been thinking about all this."

She did not say a word about her own wedding, for she did not like to, but her father knew and said, "You shall have the mules, my love, and whatever else you have a mind for. Be off with you, and the men shall get you a good strong wagon with a body to it that will hold all your clothes."

On this he gave his orders to the servants, who got the wagon out, harnessed the mules, and put them to, while the girl brought the clothes down from the linen room and placed them on the wagon. Her mother prepared her a basket of provisions with all sorts of good things, and a goat skin full of wine; the girl now got into the wagon, and her mother gave her also a golden cruse of oil, that she and her women might anoint themselves. Then she took the whip and reins and lashed the mules on, whereon they set off, and their hoofs clattered on the road. They pulled without flagging, and carried not only Nausicaa and her wash of clothes, but the maids also who were with her.

When they reached the waterside they went to the washing cisterns, through which there ran at all times enough pure water to wash any quantity of linen, no matter how dirty. Here they unharnessed the mules and turned them out to feed on the sweet juicy herbage that grew by the waterside. They took the clothes out of the wagon, put them in the water, and vied with one another in treading them in the pits to get the dirt out. After they had washed them and got them quite clean, they laid them out by the sea side, where the waves had raised a high beach of shingle, and set about washing themselves and anointing themselves with olive oil. Then they got their dinner by the side of the stream, and waited for the sun to finish drying the clothes. When they had done dinner they threw off the veils that covered their heads and began to play at ball, while Nausicaa sang for them. As the huntress Artemis goes forth upon the mountains of Taygetus or Erymanthus to hunt wild boars or deer, and the wood nymphs, daughters of Aegis-bearing Zeus, take their sport along with her (then is Leto proud at seeing her daughter stand a full head taller than the others, and eclipse the loveliest amid a whole bevy of beauties), even so did the girl outshine her handmaids.

When it was time for them to start home, and they were folding the clothes and putting them into the wagon, Athena began to consider how Odysseus should wake up and see the handsome girl who was to conduct him to the city of the Phaeacians. The girl, therefore, threw a ball at one of the maids, which missed her and fell into deep water. On this they all shouted, and the noise they made woke Odysseus, who sat up in his bed of leaves and began to wonder what it might all be.

"Alas," said he to himself, "what kind of people have I come amongst? Are they cruel, savage, and uncivilized, or hospitable and humane? I seem to hear the voices of young women, and they sound like those of the nymphs that haunt mountain tops, or springs of rivers and meadows of green grass. At any rate I am among a race of men and women. Let me try if I cannot manage to get a look at them."

As he said this he crept from under his bush, and broke off a bough covered with thick leaves to hide his nakedness. He looked like some lion of the wilderness that stalks about exulting in his strength and defying both wind and rain; his eyes glare as he prowls in quest of oxen, sheep, or deer, for he is famished, and will dare break even into a well fenced homestead, trying to get at the sheep—even such did Odysseus seem to the young women, as he drew near to them all naked as he was, for he was in great want.† On seeing one so unkempt and so begrimed with salt water, the others scampered off along the spits that jutted out into the sea, but the daughter of Alcinous stood firm, for Athena put courage into her heart and took away all fear from her. She stood right in front of Odysseus, and he doubted whether he should go up to her, throw himself at her feet, and embrace her knees as a suppliant, or stay where he was and entreat her to give him some clothes and show him the way to the town. In the end he deemed it best to entreat her from a distance in case the girl should take offense at his coming near enough to clasp her knees,† so he addressed her in honeyed and persuasive language.

"O queen," he said, "I implore your aid—but tell me, are you a goddess or are you a mortal woman? If you are a goddess and dwell in heaven, I can only conjecture that you are Zeus' daughter Artemis, for your face and figure resemble none but hers; if on the other hand you are a mortal and live on earth, thrice happy are your father and mother—thrice happy, too, are your brothers and sisters; how proud and delighted they must feel when they see so fair a scion as yourself going out to a dance; most happy, however, of all will he be whose wedding gifts have been the richest, and who takes you to his own home. I never yet saw any one so beautiful, neither man nor woman, and am lost in admiration as I behold you. I can only compare you to a young palm tree which I saw when I was at Delos growing near the altar of Apollo—for I was there, too, with much people after me, when I was on that journey which has been the source of all my troubles. Never yet did such a young plant shoot out of the ground as that was, and I admired and wondered at it exactly as I now admire and wonder at yourself. I dare not clasp your knees, but I am in great distress; yesterday made the twentieth day that I had been tossing about upon the sea. The winds and waves have taken me all the way from the Ogygian island, and now fate has flung me upon this coast that I may endure still further suffering; for I do not think that I have yet come to the end of it, but rather that heaven has still much evil in store for me.

"And now, O queen, have pity upon me, for you are the first person I have met, and I know no one else in this country. Show me the way to your town, and let me have anything that you may have brought hither to wrap your clothes in. May heaven grant you in all things your heart's desire—husband, house, and a happy, peaceful home; for there is nothing better in this world than that man and wife should be of one mind in a house. It discomfits their enemies, makes the hearts of their friends glad, and they themselves know more about it than anyone."

To this Nausicaa answered, "Stranger, you appear to be a sensible, well-disposed person. There is no accounting for luck; Zeus gives prosperity to rich and poor just as he chooses, so you must take what he has seen fit to send you, and make the best of it.[†] Now, however, that you have come to this our country, you shall not want for clothes nor for anything else that a foreigner in distress may reasonably look for. I will show you the way to the town, and will tell you the name of our people; we are called Phaeacians, and I am daughter to Alcinous, in whom the whole power of the state is vested."

Then she called her maids and said, "Stay where you are, you girls. Can you not see a man without running away from him? Do you take him for a robber or a murderer? Neither he nor anyone else can come here to do us Phaeacians any harm, for we are dear to the gods, and live apart on a land's end that juts into the sounding sea, and have nothing to do with any other people. This is only some poor man who has lost his way, and we must be kind to him, for strangers and foreigners in distress are under Zeus' protection,[†] and will take what they can get and be thankful; so, girls, give the poor fellow something to eat and drink, and wash him in the stream at some place that is sheltered from the wind."

On this the maids left off running away and began calling one another back. They made Odysseus sit down in the shelter as Nausicaa had told them, and brought him a shirt and cloak. They also brought him the little golden cruse of oil, and told him to go and wash in the stream. But Odysseus said, "Young women, please to stand a little on one side that I may wash the brine from my shoulders and anoint myself with oil, for it is long enough since my skin has had a drop of oil upon it. I cannot wash as long as you all keep standing there. I am ashamed to bare myself before a number of finely tressed young women."

Then they stood on one side and went to tell the girl, while Odysseus washed himself in the stream and scrubbed the brine from his back and from his broad shoulders. When he had thoroughly washed himself, and had got the brine out of his hair, he anointed himself with oil, and put on the clothes which the girl had given him; Athena then made him look taller and stronger than before, she also made the hair grow thick on the top of his head, and flow down in curls like hyacinth blossoms; she glorified him about the head and shoulders as a skilful workman who has studied art of all kinds under Hephaestus and Athena enriches a piece of silver plate by gilding it—and his work is full of beauty. Then he went and sat down a little way off upon the beach, looking quite young and handsome,[†] and the girl gazed on him with admiration; then she said to her maids:

"Hush, my dears, for I want to say something. I believe the gods who live in heaven have sent this man to the Phaeacians. When I first saw him I thought him plain, but now his appearance is like that of the gods who dwell in heaven. I should like my future husband to be just such another as he is, if he would only stay here and not want to go away. However, give him something to eat and drink."

They did as they were told, and set food before Odysseus, who ate and drank ravenously, for it was long since he had had food of any kind. Meanwhile, Nausicaa bethought her of another matter. She got the linen folded and placed in the wagon, she then yoked the mules, and, as she took her seat, she called Odysseus:

"Stranger," said she, "rise and let us be going back to the town; I will introduce you at the house of my excellent father, where I can tell you that you will meet all the best people among the Phaeacians. But be sure and do as I bid you, for you seem to be a sensible person. As long as we are going past the fields and farm lands, follow briskly behind the wagon along with the maids and I will lead the way myself. Presently, however, we shall come to the town, where you will find a high wall running all round it, and a good harbor on either side with a narrow entrance into the city, and the ships will be drawn up by the road side, for everyone has a place where his own ship can lie. You will see the market place with a temple of Poseidon in the middle of it, and paved with large stones bedded in the earth. Here people deal in ship's gear of all kinds, such as cables and sails, and here, too, are the places where oars are made, for the Phaeacians are not a nation of archers; they know nothing about bows and arrows, but are a sea-faring folk, and pride themselves on their masts, oars, and ships, with which they travel far over the sea.

"I am afraid of the gossip and scandal that may be set on foot against me later on;[†] for the people here are very ill-natured, and some low fellow, if he met us, might say, 'Who is this fine-looking stranger that is going about with Nausicaa? Where did she find him? I suppose she is going to marry him. Perhaps he is a vagabond sailor whom she has taken from some foreign vessel, for we have no neighbors; or some god has at last come down from heaven in answer to her prayers, and she is going to live with him all the rest of her life. It would be a good thing if she would take herself off and find a husband somewhere else, for she will not look at one of the many excellent young Phaeacians who are in love with her.' This is the kind of disparaging remark that would be made about me, and I could not complain, for I should myself be scandalized at seeing any other girl do the like, and go about with men in spite of everybody, while her father and mother were still alive, and without having been married in the face of all the world.

"If, therefore, you want my father to give you an escort and to help you home, do as I bid you; you will see a beautiful grove of poplars by the road side dedicated to Athena; it has a well in it and a meadow all round it. Here my father has a field of rich garden ground, about as far from the town as a man's voice will carry. Sit down there and wait for a while till the rest of us can get into the town and reach my father's house. Then, when you think we must have done this, come into the town and ask the way to the house of my father Alcinous. You will have no difficulty in finding it; any child will point it out to you, for no one else in the whole town has anything like such a fine house as he has. When you have got past the gates and through the outer court, go right across the inner court till you come to my mother. You will find her sitting by the fire and spinning her purple wool by firelight. It is a fine sight to see her as she leans back against one of the bearing-posts with her maids all ranged behind her. Close to her seat stands that of my father, on which he sits like an immortal god. Never mind him, but go up to my mother, and lay your hands upon her knees if you would get home quickly. If you can gain her over, you may hope to see your own country again, no matter how distant it may be."

So saying she lashed the mules with her whip and they left the river. The mules drew well, and their hoofs went up and down upon the road. She was careful not to go too fast for Odysseus and the maids who were following on foot along with the wagon, so she plied her whip with judgement. As the sun was going down they came to the sacred grove of Athena, and there Odysseus sat down and prayed to the mighty daughter of Zeus.

"Hear me," he cried, "daughter of Aegis-bearing Zeus, unweariable, hear me now, for you gave no heed to my prayers when Poseidon was wrecking me.[†] Now, therefore, have pity upon me and grant that I may find friends and be hospitably received by the Phaeacians."

Thus did he pray, and Athena heard his prayer, but she would not show herself to him openly, for she was afraid of her uncle Poseidon, who was still furious in his endeavors to prevent Odysseus from getting home.

BOOK VII

Reception of Odysseus at the palace of King Alcinous.

T HUS, THEN, DID Odysseus wait and pray; but the girl drove on to the town. When she reached her father's house she drew up at the gateway, and her brothers—comely as the gods—gathered round her, took the mules out of the wagon, and carried the clothes into the house, while she went to her own room, where an old servant, Eurymedusa of Apeira, lit the fire for her. This old woman had been brought by sea from Apeira, and had been chosen as a prize for Alcinous because he was king over the Phaeacians, and the people obeyed him as though he were a god. She had been nurse to Nausicaa, and had now lit the fire for her, and brought her supper for her into her own room.

Presently Odysseus got up to go towards the town; and Athena shed a thick mist all round him to hide him in case any of the proud Phaeacians who met him should be rude to him, or ask him who he was. Then, as he was just entering the town, she came towards him in the likeness of a little girl carrying a pitcher.[†] She stood right in front of him, and Odysseus said:

"My dear, will you be so kind as to show me the house of king Alcinous? I am an unfortunate foreigner in distress, and do not know one in your town and country."

Then Athena said, "Yes, father stranger, I will show you the house you want, for Alcinous lives quite close to my own father. I will go before you and show the way, but say not a word as you go, and do not look at any man, nor ask him questions; for the people here cannot abide strangers, and do not like men who come from some other place. They are a sea-faring folk, and sail the seas by the grace of Poseidon in ships that glide along like thought, or as a bird in the air."

On this she led the way, and Odysseus followed in her steps; but not one of the Phaeacians could see him as he passed through the city in the midst of them; for the great goddess Athena in her good will towards him had hidden him in a thick cloud of darkness. He admired their harbors, ships, places of assembly, and the lofty walls of the city, which, with the palisade on top of them, were very striking, and when they reached the king's house Athena said:

"This is the house, father stranger, which you would have me show you. You will find a number of great people sitting at table, but do not be afraid;† go straight in, for the bolder a man is the more likely he is to carry his point, even though he is a stranger. First find the queen. Her name is Arete, and she comes of the same family as her husband Alcinous. They both descend originally from Poseidon, who was father to Nausithous by Periboea, a woman of great beauty. Periboea was the youngest daughter of Eurymedon, who at one time reigned over the giants, but he ruined his ill-fated people and lost his own life to boot.

"Poseidon, however, lay with his daughter, and she had a son by him, the great Nausithous, who reigned over the Phaeacians. Nausithous had two sons Rhexenor and Alcinous;† Apollo killed the first of them while he was still a bridegroom and without male issue; but he left a daughter Arete, whom Alcinous married, and honors as no other woman is honored of all those that keep house along with their husbands.

"Thus she both was, and still is, respected beyond measure by her children, by Alcinous himself, and by the whole people, who look upon her as a goddess, and greet her whenever she goes about the city, for she is a thoroughly good woman both in head and heart, and when any women are friends of hers, she will help their husbands also to settle their disputes. If you can gain her good will, you may have every hope of seeing your friends again, and getting safely back to your home and country."

Then Athena left Scheria and went away over the sea. She went to Marathon and to the spacious streets of Athens, where she entered the abode of Erechtheus; but Odysseus went on to the house of Alcinous, and he pondered much as he paused a while before reaching the threshold of bronze, for the splendor of the palace was like that of the sun or moon. The walls on either side were of bronze from end to end, and the cornice was of blue enamel. The doors were gold, and hung on pillars of silver that rose from a floor of bronze, while the lintel was silver and the hook of the door was of gold.

On either side there stood gold and silver mastiffs which Hephaestus, with his consummate skill, had fashioned expressly to keep watch over the palace of king Alcinous; so they were immortal and could never grow old. Seats were ranged all along the wall, here and there from one end to the other, with coverings of fine woven work which the women of the house had made. Here the chief persons of the Phaeacians used to sit and eat and drink, for there was abundance at all seasons; and there were golden figures of young men with lighted torches in their hands, raised on pedestals, to give light by night to those who were at table. There are fifty maid servants in the house, some of whom are always grinding rich yellow grain at the mill, while others work at the loom, or sit and spin, and their shuttles go backwards and forwards like the fluttering of aspen leaves, while the linen is so closely woven that it will turn oil. As the Phaeacians are the best sailors in the world, so their women excel all others in weaving, for Athena has taught them all manner of useful arts, and they are very intelligent.

Outside the gate of the outer court there is a large garden of about four acres with a wall all round it. It is full of beautiful trees—pears, pomegranates, and the most delicious apples. There are luscious figs also, and olives in full growth. The fruits never rot nor fail all the year round, neither winter nor summer, for the air is so soft that a new crop ripens before the old has dropped. Pear grows on pear, apple on apple, and fig on fig, and so also with the grapes, for there is an excellent vineyard: on the level ground of a part of this, the grapes are being made into raisins; in another part they are being gathered; some are being trodden in the wine tubs, others further on have shed their blossom and are beginning to show fruit, others again are just changing color. In the furthest part of the ground there are beautifully arranged beds of flowers that are in bloom all the year round. Two streams go through it, the one turned in ducts throughout the whole garden, while the other is carried under the ground of the outer court to the house itself, and the town's people draw water from it. Such, then, were the splendours with which the gods had endowed the house of king Alcinous.

So here Odysseus stood for a while and looked about him, but when he had looked long enough he crossed the threshold and went within the precincts of the house. There he found all the chief people among the Phaeacians making their drink offerings to Hermes, which they always did the last thing before going away for the night. He went straight through the court, still hidden by the cloak of darkness in which Athena had enveloped him, till he reached Arete and King Alcinous; then he laid his hands upon the knees of the queen, and at that moment the miraculous darkness fell away from him and he became visible. Everyone was speechless with surprise at seeing a man there, but Odysseus began at once with his petition.

"Queen Arete," he exclaimed, "daughter of great Rhexenor, in my distress I humbly pray you, as also your husband and these your guests (whom may heaven prosper with long life and happiness, and may they leave their possessions to their children, and all the honors conferred upon them by the state) to help me home to my own country as soon as possible; for I have been long in trouble and away from my friends."

Then he sat down on the hearth among the ashes and they all held their peace, till presently the old hero Echeneus, who was an excellent speaker and an elder among the Phaeacians, plainly and in all honesty addressed them thus:

"Alcinous," said he, "it is not creditable to you that a stranger should be seen sitting among the ashes of your hearth; everyone is waiting to hear what you are about to say; tell him, then, to rise and take a seat on a stool inlaid with silver, and bid your servants mix some wine and water that we may make a drink offering to Zeus the lord of thunder, who takes all well disposed suppliants under his protection; and let the housekeeper give him some supper, of whatever there may be in the house."[†]

When Alcinous heard this he took Odysseus by the hand, raised him from the hearth, and bade him take the seat of Laodamas, who had been sitting beside him, and was his favorite son. A maid servant then brought him water in a beautiful golden ewer and poured it into a silver basin for him to wash his hands, and she drew a clean table beside him; an upper servant brought him bread and offered him many good things of what there was in the house, and Odysseus ate and drank. Then Alcinous said to one of the servants, "Pontonous, mix a cup of wine and hand it round that we may make drink-offerings to Zeus the lord of thunder, who is the protector of all well-disposed suppliants."

Pontonous then mixed wine and water, and handed it round after giving every man his drink-offering. When they had made their offerings, and had drunk each as much as he was minded, Alcinous said:

"Aldermen and town councillors of the Phaeacians, hear my words. You have had your supper, so now go home to bed. To-morrow morning I shall invite a still larger number of aldermen, and will give a sacrificial banquet in honor of our guest; we can then discuss the question of his escort, and consider how we may at once send him back rejoicing to his own country without trouble or inconvenience to himself, no matter how distant it may be. We must see that he comes to no harm while on his homeward journey, but when he is once at home he will have to take the luck he was born with for better or worse like other people. It is possible, however, that the stranger is one of the immortals who has come down from heaven to visit us; but in this case the gods are departing from their usual practice, for hitherto they have made themselves perfectly clear to us when we have been offering them hecatombs. They come and sit at our feasts just like one of our selves, and if any solitary wayfarer happens to stumble upon some one or other of them, they affect no concealment, for we are as near of kin to the gods as the Cyclopes and the savage giants are."

Then Odysseus said: "Pray, Alcinous, do not take any such notion into your head. I have nothing of the immortal about me, neither in body nor mind, and most resemble those among you who are the most afflicted. Indeed, were I to tell you all that heaven has seen fit to lay upon me, you would say that I was still worse off than they are. Nevertheless, let me sup in spite of sorrow, for an empty stomach is a very importunate thing, and thrusts itself on a man's notice no matter how dire is his distress. I am in great trouble, yet it insists that I shall eat and drink, bids me lay aside all memory of my sorrows and dwell only on the due replenishing of itself. As for yourselves, do as you propose, and at break of day set about helping me to get home. I shall be content to die if I may first once more behold my property, my bondsmen, and all the greatness of my house."

Thus did he speak. Everyone approved his saying, and agreed that he should have his escort inasmuch as he had spoken reasonably. Then when they had made their drink offerings, and had drunk each as much as he was minded they went home to bed every man in his own abode, leaving Odysseus in the cloister with Arete and Alcinous while the servants were taking the things away after supper. Arete was the first to speak, for she recognized the shirt, cloak, and good clothes that Odysseus was wearing, as the work of herself and of her maids; so she said, "Stranger, before we go any further, there is a question I should like to ask you. Who, and whence are you, and who gave you those clothes? Did you not say you had come here from beyond the sea?"

And Odysseus answered, "It would be a long story Madam, were I to relate in full the tale of my misfortunes, for the hand of heaven has been laid heavy upon me; but as regards your question, there is an island far away in the sea which is called 'the Ogygian.' Here dwells the cunning and powerful goddess Calypso, daughter of Atlas. She lives by herself far from all neighbors human or divine. Fortune, however, brought me to her hearth all desolate and alone, for Zeus struck my ship with his thunderbolts, and broke it up in mid-ocean. My brave comrades were drowned every man of them, but I stuck to the keel and was carried hither and thither for the space of nine days, till at last during the darkness of the tenth night the gods brought me to the Ogygian island where the great goddess Calypso lives. She took me in and treated me with the utmost kindness; indeed she wanted to make me immortal that I might never grow old, but she could not persuade me to let her do so.

"I stayed with Calypso seven years straight on end, and watered the good clothes she gave me with my tears during the whole time; but at last when the eighth year came round she bade me depart of her own free will, either because Zeus had told her she must, or because she had changed her mind. She sent me from her island on a raft, which she provisioned with abundance of bread and wine. Moreover she gave me good stout clothing, and sent me a wind that blew both warm and fair. Days seven and ten did I sail over the sea, and on the eighteenth I caught sight of the first outlines of the mountains upon your coast—and glad indeed was I to set eyes upon them. Nevertheless there was still much trouble in store for me, for at this point Poseidon would let me go no further, and raised a great storm against me; the sea was so terribly high that I could no longer keep to my raft, which went to pieces under the fury of the gale, and I had to swim for it, till wind and current brought me to your shores.

"There I tried to land, but could not, for it was a bad place and the waves dashed me against the rocks, so I again took to the sea and swam on till I came to a river that seemed the most likely landing place, for there were no rocks and it was sheltered from the wind. Here, then, I got out of the water and gathered my senses together again. Night was coming on, so I left the river, and went into a thicket, where I covered myself all over with leaves, and presently heaven sent me off into a very deep sleep. Sick and sorry as I was I slept among the leaves all night, and through the next day till afternoon, when I woke as the sun was westering, and saw your daughter's maid servants playing upon the beach, and your daughter among them looking like a goddess. I besought her aid, and she proved to be of an excellent disposition, much more so than could be expected from so young a person—for young people are apt to be thoughtless. She gave me much bread and wine, and when she had had me washed in the river she also gave me the clothes in which you see me. Now, therefore, though it has pained me to do so, I have told you the whole truth."

Then Alcinous said, "Stranger, it was very wrong of my daughter not to bring you on at once to my house along with the maids, seeing that she was the first person whose aid you asked."

"Pray do not scold her," replied Odysseus; "she is not to blame. She did tell me to follow along with the maids, but I was ashamed and afraid, for I thought you might perhaps be displeased if you saw me. Every human being is sometimes a little suspicious and irritable."

"Stranger," replied Alcinous, "I am not the kind of man to get angry about nothing; it is always better to be reasonable; but by Father Zeus, Athena, and Apollo, now that I see what kind of person you are, and how much you think as I do, I wish you would stay here, marry my daughter, and become my son-in-law. If you will stay I will give you a house and an estate, but no one (heaven forbid) shall keep you here against your own wish, and that you may be sure of this I will attend tomorrow to the matter of your escort. You can sleep during the whole voyage if you like, and the men shall sail you over smooth waters either to your own home, or wherever you please, even though it be a long way further off than Euboea, which those of my people who saw it when they took yellow-haired Rhadamanthus to see Tityus the son of Gaia, tell me is the furthest of any place—and yet they did the whole voyage in a single day without distressing themselves, and came back again afterwards. You will thus see how much my ships excel all others, and what magnificent oarsmen my sailors are."

Then was Odysseus glad and prayed aloud saying, "Father Zeus, grant that Alcinous may do all as he has said, for so he will win an imperishable name among mankind, and at the same time I shall return to my country."

Thus did they converse. Then Arete told her maids to set a bed in the room that was in the gatehouse, and make it with good red rugs, and to spread coverlets on the top of them with woollen cloaks for Odysseus to wear. The maids went out with torches in their hands, and when they had made the bed they came up to Odysseus and said, "Rise, sir stranger, and come with us for your bed is ready," and glad indeed was he to go to his rest.

So Odysseus slept in a bed placed in a room over the echoing gateway; but Alcinous lay in the inner part of the house, with the queen his wife by his side.

B O O K *8* V I I I

Banquet in the house of Alcinous
The games

NOW WHEN THE child of morning, rosy-fingered Dawn, appeared, Alcinous and Odysseus both rose, and Alcinous led the way to the Phaeacian place of assembly, which was near the ships. When they got there they sat down side by side on a seat of polished stone, while Athena took the form of one of Alcinous' servants,† and went round the town in order to help Odysseus to get home. She went up to the citizens, man by man, and said, "Aldermen and town councillors of the Phaeacians, come to the assembly all of you and listen to the stranger who has just come off a long voyage to the house of King Alcinous; he looks like an immortal god."

With these words she made them all want to come, and they flocked to the assembly till seats and standing room were alike crowded. Everyone was struck with the appearance of Odysseus, for Athena had beautified him about the head and shoulders, making him look taller and stouter† than he really was, that he might impress the Phaeacians favorably as being a very remarkable man, and might come off well in the many trials of skill to which they would challenge him. Then, when they were got together, Alcinous spoke:

"Hear me," said he, "aldermen and town councillors of the Phaeacians, that I may speak even as I am minded. This stranger, whoever he may be, has found his way to my house from somewhere or other either East or West. He wants an escort and wishes to have the matter settled. Let us then get one ready for him, as we have done for others before him; indeed, no one who ever yet came to my house has been able to complain of me for not speeding on his way soon enough. Let us draw a ship into the sea—one that has never yet made a voyage—and man her with two and fifty of our smartest young sailors. Then when you have made fast your oars each by his own seat, leave the ship and come to my house to prepare a feast. I am giving these instructions to the young men who will form the crew, for as regards you aldermen and town councillors, you will join me in entertaining our guest in the cloisters.† I can take no excuses, and we will have Demodocus to sing to us; for there is no bard like him whatever he may choose to sing about."

Alcinous then led the way, and the others followed after, while a servant went to fetch Demodocus. The fifty-two picked oarsmen went to the sea shore as they had been told, and when they got there they drew the ship into the water, got her mast and sails inside her, bound the oars to the thole-pins with twisted thongs of leather, all in due course, and spread the white sails aloft. They moored the vessel a little way out from land, and then came on shore and went to the house of King Alcinous. The out houses, yards, and all the precincts were filled with crowds of men in great multitudes both old and young; and Alcinous killed them a dozen sheep, eight full grown pigs, and two oxen. These they skinned and dressed so as to provide a magnificent banquet.

A servant presently led in the famous bard Demodocus, whom the muse had dearly loved, but to whom she had given both good and evil, for though she had endowed him with a divine gift of song, she had robbed him of his eyesight.† Pontonous set a seat for him among the guests, leaning it up against a bearing-post. He hung the lyre for him on a peg over his head, and showed him where he was to feel for it with his hands. He also set a fair table with a basket of victuals by his side, and a cup of wine from which he might drink whenever he was so disposed.

The company then laid their hands upon the good things that were before them, but as soon as they had had enough to eat and drink, the muse inspired Demodocus to sing the feats of heroes, and more especially a matter that was then in the mouths of all men, to wit, the quarrel between Odysseus and Achilles, and the fierce words that they heaped on one another as they sat together at a banquet. But Agamemnon was glad when he heard his chieftains quarrelling with one another,† for Apollo had foretold him this at Pytho when he crossed the stone floor to consult the oracle. Here was the beginning of the evil that by the will of Zeus fell both upon Danaans and Trojans.

Thus sang the bard, but Odysseus drew his purple mantle over his head and covered his face, for he was ashamed to let the Phaeacians see that he was weeping. When the bard left off singing he wiped the tears from his eyes, uncovered his face, and, taking his cup, made a drink-offering to the gods; but when the Phaeacians pressed Demodocus to sing further, for they delighted in his lays, then Odysseus again drew his mantle over his head and wept bitterly.

No one noticed his distress except Alcinous, who was sitting near him, and heard the heavy sighs that he was heaving. So he at once said, "Aldermen and town councillors of the Phaeacians, we have had enough now, both of the feast, and of the minstrelsy that is its due accompaniment; let us proceed therefore to the athletic sports, so that our guest on his return home may be able to tell his friends how much we surpass all other nations as boxers, wrestlers, jumpers, and runners."

With these words he led the way, and the others followed after. A servant hung Demodocus' lyre on its peg for him, led him out of the cloister, and set him on the same way as that along which all the chief men of the Phaeacians were going to see the sports; a crowd of several thousands of people followed them, and there were many excellent competitors for all the prizes. Acroneos, Ocyalus, Elatreus, Nauteus, Prymneus, Anchialus, Eretmeus, Ponteus, Proreus, Thoon, Anabesineus, and Amphialus son of Polyneus son of Tecton. There was also Euryalus son of Naubolus, who was like Ares himself, and was the best looking man among the Phaeacians except Laodamas. Three sons of Alcinous, Laodamas, Halios, and Clytoneus, competed also.

The foot races came first. The course was set out for them from the starting post, and they raised a dust upon the plain as they all flew forward at the same moment. Clytoneus came in first by a long way; he left everyone else behind him by the length of the furrow that a couple of mules can plough in a fallow field. They then turned to the painful art of wrestling, and here Euryalus proved to be the best man. Amphialus excelled all the others in jumping, while at throwing the disc there was no one who could approach Elatreus. Alcinous' son Laodamas was the best boxer, and he it was who presently said, when they had all been diverted with the games, "Let us ask the stranger whether he excels in any of these sports; he seems very powerfully built; his thighs, calves, hands, and neck are of prodigious strength, nor is he at all old, but he has suffered much lately, and there is nothing like the sea for making havoc with a man, no matter how strong he is."

"You are quite right, Laodamas," replied Euryalus, "go up to your guest and speak to him about it yourself."

When Laodamas heard this he made his way into the middle of the crowd and said to Odysseus, "I hope, Sir, that you will enter yourself for some one or other of our competitions if you are skilled in any of them—and you must have gone in for many a one before now. There is nothing that does anyone so much credit all his life long as the showing himself a proper man with his hands and feet. Have a try therefore at something, and banish all sorrow from your mind. Your return home will not be long delayed, for the ship is already drawn into the water, and the crew is found."

Odysseus answered, "Laodamas, why do you taunt me in this way? my mind is set rather on cares than contests; I have been through infinite trouble, and am come among you now as a suppliant, praying your king and people to further me on my return home."

Then Euryalus reviled him outright and said, "I gather, then, that you are unskilled in any of the many sports that men generally delight in. I suppose you are one of those grasping traders that go about in ships as captains or merchants, and who think of nothing but of their outward freights and homeward cargoes.[†] There does not seem to be much of the athlete about you."

"For shame, Sir," answered Odysseus, fiercely, "you are an insolent fellow—so true is it that the gods do not grace all men alike in speech, person, and understanding. One man may be of weak presence, but heaven has adorned this with such a good conversation that he charms everyone who sees him; his honeyed moderation carries his hearers with him so that he is leader in all assemblies of his fellows, and wherever he goes he is looked up to. Another may be as handsome as a god, but his good looks are not crowned with discretion. This is your case. No god could make a finer looking fellow than you are, but you are a fool. Your ill-judged remarks have made me exceedingly angry, and you are quite mistaken, for I excel in a great many athletic exercises; indeed, so long as I had youth and strength, I was among the first athletes of the age. Now, however, I am worn out by labor and sorrow, for I have gone through much both on the field of battle and by the waves of the weary sea; still, in spite of all this I will compete, for your taunts have stung me to the quick."[†]

So he hurried up without even taking his cloak off, and seized a disc, larger, more massive and much heavier than those used by the Phaeacians when disc-throwing among themselves. Then, swinging it back, he threw it from his brawny hand, and it made a humming sound in the air as he did so. The Phaeacians quailed beneath the rushing of its flight as it sped gracefully from his hand, and flew beyond any mark that had been made yet. Athena, in the form of a man, came and marked the place where it had fallen.[†] "A blind man, Sir," said she, "could easily tell your mark by groping for it—it is so far ahead of any other. You may make your mind easy about this contest, for no Phaeacian can come near to such a throw as yours."

Odysseus was glad when he found he had a friend among the lookers-on, so he began to speak more pleasantly. "Young men," said he, "come up to that throw if you can, and I will throw another disc as heavy or even heavier. If anyone wants to have a bout with me let him come on, for I am exceedingly angry; I will box, wrestle, or run, I do not care what it is, with any man of you all except Laodamas, but not with him because I am his guest, and one cannot compete with one's own personal friend. At least I do not think it a prudent or a sensible thing for a guest to challenge his host's family at any game, especially when he is in a foreign country.[†] He will cut the ground from under his own feet if he does; but I make no exception as regards anyone else, for I want to have the matter out and know which is the best man. I am a good hand at every kind of athletic sport known among mankind. I am an excellent archer. In battle I am always the first to bring a man down with my arrow, no matter how many more are taking aim at him alongside of me. Philoctetes was the only man who could shoot better than I could when we Achaeans were before Troy and in practice. I far excel everyone else in the whole world, of those who still eat bread upon the face of the earth, but I should not like to shoot against the mighty dead, such as Heracles, or Eurytus the Oechalian—men who could shoot against the gods themselves. This in fact was how Eurytus came prematurely by his end, for Apollo was angry with him and killed him because he challenged him as an archer. I can throw a dart farther than anyone else can shoot an arrow. Running is the only point in respect of which I am afraid some of the Phaeacians might beat me, for I have been brought down very low at sea; my provisions ran short, and therefore I am still weak."

They all held their peace except King Alcinous, who began, "Sir, we have had much pleasure in hearing all that you have told us, from which I understand that you are willing to show your prowess, as having been displeased with some insolent remarks that have been made to you by one of our athletes, and which could never have been uttered by anyone who knows how to talk with propriety. I hope you will apprehend my meaning, and will explain to any one of your chief men who may be dining with yourself and your family when you get home, that we have an hereditary aptitude for accomplishments of all kinds. We are not particularly remarkable for our boxing, nor yet as wrestlers, but we are singularly fleet of foot and are excellent sailors. We are extremely fond of good dinners, music, and dancing; we also like frequent changes of linen, warm baths, and good beds, so now, please, some of you who are the best dancers set about dancing, that our guest on his return home may be able to tell his friends how much we surpass all other nations as sailors, runners, dancers, and minstrels. Demodocus has left his lyre at my house, so run some one or other of you and fetch it for him."

On this a servant hurried off to bring the lyre from the king's house, and the nine men who had been chosen as stewards stood forward. It was their business to manage everything connected with the sports, so they made the ground smooth and marked a wide space for the dancers. Presently the servant came back with Demodocus' lyre, and he took his place in the midst of them, whereon the best young dancers in the town began to foot and trip it so nimbly that Odysseus was delighted with the merry twinkling of their feet.

Meanwhile the bard began to sing the loves of Ares and Aphrodite, and how they first began their intrigue in the house of Hephaestus. Ares made Aphrodite many presents, and defiled King Hephaestus' marriage bed, so the sun, who saw what they were about, told Hephaestus. Hephaestus was very angry when he heard such dreadful news, so he went to his smithy brooding mischief, got his great anvil into its place, and began to forge some chains which none could either unloose or break, so that they might stay there in that place. When he had finished his snare he went into his bedroom and festooned the bed-posts all over with chains like cobwebs; he also let many hang down from the great beam of the ceiling. Not even a god could see them so fine and subtle were they. As soon as he had spread the chains all over the bed, he made as though he were setting out for the fair state of Lemnos, which of all places in the world was the one he was most fond of. But Ares kept no blind look out, and as soon as he saw him start, hurried off to his house, burning with love for Aphrodite.

Now Aphrodite was just come in from a visit to her father Zeus, and was about sitting down when Ares came inside the house, and said as he took her hand in his own, "Let us go to the couch of Hephaestus: he is not at home, but is gone off to Lemnos among the Sintians, whose speech is barbarous."

She was nothing loth, so they went to the couch to take their rest, whereon they were caught in the toils which cunning Hephaestus had spread for them, and could neither get up nor stir hand or foot, but found too late that they were in a trap.† Then Hephaestus came up to them, for he had turned back before reaching Lemnos, when his scout the sun told him what was going on. He was in a furious passion, and stood in the vestibule making a dreadful noise as he shouted to all the gods.

"Father Zeus," he cried, "and all you other blessed gods who live for ever, come here and see the ridiculous and disgraceful sight that I will show you. Zeus' daughter Aphrodite is always dishonoring me because I am lame. She is in love with Mars, who is handsome and clean built, whereas I am a cripple— but my parents are to blame for that, not I; they ought never to have begotten me. Come and see the pair together asleep on my bed. It makes me furious to look at them. They are very fond of one another, but I do not think they will lie there longer than they can help, nor do I think that they will sleep much; there, however, they shall stay till her father has repaid me the sum I gave him for his baggage of a daughter, who is fair but not honest."

On this the gods gathered to the house of Hephaestus. Earth-encircling Poseidon came, and Hermes the bringer of luck, and King Apollo, but the goddesses stayed at home all of them for shame. Then the givers of all good things stood in the doorway, and the blessed gods roared with inextinguishable laughter, as they saw how cunning Hephaestus had been, whereon one would turn towards his neighbor saying:

"Ill deeds do not prosper, and the weak confound the strong. See how limping Hephaestus, lame as he is, has caught Ares who is the fleetest god in heaven; and now Ares will be cast in heavy damages."

Thus did they converse, but King Apollo said to Hermes, "Messenger

Hermes, giver of good things, you would not care how strong the chains were, would you, if you could sleep with Aphrodite?"

"King Apollo," answered Hermes, "I only wish I might get the chance, though there were three times as many chains—and you might look on, all of you, gods and goddesses, but I would sleep with her if I could."

The immortal gods burst out laughing as they heard him, but Poseidon took it all seriously, and kept on imploring Hephaestus to set Ares free again. "Let him go," he cried, "and I will undertake, as you require, that he shall pay you all the damages that are held reasonable among the immortal gods."

"Do not," replied Hephaestus, "ask me to do this; a bad man's bond is bad security; what remedy could I enforce against you if Ares should go away and leave his debts behind him along with his chains?"

"Hephaestus," said Poseidon, "if Ares goes away without paying his damages, I will pay you myself." So Hephaestus answered, "In this case I cannot and must not refuse you."

Thereon he loosed the bonds that bound them, and as soon as they were free they scampered off, Ares to Thrace and laughter-loving Aphrodite to Cyprus and to Paphos, where is her grove and her altar fragrant with burnt offerings. Here the Graces bathed her, and anointed her with oil of ambrosia such as the immortal gods make use of, and they clothed her in raiment of the most enchanting beauty.

Thus sang the bard, and both Odysseus and the seafaring Phaeacians were charmed as they heard him.

Then Alcinous told Laodamas and Halius to dance alone, for there was no one to compete with them. So they took a red ball which Polybus had made for them, and one of them bent himself backwards and threw it up towards the clouds, while the other jumped from off the ground and caught it with ease before it came down again. When they had done throwing the ball straight up into the air they began to dance, and at the same time kept on throwing it backwards and forwards to one another, while all the young men in the ring applauded and made a great stamping with their feet. Then Odysseus said:

"King Alcinous, you said your people were the nimblest dancers in the world, and indeed they have proved themselves to be so. I was astonished as I saw them."

The king was delighted at this, and exclaimed to the Phaeacians, "Aldermen and town councillors, our guest seems to be a person of singular judgement; let us give him such proof of our hospitality as he may reasonably expect. There are twelve chief men among you, and counting myself there are thirteen; contribute, each of you, a clean cloak, a shirt, and a talent of fine gold; let us give him all this in a lump down at once, so that when he gets his supper he may do so with a light heart. As for Euryalus he will have to make a formal apology and a present too, for he has been rude."

Thus did he speak. The others all of them applauded his saying, and sent their servants to fetch the presents. Then Euryalus said, "King Alcinous, I will give the stranger all the satisfaction you require. He shall have my sword, which is of bronze, all but the hilt, which is of silver. I will also give him the scabbard of newly sawn ivory into which it fits. It will be worth a great deal to him."†

As he spoke he placed the sword in the hands of Odysseus and said, "Good luck to you, father stranger; if anything has been said amiss may the winds blow it away with them, and may heaven grant you a safe return, for I understand you have been long away from home, and have gone through much hardship."

To which Odysseus answered, "Good luck to you too my friend, and may the gods grant you every happiness. I hope you will not miss the sword you have given me along with your apology."

With these words he girded the sword about his shoulders and towards sundown the presents began to make their appearance, as the servants of the donors kept bringing them to the house of King Alcinous; here his sons received them, and placed them under their mother's charge. Then Alcinous led the way to the house and bade his guests take their seats.

"Wife," said he, turning to Queen Arete, "Go, fetch the best chest we have, and put a clean cloak and shirt in it. Also, set a copper on the fire and heat some water; our guest will take a warm bath; see also to the careful packing of the presents that the noble Phaeacians have made him; he will thus better enjoy both his supper and the singing that will follow. I shall myself give him this golden goblet—which is of exquisite workmanship—that he may be reminded of me for the rest of his life whenever he makes a drink offering to Zeus, or to any of the gods."†

Then Arete told her maids to set a large tripod upon the fire as fast as they could, whereon they set a tripod full of bath water on to a clear fire; they threw on sticks to make it blaze, and the water became hot as the flame played about the belly of the tripod. Meanwhile Arete brought a magnificent chest from her own room, and inside it she packed all the beautiful presents of gold and raiment which the Phaeacians had brought. Lastly she added a cloak and a good shirt from Alcinous, and said to Odysseus:

"See to the lid yourself, and have the whole bound round at once, for fear anyone should rob you by the way when you are asleep in your ship."

When Odysseus heard this he put the lid on the chest and made it fast with a bond that Circe† had taught him. He had done so before an upper servant told him to come to the bath and wash himself. He was very glad of a warm bath, for he had had no one to wait upon him ever since he left the house of Calypso, who as long as he remained with her had taken as good care of him as though he had been a god. When the servants had done washing and anointing him with oil, and had given him a clean cloak and shirt, he left the bath room and joined the guests who were sitting over their wine. Lovely Nausicaa stood by one of the bearing-posts supporting the roof of the cloister, and admired him as she saw him pass. "Farewell stranger," said she, "do not forget me when you are safe at home again, for it is to me first that you owe a ransom for having saved your life."

And Odysseus said, "Nausicaa, daughter of great Alcinous, may Zeus the mighty husband of Hera, grant that I may reach my home; so shall I bless you as my guardian angel all my days, for it was you who saved me."

When he had said this, he seated himself beside Alcinous. Supper was then served, and the wine was mixed for drinking. A servant led in the favorite bard Demodocus, and set him in the midst of the company, near one of the bearing-posts supporting the cloister, that he might lean against it. Then Odysseus cut off a piece of roast pork with much fat (for there was abundance left on the joint) and said to a servant, "Take this piece of pork over to Demodocus and tell him to eat it;[†] for all the pain his lays may cause me I will salute him none the less; bards are honored and respected throughout the world, for the muse teaches them their songs and loves them."

The servant carried the pork in his fingers over to Demodocus, who took it and was very much pleased. They then laid their hands on the good things that were before them, and as soon as they had had to eat and drink, Odysseus said to Demodocus, "Demodocus, there is no one in the world whom I admire more than I do you. You must have studied under the Muse, Zeus' daughter, and under Apollo, so accurately do you sing the return of the Achaeans with all their sufferings and adventures. If you were not there yourself, you must have heard it all from someone who was. Now, however, change your song and tell us of the wooden horse which Epeus made with the assistance of Athena, and which Odysseus got by stratagem into the fort of Troy after freighting it with the men who afterwards sacked the city.[†] If you will sing this tale aright I will tell all the world how magnificently heaven has endowed you."

The bard inspired of heaven took up the story at the point where some of the Argives set fire to their tents and sailed away while others, hidden within the horse, were waiting with Odysseus in the Trojan place of assembly. For the Trojans themselves had drawn the horse into their fortress, and it stood there while they sat in council round it, and were in three minds as to what they should do. Some were for breaking it up then and there; others would have it dragged to the top of the rock on which the fortress stood, and then thrown down the precipice; while yet others were for letting it remain as an offering and propitiation for the gods. And this was how they settled it in the end, for the city was doomed when it took in that horse, within which were all the bravest of the Argives waiting to bring death and destruction on the Trojans. Anon he sang how the sons of the Achaeans issued from the horse, and sacked the town, breaking out from their ambuscade. He sang how they overran the city hither and thither and ravaged it, and how Odysseus went raging like Ares along with Menelaus to the house of Deiphobus. It was there that the fight raged most furiously, nevertheless by Athena's help he was victorious.[†]

All this he told, but Odysseus was overcome as he heard him, and his cheeks were wet with tears. He wept as a woman weeps when she throws herself on the body of her husband who has fallen before his own city and people, fighting bravely in defense of his home and children. She screams aloud and flings her arms about him as he lies gasping for breath and dying, but her enemies beat her from behind about the back and shoulders, and carry her off into slavery, to a life of labor and sorrow, and the beauty fades from her cheeks—even so piteously did Odysseus weep, but none of those present perceived his tears except Alcinous, who was sitting near him, and could hear the sobs and sighs that he was heaving.[†] The king, therefore, at once rose and said:

"Aldermen and town councillors of the Phaeacians, let Demodocus cease his song, for there are those present who do not seem to like it. From the moment that we had done supper and Demodocus began to sing, our guest has been all the time groaning and lamenting. He is evidently in great trouble, so let the bard leave off, that we may all enjoy ourselves, hosts and guest alike. This will be much more as it should be, for all these festivities, with the escort and the presents that we are making with so much good will are wholly in his honor, and anyone with even a moderate amount of right feeling knows that he ought to treat a guest and a suppliant as though he were his own brother.

"Therefore, Sir, do you on your part affect no more concealment nor reserve in the matter about which I shall ask you; it will be more polite in you to give me a plain answer; tell me the name by which your father and mother over yonder used to call you, and by which you were known among your neighbors and fellow-citizens. There is no one, neither rich nor poor, who is absolutely without any name whatever, for people's fathers and mothers give them names as soon as they are born. Tell me also your country, nation, and city, that our ships may shape their purpose accordingly and take you there. For the Phaeacians have no pilots; their vessels have no rudders as those of other nations have, but the ships themselves understand what it is that we are thinking about and want; they know all the cities and countries in the whole world, and can traverse the sea just as well even when it is covered with mist and cloud, so that there is no danger of being wrecked or coming to any harm. Still I do remember hearing my father say that Poseidon was angry with us for being too easy-going in the matter of giving people escorts. He said that one of these days he should wreck a ship of ours as it was returning from having escorted someone, and bury our city under a high mountain.[†] This is what

B O O K 9 I X

Odysseus declares himself and begins his story
The Cicons, Lotophagi, and Cyclopes

AND ODYSSEUS ANSWERED, "King Alcinous, it is a good thing to hear a bard with such a divine voice as this man has. There is nothing better or more delightful than when a whole people make merry together, with the guests sitting orderly to listen, while the table is loaded with bread and meats, and the cup-bearer draws wine and fills his cup for every man. This is indeed as fair a sight as a man can see. Now, however, since you are inclined to ask the story of my sorrows, and rekindle my own sad memories in respect of them, I do not know how to begin, nor yet how to continue and conclude my tale, for the hand of heaven has been laid heavily upon me.

"Firstly, then, I will tell you my name that you too may know it, and one day, if I outlive this time of sorrow, may become my guests though I live so far away from all of you. I am Odysseus son of Laertes, renowned among mankind for all manner of subtlety, so that my fame ascends to heaven. I live in Ithaca, where there is a high mountain called Neritum, covered with forests; and not far from it there is a group of islands very near to one another—Dulichium, Same, and the wooded island of Zacynthus. It lies squat on the horizon, all highest up in the sea towards the sunset, while the others lie away from it towards dawn. It is a rugged island, but it breeds brave men, and my eyes know none that they better love to look upon. The goddess Calypso kept me with her in her cave, and wanted me to marry her, as did also the cunning Aeaean goddess Circe; but they could neither of them persuade me, for there is nothing dearer to a man than his own country and his parents, and

91

however splendid a home he may have in a foreign country, if it be far from
father or mother, he does not care about it. Now, however, I will tell you of
the many hazardous adventures which by Zeus' will I met with on my return
from Troy.

"When I had set sail thence the wind took me first to Ismarus, which
is the city of the Cicons. There I sacked the town and put the people to the
sword. We took their wives and also much booty, which we divided equitably
amongst us, so that none might have reason to complain. I then said that we
had better make off at once, but my men very foolishly would not obey me,
so they stayed there drinking much wine and killing great numbers of sheep
and oxen on the sea shore. Meanwhile the Cicons cried out for help to other
Cicons who lived inland. These were more in number, and stronger, and they
were more skilled in the art of war, for they could fight, either from chariots or
on foot as the occasion served; in the morning, therefore, they came as thick
as leaves and bloom in summer, and the hand of heaven was against us, so
that we were hard pressed.[†] They set the battle in array near the ships, and the
hosts aimed their bronze-shod spears at one another. So long as the day waxed
and it was still morning, we held our own against them, though they were
more in number than we; but as the sun went down, towards the time when
men loose their oxen, the Cicons got the better of us, and we lost half a dozen
men from every ship we had; so we got away with those that were left.

"Thence we sailed onward with sorrow in our hearts, but glad to have
escaped death though we had lost our comrades, nor did we leave till we had
thrice invoked each one of the poor fellows who had perished by the hands of
the Cicons. Then Zeus raised the North wind against us till it blew a hurricane,
so that land and sky were hidden in thick clouds, and night sprang forth out of
the heavens. We let the ships run before the gale, but the force of the wind tore
our sails to tatters, so we took them down for fear of shipwreck, and rowed
our hardest towards the land. There we lay two days and two nights suffering
much alike from toil and distress of mind, but on the morning of the third day
we again raised our masts, set sail, and took our places, letting the wind and
steersmen direct our ship. I should have got home at that time unharmed had
not the North wind and the currents been against me as I was doubling Cape
Malea, and set me off my course hard by the island of Cythera.

"I was driven thence by foul winds for a space of nine days upon the sea,
but on the tenth day we reached the land of the Lotus-eaters, who live on a
food that comes from a kind of flower. Here we landed to take in fresh water,
and our crews got their mid-day meal on the shore near the ships. When
they had eaten and drunk I sent two of my company to see what manner of
men the people of the place might be, and they had a third man under them.
They started at once, and went about among the Lotus-eaters, who did them
no hurt, but gave them to eat of the lotus, which was so delicious that those

who ate of it left off caring about home, and did not even want to go back and say what had happened to them, but were for staying and munching lotus with the Lotus-eaters without thinking further of their return;† nevertheless, though they wept bitterly I forced them back to the ships and made them fast under the benches. Then I told the rest to go on board at once, lest any of them should taste of the lotus and leave off wanting to get home, so they took their places and smote the grey sea with their oars.

"We sailed hence, always in much distress, till we came to the land of the lawless and inhuman Cyclopes.† Now the Cyclopes neither plant nor plough, but trust in providence, and live on such wheat, barley, and grapes as grow wild without any kind of tillage, and their wild grapes yield them wine as the sun and the rain may grow them. They have no laws nor assemblies of the people, but live in caves on the tops of high mountains; each is lord and master in his family, and they take no account of their neighbors.

"Now off their harbor there lies a wooded and fertile island not quite close to the land of the Cyclopes, but still not far. It is over-run with wild goats, that breed there in great numbers and are never disturbed by foot of man; for sportsmen—who as a rule will suffer so much hardship in forest or among mountain precipices—do not go there, nor yet again is it ever ploughed or fed down, but it lies a wilderness untilled and unsown from year to year, and has no living thing upon it but only goats. For the Cyclopes have no ships, nor yet shipwrights who could make ships for them; they cannot therefore go from city to city, or sail over the sea to one another's country as people who have ships can do; if they had had these they would have colonized the island, for it is a very good one, and would yield everything in due season. There are meadows that in some places come right down to the sea shore, well watered and full of luscious grass; grapes would do there excellently; there is level land for ploughing, and it would always yield heavily at harvest time, for the soil is deep. There is a good harbor where no cables are wanted, nor yet anchors, nor need a ship be moored, but all one has to do is to beach one's vessel and stay there till the wind becomes fair for putting out to sea again. At the head of the harbor there is a spring of clear water coming out of a cave, and there are poplars growing all round it.

"Here we entered, but so dark was the night that some god must have brought us in, for there was nothing whatever to be seen. A thick mist hung all round our ships; the moon was hidden behind a mass of clouds so that no one could have seen the island if he had looked for it, nor were there any breakers to tell us we were close in shore before we found ourselves upon the land itself; when, however, we had beached the ships, we took down the sails, went ashore and camped upon the beach till daybreak.

"When the child of morning, rosy-fingered Dawn appeared, we admired the island and wandered all over it, while the nymphs Zeus' daughters roused the wild goats that we might get some meat for our dinner. On this we fetched our spears and bows and arrows from the ships, and dividing ourselves into three bands began to shoot the goats. Heaven sent us excellent sport; I had twelve ships with me, and each ship got nine goats, while my own ship had ten; thus through the livelong day to the going down of the sun we ate and drank our fill, and we had an abundance of wine left, for each one of us had taken many jars full when we sacked the city of the Cicons, and this had not yet run out. While we were feasting we kept turning our eyes towards the land of the Cyclopes, which was close by, and saw the smoke of their stubble fires. We could almost fancy we heard their voices and the bleating of their sheep and goats, but when the sun went down and it came on dark, we camped down upon the beach, and next morning I called a council.

" 'Stay here, my brave fellows,' said I, 'all the rest of you, while I go with my ship and exploit these people myself: I want to see if they are uncivilized savages, or a hospitable and humane race.'

"I went on board, bidding my men to do so also and loose the hawsers; so they took their places and smote the grey sea with their oars. When we got to the land, which was not far, there, on the face of a cliff near the sea, we saw a great cave overhung with laurels. It was a station for a great many sheep and goats, and outside there was a large yard, with a high wall round it made of stones built into the ground and of trees both pine and oak. This was the abode of a huge monster who was then away from home shepherding his flocks. He would have nothing to do with other people, but led the life of an outlaw. He was a horrid creature, not like a human being at all, but resembling rather some crag that stands out boldly against the sky on the top of a high mountain.[†]

"I told my men to draw the ship ashore, and stay where they were, all but the twelve best among them, who were to go along with myself. I also took a goatskin of sweet black wine which had been given me by Maron, son of Euanthes, who was priest of Apollo the patron god of Ismarus, and lived within the wooded precincts of the temple. When we were sacking the city we respected him, and spared his life, as also his wife and child; so he made me some presents of great value—seven talents of fine gold, and a bowl of silver, with twelve jars of sweet wine, unblended, and of the most exquisite flavour. Not a man nor maid in the house knew about it, but only himself, his wife, and one housekeeper: when he drank it he mixed twenty parts of water to one of wine, and yet the fragrance from the mixing-bowl was so exquisite that it was impossible to refrain from drinking. I filled a large skin with this wine, and took a wallet full of provisions with me, for my mind warned me that I might have to deal with some savage who would be of great strength, and would respect neither right nor law.

"We soon reached his cave, but he was out shepherding, so we went inside and took stock of all that we could see. His cheese-racks were loaded with cheeses, and he had more lambs and kids than his pens could hold. They were kept in separate flocks; first there were the hoggets, then the oldest of the younger lambs and lastly the very young ones all kept apart from one another; as for his dairy, all the vessels, bowls, and milk pails into which he milked, were swimming with whey. When they saw all this, my men begged me to let them first steal some cheeses, and make off with them to the ship; they would then return, drive down the lambs and kids, put them on board and sail away with them. It would have been indeed better if we had done so but I would not listen to them, for I wanted to see the owner himself, in the hope that he might give me a present. When, however, we saw him my poor men found him ill to deal with.

"We lit a fire, offered some of the cheeses in sacrifice, ate others of them, and then sat waiting till the Cyclops should come in with his sheep.† When he came, he brought in with him a huge load of dry firewood to light the fire for his supper, and this he flung with such a noise on to the floor of his cave that we hid ourselves for fear at the far end of the cavern. Meanwhile he drove all the ewes inside, as well as the she-goats that he was going to milk, leaving the males, both rams and he-goats, outside in the yards. Then he rolled a huge stone to the mouth of the cave—so huge that two and twenty strong four-wheeled wagons would not be enough to draw it from its place against the doorway. When he had so done he sat down and milked his ewes and goats, all in due course, and then let each of them have her own young. He curdled half the milk and set it aside in wicker strainers, but the other half he poured into bowls that he might drink it for his supper. When he had got through with all his work, he lit the fire, and then caught sight of us, whereon he said:

" 'Strangers, who are you? Where do sail from? Are you traders, or do you sail the sea as rovers, with your hands against every man, and every man's hand against you?'

"We were frightened out of our senses by his loud voice and monstrous form, but I managed to say, 'We are Achaeans on our way home from Troy, but by the will of Zeus, and stress of weather, we have been driven far out of our course. We are the people of Agamemnon, son of Atreus, who has won infinite renown throughout the whole world, by sacking so great a city and killing so many people. We therefore humbly pray you to show us some hospitality, and otherwise make us such presents as visitors may reasonably expect. May your excellency fear the wrath of heaven, for we are your suppliants, and Zeus takes all respectable travelers under his protection, for he is the avenger of all suppliants and foreigners in distress.'

"To this he gave me but a pitiless answer, 'Stranger,' said he, 'you are a fool, or else you know nothing of this country. Talk to me, indeed, about fearing the gods or shunning their anger? We Cyclopes do not care about Zeus or any of your blessed gods, for we are ever so much stronger than they. I shall not spare either yourself or your companions out of any regard for Zeus, unless I am in the humor for doing so. And now tell me where you made your ship fast when you came on shore. Was it round the point, or is she lying straight off the land?'

"He said this to draw me out, but I was too cunning to be caught in that way, so I answered with a lie; 'Poseidon,' said I, 'sent my ship on to the rocks at the far end of your country, and wrecked it. We were driven on to them from the open sea, but I and those who are with me escaped the jaws of death.'

"The cruel wretch vouchsafed me not one word of answer, but with a sudden clutch he gripped up two of my men at once and dashed them down upon the ground as though they had been puppies. Their brains were shed upon the ground, and the earth was wet with their blood. Then he tore them limb from limb and supped upon them. He gobbled them up like a lion in the wilderness, flesh, bones, marrow, and entrails, without leaving anything uneaten.† As for us, we wept and lifted up our hands to heaven on seeing such a horrid sight, for we did not know what else to do; but when the Cyclops had filled his huge paunch, and had washed down his meal of human flesh with a drink of neat milk, he stretched himself full length upon the ground among his sheep, and went to sleep. I was at first inclined to seize my sword, draw it, and drive it into his vitals, but I reflected that if I did we should all certainly be lost, for we should never be able to shift the stone which the monster had put in front of the door. So we stayed sobbing and sighing where we were till morning came.

"When the child of morning, rosy-fingered dawn, appeared, he again lit his fire, milked his goats and ewes, all quite rightly, and then let each have her own young one; as soon as he had got through with all his work, he clutched up two more of my men, and began eating them for his morning's meal. Presently, with the utmost ease, he rolled the stone away from the door and drove out his sheep, but he at once put it back again—as easily as though he were merely clapping the lid on to a quiver full of arrows. As soon as he had done so he shouted, and cried 'Shoo, shoo,' after his sheep to drive them on to the mountain; so I was left to scheme some way of taking my revenge and covering myself with glory.†

"In the end I deemed it would be the best plan to do as follows: The Cyclops had a great club which was lying near one of the sheep pens; it was of green olive wood, and he had cut it intending to use it for a staff as soon as it should be dry. It was so huge that we could only compare it to the mast of a twenty-oared merchant vessel of large burden, and able to venture out into open sea. I went up to this club and cut off about six feet of it; I then gave this piece to the men and told them to fine it evenly off at one end, which they proceeded to do, and lastly I brought it to a point myself, charring the end in the fire to make it harder. When I had done this I hid it under dung, which was lying about all over the cave, and told the men to cast lots which of them should venture along with myself to lift it and bore it into the monster's eye while he was asleep. The lot fell upon the very four whom I should have chosen, and I myself made five. In the evening the wretch came back from shepherding, and drove his flocks into the cave—this time driving them all inside, and not leaving any in the yards; I suppose some fancy must have taken him, or a god must have prompted him to do so. As soon as he had put the stone back to its place against the door, he sat down, milked his ewes and his goats all quite rightly, and then let each have her own young one; when he had got through with all this work, he gripped up two more of my men, and made his supper off them. So I went up to him with an ivy-wood bowl of black wine in my hands:

" 'Look here, Cyclops,' said I, 'you have been eating a great deal of man's flesh, so take this and drink some wine, that you may see what kind of liquor we had on board my ship. I was bringing it to you as a drink-offering, in the hope that you would take compassion upon me and further me on my way home, whereas all you do is to go on ramping and raving most intolerably. You ought to be ashamed of yourself; how can you expect people to come see you any more if you treat them in this way?'

"He then took the cup and drank. He was so delighted with the taste of the wine that he begged me for another bowl full. 'Be so kind,' he said, 'as to give me some more, and tell me your name at once. I want to make you a present that you will be glad to have. We have wine even in this country, for our soil grows grapes and the sun ripens them, but this drinks like Nectar and Ambrosia all in one.'

"I then gave him some more; three times did I fill the bowl for him, and three times did he drain it without thought or heed; then, when I saw that the wine had got into his head, I said to him as plausibly as I could: 'Cyclops, you ask my name and I will tell it you; give me, therefore, the present you promised me; my name is Noman; this is what my father and mother and my friends have always called me.'†

"But the cruel wretch said, 'Then I will eat all Noman's comrades before Noman himself, and will keep Noman for the last. This is the present that I will make him.'

"As he spoke he reeled, and fell sprawling face upwards on the ground. His great neck hung heavily backwards and a deep sleep took hold upon him. Presently he turned sick, and threw up both wine and the gobbets of human flesh on which he had been gorging, for he was very drunk. Then I thrust the beam of wood far into the embers to heat it, and encouraged my men lest any of them should turn faint-hearted. When the wood, green though it was, was about to blaze, I drew it out of the fire glowing with heat, and my men gathered round me, for heaven had filled their hearts with courage. We drove the sharp end of the beam into the monster's eye, and bearing upon it with all my weight I kept turning it round and round as though I were boring a hole in a ship's plank with an auger,† which two men with a wheel and strap can keep on turning as long as they choose. Even thus did we bore the red hot beam into his eye, till the boiling blood bubbled† all over it as we worked it round and round, so that the steam from the burning eyeball scalded his eyelids and eyebrows, and the roots of the eye sputtered in the fire. As a blacksmith plunges an axe or hatchet into cold water to temper it—for it is this that gives strength to the iron—and it makes a great hiss as he does so, even thus did the Cyclops' eye hiss round the beam of olive wood, and his hideous yells made the cave ring again. We ran away in a fright, but he plucked the beam all besmirched with gore from his eye, and hurled it from him in a frenzy of rage and pain, shouting as he did so to the other Cyclopes who lived on the bleak headlands near him; so they gathered from all quarters round his cave when they heard him crying, and asked what was the matter with him.

" 'What ails you, Polyphemus,' said they, 'that you make such a noise, breaking the stillness of the night, and preventing us from being able to sleep? Surely no man is carrying off your sheep? Surely no man is trying to kill you either by fraud or by force?'

"But Polyphemus shouted to them from inside the cave, 'Noman is killing me by fraud; no man is killing me by force.'

" 'Then,' said they, 'if no man is attacking you, you must be ill; when Zeus makes people ill, there is no help for it, and you had better pray to your father Poseidon.'

"Then they went away, and I laughed inwardly at the success of my clever stratagem, but the Cyclops, groaning and in an agony of pain, felt about with his hands till he found the stone and took it from the door; then he sat in the doorway and stretched his hands in front of it to catch anyone going out with the sheep, for he thought I might be foolish enough to attempt this.

"As for myself I kept on puzzling to think how I could best save my own life and those of my companions; I schemed and schemed, as one who knows that his life depends upon it, for the danger was very great. In the end I deemed that this plan would be the best; the male sheep were well grown, and carried a heavy black fleece, so I bound them noiselessly in threes together, with some of the withies on which the wicked monster used to sleep. There was to be a man under the middle sheep, and the two on either side were to cover him, so that there were three sheep to each man. As for myself there was a ram finer than any of the others, so I caught hold of him by the back, esconced myself in the thick wool under his belly, and hung on patiently to his fleece, face upwards, keeping a firm hold on it all the time.

"Thus, then, did we wait in great fear of mind till morning came, but when the child of morning, rosy-fingered Dawn, appeared, the male sheep hurried out to feed, while the ewes remained bleating about the pens waiting to be milked, for their udders were full to bursting; but their master in spite of all his pain felt the backs of all the sheep as they stood upright, without being sharp enough to find out that the men were underneath their bellies. As the ram was going out, last of all, heavy with its fleece and with the weight of my crafty self, Polyphemus laid hold of it and said:

" 'My good ram, what is it that makes you the last to leave my cave this morning? You are not wont to let the ewes go before you, but lead the mob with a run whether to flowery meadow or bubbling fountain, and are the first to come home again at night; but now you lag last of all. Is it because you know your master has lost his eye, and are sorry because that wicked Noman and his horrid crew has got him down in his drink and blinded him? But I will have his life yet. If you could understand and talk, you would tell me where the wretch is hiding, and I would dash his brains upon the ground till they flew all over the cave. I should thus have some satisfaction for the harm this no-good Noman has done me.'

"As he spoke he drove the ram outside, but when we were a little way out from the cave and yards, I first got from under the ram's belly, and then freed my comrades; as for the sheep, which were very fat, by constantly heading them in the right direction we managed to drive them down to the ship. The crew rejoiced greatly at seeing those of us who had escaped death, but wept for the others whom the Cyclops had killed. However, I made signs to them by nodding and frowning that they were to hush their crying, and told them to get all the sheep on board at once and put out to sea; so they went aboard, took their places, and smote the grey sea with their oars.† Then, when I had got as far out as my voice would reach, I began to jeer at the Cyclops.

" 'Cyclops,' said I, 'you should have taken better measure of your man before eating up his comrades in your cave. You wretch, eat up your visitors in your own house? You might have known that your sin would find you out, and now Zeus and the other gods have punished you.'

"He got more and more furious as he heard me, so he tore the top from off a high mountain, and flung it just in front of my ship so that it was within a little of hitting the end of the rudder. The sea quaked as the rock fell into it, and the wash of the wave it raised carried us back towards the mainland, and forced us towards the shore. But I snatched up a long pole and kept the ship off, making signs to my men by nodding my head, that they must row for their lives, whereon they laid out with a will. When we had got twice as far as we were before, I was for jeering at the Cyclops again, but the men begged and prayed of me to hold my tongue.†

" 'Do not,' they exclaimed, 'be mad enough to provoke this savage creature further; he has thrown one rock at us already which drove us back again to the mainland, and we thought it would have been the death of us; if he had then heard any further sound of voices he would have pounded our heads and our ship's timbers into a jelly with the rugged rocks he would have heaved at us, for he can throw them a long way.'

"But I would not listen to them, and shouted out to him in my rage, 'Cyclops, if anyone asks you who it was that put your eye out and spoiled your beauty, say it was the valiant warrior Odysseus, son of Laertes, who lives in Ithaca.'

"On this he groaned, and cried out, 'Alas, alas, then the old prophecy about me is coming true. There was a prophet here, at one time, a man both brave and of great stature, Telemus son of Eurymus, who was an excellent seer, and did all the prophesying for the Cyclopes till he grew old; he told me that all this would happen to me some day, and said I should lose my sight by the hand of Odysseus. I have been all along expecting someone of imposing presence and superhuman strength, whereas he turns out to be a little insignificant weakling,[†] who has managed to blind my eye by taking advantage of me in my drink; come here, then, Odysseus, that I may make you presents to show my hospitality, and urge Poseidon to help you forward on your journey—for Poseidon and I are father and son. He, if he so will, shall heal me, which no one else neither god nor man can do.'

"Then I said, 'I wish I could be as sure of killing you outright and sending you down to the house of Hades, as I am that it will take more than Poseidon to cure that eye of yours.'[†]

"On this he lifted up his hands to the firmament of heaven and prayed, saying, 'Hear me, great Poseidon; if I am indeed your own true begotten son, grant that Odysseus may never reach his home alive; or if he must get back to his friends at last, let him do so late and in sore plight after losing all his men let him reach his home in another man's ship and find trouble in his house.'

"Thus did he pray, and Poseidon heard his prayer. Then he picked up a rock much larger than the first, swung it aloft and hurled it with prodigious force. It fell just short of the ship, but was within a little of hitting the end of the rudder. The sea quaked as the rock fell into it, and the wash of the wave it raised drove us onwards on our way towards the shore of the island.

"When at last we got to the island where we had left the rest of our ships, we found our comrades lamenting us, and anxiously awaiting our return. We ran our vessel upon the sands and got out of her on to the sea shore; we also landed the Cyclops' sheep, and divided them equitably amongst us so that none might have reason to complain. As for the ram, my companions agreed that I should have it as an extra share; so I sacrificed it on the sea shore, and burned its thigh bones to Zeus, who is the lord of all. But he heeded not my sacrifice, and only thought how he might destroy both my ships and my comrades.

BOOK X

Aeolus
The Laestrygones
Circe

"THENCE WE WENT on to the Aeolian island where lives Aeolus son
of Hippotas, dear to the immortal gods. It is an island that floats (as it
were) upon the sea, iron bound with a wall that girds it. Now, Aeolus
has six daughters and six lusty sons, so he made the sons marry the daughters,
and they all live with their dear father and mother, feasting and enjoying every
conceivable kind of luxury. All day long the atmosphere of the house is loaded
with the savor of roasting meats till it groans again, yard and all;† but by night
they sleep on their well made bedsteads, each with his own wife between the
blankets. These were the people among whom we had now come.

"Aeolus entertained me for a whole month asking me questions all the time
about Troy, the Argive fleet, and the return of the Achaeans. I told him exactly
how everything had happened, and when I said I must go, and asked him to
further me on my way, he made no sort of difficulty, but set about doing so at
once. Moreover, he flayed me a prime ox-hide to hold the ways of the roaring
winds, which he shut up in the hide as in a sack—for Zeus had made him
captain over the winds, and he could stir or still each one of them according to
his own pleasure. He put the sack in the ship and bound the mouth so tightly
with a silver thread that not even a breath of a side-wind could blow from any
quarter. The West wind which was fair for us did he alone let blow as it chose;
but it all came to nothing, for we were lost through our own folly.†

"Nine days and nine nights did we sail, and on the tenth day our native land showed on the horizon. We got so close in that we could see the stubble fires burning, and I, being then dead beat, fell into a light sleep, for I had never let the rudder out of my own hands, that we might get home the faster. On this the men fell to talking among themselves, and said I was bringing back gold and silver in the sack that Aeolus had given me. 'Bless my heart,' would one turn to his neighbor, saying, 'how this man gets honored and makes friends to whatever city or country he may go. See what fine prizes he is taking home from Troy, while we, who have traveled just as far as he has, come back with hands as empty as we set out with—and now Aeolus has given him ever so much more. Quick—let us see what it all is, and how much gold and silver there is in the sack he gave him.'

"Thus they talked and evil counsels prevailed. They loosed the sack, whereupon the wind flew howling forth and raised a storm that carried us weeping out to sea and away from our own country. Then I awoke, and knew not whether to throw myself into the sea or to live on and make the best of it; but I bore it, covered myself up, and lay down in the ship, while the men lamented bitterly as the fierce winds bore our fleet back to the Aeolian island.

"When we reached it we went ashore to take in water, and dined hard by the ships. Immediately after dinner I took a herald and one of my men and went straight to the house of Aeolus, where I found him feasting with his wife and family; so we sat down as suppliants on the threshold. They were astounded when they saw us and said, 'Odysseus, what brings you here? What god has been ill-treating you? We took great pains to further you on your way home to Ithaca, or wherever it was that you wanted to go to.'

"Thus did they speak, but I answered sorrowfully, 'My men have undone me; they, and cruel sleep, have ruined me. My friends, mend me this mischief, for you can if you will.'

"I spoke as movingly as I could, but they said nothing, till their father answered, 'Vilest of mankind, get you gone at once out of the island; him whom heaven hates will I in no wise help. Be off, for you come here as one abhorred of heaven.'† And with these words he sent me sorrowing from his door.

"Thence we sailed sadly on till the men were worn out with long and fruitless rowing, for there was no longer any wind to help them. Six days, night and day did we toil, and on the seventh day we reached the rocky stronghold of Lamus—Telepylus, the city of the Laestrygonians, where the shepherd who is driving in his sheep and goats to be milked salutes him who is driving out his flock to feed and this last answers the salute. In that country a man who could do without sleep might earn double wages, one as a herdsman of cattle, and another as a shepherd, for they work much the same by night as they do by day.

"When we reached the harbor we found it land-locked under steep cliffs, with a narrow entrance between two headlands. My captains took all their ships inside, and made them fast close to one another, for there was never so much as a breath of wind inside, but it was always dead calm. I kept my own ship outside, and moored it to a rock at the very end of the point; then I climbed a high rock to reconnoitre, but could see no sign neither of man nor cattle, only some smoke rising from the ground. So I sent two of my company with an attendant to find out what sort of people the inhabitants were.

"The men when they got on shore followed a level road by which the people draw their firewood from the mountains into the town, till presently they met a young woman who had come outside to fetch water, and who was daughter to a Laestrygonian named Antiphates. She was going to the fountain Artacia from which the people bring in their water, and when my men had come close up to her, they asked her who the king of that country might be, and over what kind of people he ruled; so she directed them to her father's house, but when they got there they found his wife to be a giantess as huge as a mountain, and they were horrified at the sight of her.

"She at once called her husband Antiphates from the place of assembly, and forthwith he set about killing my men. He snatched up one of them, and began to make his dinner off him then and there, whereon the other two ran back to the ships as fast as ever they could. But Antiphates raised a hue-and-cry after them, and thousands of sturdy Laestrygonians sprang up from every quarter—ogres, not men. They threw vast rocks at us from the cliffs as though they had been mere stones, and I heard the horrid sound of the ships crunching up against one another, and the death cries of my men, as the Laestrygonians speared them like fishes and took them home to eat them. While they were thus killing my men within the harbor I drew my sword, cut the cable of my own ship, and told my men to row with all their might if they too would not fare like the rest; so they laid out for their lives, and we were thankful enough when we got into open water out of reach of the rocks they hurled at us. As for the others there was not one of them left.

"Thence we sailed sadly on, glad to have escaped death, though we had lost our comrades,[†] and came to the Aeaean island, where Circe lives—a great and cunning goddess who is own sister to the magician Aeetes—for they are both children of the sun by Perse, who is daughter to Oceanus. We brought our ship into a safe harbor without a word, for some god guided us thither, and having landed we lay there for two days and two nights, worn out in body and mind. When the morning of the third day came I took my spear and my sword, and went away from the ship to reconnoitre, and see if I could discover signs of human handiwork, or hear the sound of voices. Climbing to the top of a high look-out I espied the smoke of Circe's house rising upwards amid a dense forest of trees, and when I saw this I doubted whether, having seen the smoke, I would not go on at once and find out more, but in the end I deemed it best to go back to the ship, give the men their dinners, and send some of them instead of going myself.

"When I had nearly got back to the ship some god took pity upon my solitude, and sent a fine antlered stag right into the middle of my path. He was coming down his pasture in the forest to drink of the river, for the heat of the sun drove him, and as he passed I struck him in the middle of the back; the bronze point of the spear went clean through him, and he lay groaning in the dust until the life went out of him. Then I set my foot upon him, drew my spear from the wound, and laid it down; I also gathered rough grass and rushes and twisted them into a fathom or so of good stout rope, with which I bound the four feet of the noble creature together; having so done I hung him round my neck and walked back to the ship leaning upon my spear, for the stag was much too big for me to be able to carry him on my shoulder, steadying him with one hand. As I threw him down in front of the ship, I called the men and spoke cheeringly man by man to each of them. 'Look here my friends,' said I, 'we are not going to die so much before our time after all, and at any rate we will not starve so long as we have got something to eat and drink on board.' On this they uncovered their heads upon the sea shore and admired the stag, for he was indeed a splendid fellow. Then, when they had feasted their eyes upon him sufficiently, they washed their hands and began to cook him for dinner.

"Thus through the livelong day to the going down of the sun we stayed there eating and drinking our fill, but when the sun went down and it came on dark, we camped upon the sea shore. When the child of morning, rosy-fingered Dawn, appeared, I called a council and said, 'My friends, we are in very great difficulties; listen therefore to me. We have no idea where the sun either sets or rises, so that we do not even know East from West. I see no way out of it; nevertheless, we must try and find one. We are certainly on an island, for I went as high as I could this morning, and saw the sea reaching all round it to the horizon; it lies low, but towards the middle I saw smoke rising from out of a thick forest of trees.'

"Their hearts sank as they heard me, for they remembered how they had been treated by the Laestrygonian Antiphates, and by the savage ogre Polyphemus. They wept bitterly in their dismay, but there was nothing to be got by crying, so I divided them into two companies and set a captain over each; I gave one company to Eurylochus, while I took command of the other myself. Then we cast lots in a helmet, and the lot fell upon Eurylochus; so he set out with his twenty-two men, and they wept, as also did we who were left behind.

"When they reached Circe's house they found it built of cut stones, on a site that could be seen from far, in the middle of the forest. There were wild mountain wolves and lions prowling all round it—poor bewitched creatures whom she had tamed by her enchantments and drugged into subjection. They did not attack my men, but wagged their great tails, fawned upon them, and rubbed their noses lovingly against them. As hounds crowd round their master when they see him coming from dinner—for they know he will bring them something—even so did these wolves and lions with their great claws fawn upon my men, but the men were terribly frightened at seeing such strange creatures. Presently they reached the gates of the goddess' house, and as they stood there they could hear Circe within, singing most beautifully as she worked at her loom, making a web so fine, so soft, and of such dazzling colors as no one but a goddess could weave. On this Polites, whom I valued and trusted more than any other of my men, said, 'There is someone inside working at a loom and singing most beautifully; the whole place resounds with it, let us call her and see whether she is woman or goddess.'

"They called her and she came down, unfastened the door, and bade them enter. They, thinking no evil, followed her, all except Eurylochus, who suspected mischief and stayed outside. When she had got them into her house, she set them upon benches and seats and mixed them with cheese, honey, meal, and Pramnian wine, but she drugged it with wicked poisons to make them forget their homes, and when they had drunk she turned them into pigs by a stroke of her wand, and shut them up in her pig-styes. They were like pigs—head, hair, and all, and they grunted just as pigs do; but their senses were the same as before, and they remembered everything.

"Thus then were they shut up squealing, and Circe threw them some acorns and beech masts such as pigs eat, but Eurylochus hurried back to tell me about the sad fate of our comrades. He was so overcome with dismay that though he tried to speak he could find no words to do so; his eyes filled with tears and he could only sob and sigh, till at last we forced his story out of him, and he told us what had happened to the others.

" 'We went,' said he, 'as you told us, through the forest, and in the middle of it there was a fine house built with cut stones in a place that could be seen from far. There we found a woman, or else she was a goddess, working at her loom and singing sweetly; so the men shouted to her and called her, whereon she at once came down, opened the door, and invited us in. The others did not suspect any mischief so they followed her into the house, but I staid where I was, for I thought there might be some treachery. From that moment I saw them no more, for not one of them ever came out, though I sat a long time watching for them.'

"Then I took my sword of bronze and slung it over my shoulders; I also took my bow, and told Eurylochus to come back with me and show me the way. But he laid hold of me with both his hands and spoke piteously, saying, 'Sir, do not force me to go with you, but let me stay here, for I know you will not bring one of them back with you, nor even return alive yourself; let us rather see if we cannot escape at any rate with the few that are left us, for we may still save our lives.'

" 'Stay where you are, then,' answered I, 'eating and drinking at the ship, but I must go, for I am most urgently bound to do so.'†

"With this I left the ship and went up inland. When I got through the charmed grove, and was near the great house of the enchantress Circe, I met Hermes with his golden wand, disguised as a young man in the hey-day of his youth and beauty with the down just coming upon his face. He came up to me and took my hand within his own, saying, 'My poor unhappy man, whither are you going over this mountain top, alone and without knowing the way? Your men are shut up in Circe's pigstyes, like so many wild boars in their lairs. You surely do not fancy that you can set them free? I can tell you that you will never get back and will have to stay there with the rest of them. But never mind, I will protect you and get you out of your difficulty. Take this herb, which is one of great virtue, and keep it about you when you go to Circe's house, it will be a talisman to you against every kind of mischief.

" 'And I will tell you of all the wicked witchcraft that Circe will try to practice upon you. She will mix a potion for you to drink, and she will drug the meal with which she makes it, but she will not be able to charm you,† for the virtue of the herb that I shall give you will prevent her spells from working. I will tell you all about it.When Circe strikes you with her wand, draw your sword and spring upon her as though you were going to kill her. She will then be frightened, and will desire you to go to bed with her; on this you must not directly refuse her, for you want her to set your companions free, and to take good care also of yourself, but you must make her swear solemnly by all the blessed gods that she will plot no further mischief against you, or else when she has got you naked she will unman you and make you fit for nothing.'

"As he spoke he pulled the herb out of the ground and showed me what it was like. The root was black, while the flower was as white as milk; the gods call it Moly, and mortal men cannot uproot it, but the gods can do whatever they like.

"Then Hermes went back to high Olympus passing over the wooded island; but I fared onward to the house of Circe, and my heart was clouded with care as I walked along. When I got to the gates I stood there and called the goddess, and as soon as she heard me she came down, opened the door, and asked me to come in; so I followed her—much troubled in my mind. She set me on a richly decorated seat inlaid with silver, there was a footstool also under my feet, and she mixed something in a golden goblet for me to drink; but she drugged it, for she meant me mischief. When she had given it me, and I had drunk it without its charming me, she struck me with her wand.

'There now,' she cried, 'be off to the pigstye, and make your lair with the rest of them.'

"But I rushed at her with my sword drawn as though I would kill her, whereon she fell with a loud scream, clasped my knees, and spoke piteously, saying, 'Who and whence are you? from what place and people have you come? How can it be that my drugs have no power to charm you? Never yet was any man able to stand so much as a taste of the herb I gave you; you must be spell-proof; surely you can be none other than the bold hero Odysseus, who Hermes always said would come here some day with his ship while on his way home from Troy;† so be it then; sheathe your sword and let us go to bed, that we may make friends and learn to trust each other.'

"And I answered, 'Circe, how can you expect me to be friendly with you when you have just been turning all my men into pigs? And now that you have got me here myself, you mean me mischief when you ask me to go to bed with you, and will unman me and make me fit for nothing. I shall certainly not consent to go to bed with you unless you will first take your solemn oath to plot no further harm against me.'

"So she swore at once as I had told her, and when she had completed her oath then I went to bed with her.

"Meanwhile her four servants, who are her housemaids, set about their work. They are the children of the groves and fountains, and of the holy waters that run down into the sea. One of them spread a fair purple cloth over a seat, and laid a carpet underneath it. Another brought tables of silver up to the seats, and set them with baskets of gold. A third mixed some sweet wine with water in a silver bowl and put golden cups upon the tables, while the fourth brought in water and set it to boil in a large cauldron over a good fire which she had lighted. When the water in the cauldron was boiling, she poured cold into it till it was just as I liked it, and then she set me in a bath and began washing me from the cauldron about the head and shoulders, to take the tire and stiffness out of my limbs. As soon as she had done washing me and anointing me with oil, she arrayed me in a good cloak and shirt and led me to a richly decorated seat inlaid with silver; there was a footstool also under my feet. A maid servant then brought me water in a beautiful golden ewer and poured it into a silver basin for me to wash my hands, and she drew a clean table beside me; an upper servant brought me bread and offered me many things of what there was in the house, and then Circe bade me eat, but I would not, and sat without heeding what was before me, still moody and suspicious.

"When Circe saw me sitting there without eating, and in great grief, she came to me and said, 'Odysseus, why do you sit like that as though you were dumb, gnawing at your own heart, and refusing both meat and drink? Is it that you are still suspicious? You ought not to be, for I have already sworn solemnly that I will not hurt you.'

"And I said, 'Circe, no man with any sense of what is right can think of either eating or drinking in your house until you have set his friends free and let him see them. If you want me to eat and drink, you must free my men and bring them to me that I may see them with my own eyes.'

"When I had said this she went straight through the court with her wand in her hand and opened the pigstye doors. My men came out like so many prime hogs and stood looking at her, but she went about among them and anointed each with a second drug, whereon the bristles that the bad drug had given them fell off, and they became men again, younger than they were before, and much taller and better looking. They knew me at once, seized me each of them by the hand, and wept for joy till the whole house was filled with the sound of their halloa-ballooing, and Circe herself was so sorry for them that she came up to me and said, 'Odysseus, noble son of Laertes, go back at once to the sea where you have left your ship, and first draw it on to the land. Then, hide all your ship's gear and property in some cave, and come back here with your men.'

"I agreed to this, so I went back to the sea shore, and found the men at the ship weeping and wailing most piteously. When they saw me the silly blubbering fellows began frisking round me as calves break out and gambol round their mothers,† when they see them coming home to be milked after they have been feeding all day, and the homestead resounds with their low-ing. They seemed as glad to see me as though they had got back to their own rugged Ithaca, where they had been born and bred. 'Sir,' said the affectionate creatures, 'we are as glad to see you back as though we had got safe home to Ithaca; but tell us all about the fate of our comrades.'

"I spoke comfortingly to them and said, 'We must draw our ship on to the land, and hide the ship's gear with all our property in some cave; then come with me all of you as fast as you can to Circe's house, where you will find your comrades eating and drinking in the midst of great abundance.'

"On this the men would have come with me at once, but Eurylochus tried to hold them back and said, 'Alas, poor wretches that we are, what will become of us? Rush not on your ruin by going to the house of Circe, who will turn us all into pigs or wolves or lions, and we shall have to keep guard over her house. Remember how the Cyclops treated us when our comrades went inside his cave, and Odysseus with them. It was all through his sheer folly that those men lost their lives.'

"When I heard him I was in two minds whether or no to draw the keen blade that hung by my sturdy thigh and cut his head off in spite of his being a near relation of my own; but the men interceded for him and said, 'Sir, if it may so be, let this fellow stay here and mind the ship, but take the rest of us with you to Circe's house.'

"On this we all went inland, and Eurylochus was not left behind after all, but came on too, for he was frightened by the severe reprimand that I had given him.

"Meanwhile Circe had been seeing that the men who had been left behind were washed and anointed with olive oil; she had also given them woollen cloaks and shirts, and when we came we found them all comfortably at dinner in her house. As soon as the men saw each other face to face and knew one another, they wept for joy and cried aloud till the whole palace rang again. Thereon Circe came up to me and said, 'Odysseus, noble son of Laertes, tell your men to leave off crying; I know how much you have all of you suffered at sea, and how ill you have fared among cruel savages on the mainland, but that is over now, so stay here, and eat and drink till you are once more as strong and hearty as you were when you left Ithaca; for at present you are weakened both in body and mind; you keep all the time thinking of the hardships you have suffered during your travels, so that you have no more cheerfulness left in you.'

"Thus did she speak and we assented. We stayed with Circe for a whole twelvemonth feasting upon an untold quantity both of meat and wine. But when the year had passed in the waning of moons and the long days had come round, my men called me apart and said, 'Sir, it is time you began to think about going home, if so be you are to be spared to see your house and native country at all.'

"Thus did they speak and I assented. Thereon through the livelong day to the going down of the sun we feasted our fill on meat and wine, but when the sun went down and it came on dark the men laid themselves down to sleep in the covered cloisters. I, however, after I had got into bed with Circe, besought her by her knees, and the goddess listened to what I had got to say. 'Circe,' said I, 'please to keep the promise you made me about furthering me on my home-ward voyage. I want to get back and so do my men, they are always pestering me with their complaints as soon as ever your back is turned.'

"And the goddess answered, 'Odysseus, noble son of Laertes, you shall none of you stay here any longer if you do not want to, but there is another journey which you have got to take before you can sail homewards. You must go to the house of Hades and of dread Persephone to consult the ghost of the blind Theban prophet Teiresias,[†] whose reason is still unshaken. To him alone has Persephone left his understanding even in death, but the other ghosts flit about aimlessly.'

"I was dismayed when I heard this. I sat up in bed and wept, and would gladly have lived no longer to see the light of the sun, but presently when I was tired of weeping and tossing myself about, I said, 'And who shall guide me upon this voyage—for the house of Hades is a port that no ship can reach.'

" 'You will want no guide,' she answered; 'raise your mast, set your white sails, sit quite still, and the North Wind will blow you there of itself. When your ship has traversed the waters of Oceanus, you will reach the fertile shore of Persephone's country with its groves of tall poplars and willows that shed their fruit untimely; here beach your ship upon the shore of Oceanus, and go straight on to the dark abode of Hades. You will find it near the place where the rivers Pyriphlegethon and Cocytus (which is a branch of the river Styx) flow into Acheron, and you will see a rock near it, just where the two roaring rivers run into one another.

" 'When you have reached this spot, as I now tell you, dig a trench a cubit or so in length, breadth, and depth, and pour into it as a drink-offering to all the dead, first, honey mixed with milk, then wine, and in the third place water—sprinkling white barley meal over the whole. Moreover you must offer many prayers to the poor feeble ghosts, and promise them that when you get back to Ithaca you will sacrifice a barren heifer to them, the best you have, and will load the pyre with good things. More particularly you must promise that Teiresias shall have a black sheep all to himself, the finest in all your flocks.

" 'When you shall have thus besought the ghosts with your prayers, offer them a ram and a black ewe, bending their heads towards Erebus; but yourself turn away from them as though you would make towards the river. On this, many dead men's ghosts will come to you, and you must tell your men to skin the two sheep that you have just killed, and offer them as a burnt sacrifice with prayers to Hades and to Persephone. Then draw your sword and sit there, so as to prevent any other poor ghost from coming near the spilt blood before Teiresias shall have answered your questions.† The seer will presently come to you, and will tell you about your voyage—what stages you are to make, and how you are to sail the sea so as to reach your home.'

"It was day-break by the time she had done speaking, so she dressed me in my shirt and cloak. As for herself she threw a beautiful light gossamer fabric over her shoulders, fastening it with a golden girdle round her waist, and she covered her head with a mantle. Then I went about among the men every- where all over the house, and spoke kindly to each of them man by man: 'You must not lie sleeping here any longer,' said I to them, 'we must be going, for Circe has told me all about it.' And on this they did as I bade them.

"Even so, however, I did not get them away without misadventure. We had with us a certain youth named Elpenor, not very remarkable for sense or courage, who had got drunk and was lying on the house-top away from the rest of the men, to sleep off his liquor in the cool. When he heard the noise of the men bustling about, he jumped up on a sudden and forgot all about coming down by the main staircase, so he tumbled right off the roof and broke his neck, and his soul went down to the house of Hades.

"When I had got the men together I said to them, 'You think you are about to start home again, but Circe has explained to me that instead of this, we have got to go to the house of Hades and Persephone to consult the ghost of the Theban prophet Teiresias.'

"The men were broken-hearted as they heard me, and threw themselves on the ground groaning and tearing their hair,[†] but they did not mend matters by crying. When we reached the sea shore, weeping and lamenting our fate, Circe brought the ram and the ewe, and we made them fast hard by the ship. She passed through the midst of us without our knowing it, for who can see the comings and goings of a god, if the god does not wish to be seen?

B O O K X I

The visit to the dead.

"THEN, WHEN WE had got down to the sea shore we drew our ship into the water and got her mast and sails into her; we also put the sheep on board and took our places, weeping and in great distress of mind. Circe, that great and cunning goddess, sent us a fair wind that blew dead aft and staid steadily with us keeping our sails all the time well filled; so we did whatever wanted doing to the ship's gear and let her go as the wind and helmsman headed her. All day long her sails were full as she held her course over the sea, but when the sun went down and darkness was over all the earth, we got into the deep waters of the river Oceanus, where lie the land and city of the Cimmerians who live enshrouded in mist and darkness which the rays of the sun never pierce neither at his rising nor as he goes down again out of the heavens, but the poor wretches live in one long melancholy night. When we got there we beached the ship, took the sheep out of her, and went along by the waters of Oceanus till we came to the place of which Circe had told us.

"Here Perimedes and Eurylochus held the victims, while I drew my sword and dug the trench a cubit each way. I made a drink-offering to all the dead, first with honey and milk, then with wine, and thirdly with water, and I sprinkled white barley meal over the whole, praying earnestly to the poor feckless ghosts, and promising them that when I got back to Ithaca I would sacrifice a barren heifer for them, the best I had, and would load the pyre with good things. I also particularly promised that Teiresias should have a black sheep to himself, the best in all my flocks. When I had prayed sufficiently to the dead, I cut the throats of the two sheep and let the blood run into the trench, whereon the ghosts came trooping up from Erebus—brides, young bachelors, old men worn out with toil, maids who had been crossed in love, and brave men who had been killed in battle, with their armor still smirched with blood; they came from every quarter and flitted round the trench with a strange kind of screaming sound that made me turn pale with fear. When I saw them coming I told the men to be quick and flay the carcasses of the two dead sheep and make burnt offerings of them, and at the same time to repeat prayers to Hades and to Persephone; but I sat where I was with my sword drawn and would not let the poor feckless ghosts come near the blood till Teiresias should have answered my questions.

"The first ghost that came was that of my comrade Elpenor, for he had not yet been laid beneath the earth. We had left his body unwept for and unburied in Circe's house,† for we had had too much else to do. I was very sorry for him, and cried when I saw him: 'Elpenor,' said I, 'how did you come down here into this gloom and darkness? You have got here on foot quicker than I have with my ship.'

" 'Sir,' he answered with a groan, 'it was all bad luck, and my own unspeakable drunkenness. I was lying asleep on the top of Circe's house, and never thought of coming down again by the great staircase but fell right off the roof and broke my neck, so my soul came down to the house of Hades. And now I beseech you by all those whom you have left behind you, though they are not here, by your wife, by the father who brought you up when you were a child, and by Telemachus who is the one hope of your house, do what I shall now ask you. I know that when you leave this limbo you will again hold your ship for the Aeaean island. Do not go thence leaving me unmourned and unburied behind you, or I may bring heaven's anger upon you; but burn me with whatever armor I have, build a barrow for me on the sea shore, that may tell people in days to come what a poor unlucky fellow I was, and plant over my grave the oar I used to row with when I was yet alive and with my messmates.' And I said, 'My poor fellow, I will do all that you have asked of me.'

"Thus, then, did we sit and hold sad talk with one another, I on the one side of the trench with my sword held over the blood, and the ghost of my comrade saying all this to me from the other side. Then came the ghost of my dead mother Anticlea, daughter to Autolycus. I had left her alive when I set out for Troy and was moved to tears when I saw her, but even so, for all my sorrow I would not let her come near the blood till I had asked my questions of Teiresias.

"Then came also the ghost of Theban Teiresias, with his golden sceptre in his hand. He knew me and said, 'Odysseus, noble son of Laertes, why, poor man, have you left the light of day and come down to visit the dead in this sad place? Stand back from the trench and withdraw your sword that I may drink of the blood and answer your questions truly.'

"So I drew back, and sheathed my sword, and when he had drank of the blood he began with his prophecy.

" 'You want to know,' said he, 'about your return home, but heaven will make this hard for you. I do not think that you will escape the eye of Poseidon, who still nurses his bitter grudge against you for having blinded his son. Still, after much suffering you may get home if you can restrain yourself and your companions when your ship reaches the Thrinacian island, where you will find the sheep and cattle belonging to the sun, who sees and gives ear to everything. If you leave these flocks unharmed and think of nothing but of getting home, you may yet after much hardship reach Ithaca;† but if you harm them, then I forewarn you of the destruction both of your ship and of your men. Even though you may yourself escape, you will return in bad plight after losing all your men, in another man's ship, and you will find trouble in your house, which will be overrun by high-handed people, who are devouring your substance under the pretext of paying court and making presents to your wife.

" 'When you get home you will take your revenge on these suitors; and after you have killed them by force or fraud in your own house, you must take a well made oar and carry it on and on, till you come to a country where the people have never heard of the sea and do not even mix salt with their food, nor do they know anything about ships, and oars that are as the wings of a ship. I will give you this certain token which cannot escape your notice. A wayfarer will meet you and will say it must be a winnowing shovel that you have got upon your shoulder; on this you must fix the oar in the ground and sacrifice a ram, a bull, and a boar to Poseidon. Then go home and offer hecatombs to all the gods in heaven one after the other. As for yourself, death shall come to you from the sea, and your life shall ebb away very gently when you are full of years and peace of mind, and your people shall bless you. All that I have said will come true.'

" 'This,' I answered, 'must be as it may please heaven, but tell me and tell me and tell me† true, I see my poor mother's ghost close by us; she is sitting by the blood without saying a word, and though I am her own son she does not remember me and speak to me; tell me, Sir, how I can make her know me.'

" 'That,' said he, 'I can soon do. Any ghost that you let taste of the blood will talk with you like a reasonable being, but if you do not let them have any blood they will go away again.'

"On this the ghost of Teiresias went back to the house of Hades, for his prophecyings had now been spoken, but I sat still where I was until my mother came up and tasted the blood. Then she knew me at once and spoke fondly to me, saying, 'My son, how did you come down to this abode of darkness while you are still alive? It is a hard thing for the living to see these places, for between us and them there are great and terrible waters, and there is Oceanus, which no man can cross on foot, but he must have a good ship to take him. Are you all this time trying to find your way home from Troy, and have you never yet got back to Ithaca nor seen your wife in your own house?'

" 'Mother,' said I, 'I was forced to come here to consult the ghost of the Theban prophet Teiresias. I have never yet been near the Achaean land nor set foot on my native country, and I have had nothing but one long series of misfortunes from the very first day that I set out with Agamemnon for Ilius, the land of noble steeds, to fight the Trojans. But tell me, and tell me true, in what way did you die? Did you have a long illness, or did heaven vouchsafe you a gentle easy passage to eternity? Tell me also about my father, and the son whom I left behind me, is my property still in their hands, or has someone else got hold of it, who thinks that I shall not return to claim it? Tell me again what my wife intends doing, and in what mind she is; does she live with my son and guard my estate securely, or has she made the best match she could and married again?'

"My mother answered, 'Your wife still remains in your house, but she is in great distress of mind and spends her whole time in tears both night and day.†No one as yet has got possession of your fine property, and Telemachus still holds your lands undisturbed. He has to entertain largely, as of course he must, considering his position as a magistrate, and how everyone invites him; your father remains at his old place in the country and never goes near the town. He has no comfortable bed nor bedding; in the winter he sleeps on the floor in front of the fire with the men and goes about all in rags, but in summer, when the warm weather comes on again, he lies out in the vineyard on a bed of vine leaves thrown any how upon the ground. He grieves continually about your never having come home, and suffers more and more as he grows older. As for my own end it was in this wise: heaven did not take me swiftly and painlessly in my own house, nor was I attacked by any illness such as those that generally wear people out and kill them, but my longing to know what you were doing and the force of my affection for you—this it was that was the death of me.'

"Then I tried to find some way of embracing my poor mother's ghost. Thrice I sprang towards her and tried to clasp her in my arms, but each time she flitted from my embrace as it were a dream or phantom, and being touched to the quick I said to her, 'Mother, why do you not stay still when I would embrace you? If we could throw our arms around one another we might find sad comfort in the sharing of our sorrows even in the house of Hades; does Persephone want to lay a still further load of grief upon me by mocking me with a phantom only?'

"'My son,' she answered, 'most ill-fated of all mankind, it is not Persephone that is beguiling you, but all people are like this when they are dead. The sinews no longer hold the flesh and bones together; these perish in the fierceness of consuming fire as soon as life has left the body, and the soul flits away as though it were a dream. Now, however, go back to the light of day as soon as you can, and note all these things that you may tell them to your wife hereafter.'

"Thus did we converse, and soon Persephone sent up the ghosts of the wives and daughters of all the most famous men. They gathered in crowds about the blood, and I considered how I might question them severally. In the end I deemed that it would be best to draw the keen blade that hung by my sturdy thigh, and keep them from all drinking the blood at once. So they came up one after the other, and each one as I questioned her told me her race and lineage.

"The first I saw was Tyro. She was daughter of Salmoneus and wife of Cretheus the son of Aeolus. She fell in love with the river Enipeus who is much the most beautiful river in the whole world. Once when she was taking a walk by his side as usual, Poseidon, disguised as her lover, lay with her at the mouth of the river, and a huge blue wave arched itself like a mountain over them to hide both woman and god, whereon he loosed her virgin girdle and laid her in a deep slumber. When the god had accomplished the deed of love, he took her hand in his own and said, 'Tyro, rejoice in all good will; the embraces of the gods are not fruitless, and you will have fine twins about this time twelve months. Take great care of them. I am Poseidon, so now go home, but hold your tongue and do not tell anyone.'

"Then he dived under the sea, and she in due course bore Pelias and Neleus, who both of them served Zeus with all their might. Pelias was a great breeder of sheep and lived in Iolcus, but the other lived in Pylos. The rest of her children were by Cretheus, namely, Aeson, Pheres, and Amythaon, who was a mighty warrior and charioteer.

"Next to her I saw Antiope, daughter to Asopus, who could boast of having slept in the arms of even Zeus himself,[†] and who bore him two sons Amphion and Zethus. These founded Thebes with its seven gates, and built a wall all round it; for strong though they were they could not hold Thebes till they had walled it.

"Then I saw Alcmena, the wife of Amphitryon, who also bore to Zeus indomitable Heracles; and Megara who was daughter to great King Creon, and married the redoubtable son of Amphitryon.

"I also saw fair Epicaste mother of king Oedipus whose awful lot it was to marry her own son without suspecting it. He married her after having killed his father, but the gods proclaimed the whole story to the world; whereon he remained king of Thebes, in great grief for the spite the gods had borne him; but Epicaste went to the house of the mighty jailor Hades, having hanged herself for grief, and the avenging spirits haunted him as for an outraged mother—to his ruing bitterly thereafter.

"Then I saw Chloris, whom Neleus married for her beauty, having given priceless presents for her. She was youngest daughter to Amphion son of Iasus and king of Minyan Orchomenus, and was Queen in Pylos. She bore Nestor, Chromius, and Periclymenus, and she also bore that marvelously lovely woman Pero, who was wooed by all the country round; but Neleus would only give her to him who should raid the cattle of Iphicles from the grazing grounds of Phylace, and this was a hard task. The only man who would undertake to raid them was a certain excellent seer, but the will of heaven was against him, for the rangers of the cattle caught him and put him in prison; nevertheless when a full year had passed and the same season came round again, Iphicles set him at liberty, after he had expounded all the oracles of heaven. Thus, then, was the will of Zeus accomplished.

"And I saw Leda the wife of Tyndarus, who bore him two famous sons, Castor breaker of horses, and Pollux the mighty boxer. Both these heroes are lying under the earth, though they are still alive, for by a special dispensation of Zeus, they die and come to life again, each one of them every other day throughout all time, and they have the rank of gods.

"After her I saw Iphimedeia wife of Aloeus who boasted the embrace of Poseidon. She bore two sons Otus and Ephialtes, but both were short lived. They were the finest children that were ever born in this world, and the best looking, Orion only excepted; for at nine years old they were nine fathoms high, and measured nine cubits round the chest. They threatened to make war with the gods in Olympus, and tried to set Mount Ossa on the top of Mount Olympus, and Mount Pelion on the top of Ossa, that they might scale heaven itself, and they would have done it too if they had been grown up, but Apollo, son of Leto, killed both of them, before they had got so much as a sign of hair upon their cheeks or chin.

"Then I saw Phaedra, and Procris, and fair Ariadne daughter of the magician Minos, whom Theseus was carrying off from Crete to Athens, but he did not enjoy her, for before he could do so Artemis killed her in the island of Dia on account of what Dionysus had said against her.

"I also saw Maera and Clymene and hateful Eriphyle, who sold her own husband for gold. But it would take me all night if I were to name every single one of the wives and daughters of heroes whom I saw, and it is time for me to go to bed, either on board ship with my crew, or here. As for my escort, heaven and yourselves will see to it."

Here he ended, and the guests sat all of them enthralled and speechless throughout the covered cloister. Then Arete said to them:—

"What do you think of this man, O Phaeacians? Is he not tall and good looking, and is he not clever? True, he is my own guest, but all of you share in the distinction. Do not be in a hurry to send him away, nor niggardly in the presents you make to one who is in such great need, for heaven has blessed all of you with great abundance."

Then spoke the aged hero Echeneus who was one of the oldest men among them, "My friends," said he, "what our august queen has just said to us is both reasonable and to the purpose, therefore be persuaded by it; but the decision whether in word or deed rests ultimately with King Alcinous."

"The thing shall be done," exclaimed Alcinous, "as surely as I still live and reign over the Phaeacians. Our guest is indeed very anxious to get home, still we must persuade him to remain with us until to-morrow, by which time I shall be able to get together the whole sum that I mean to give him. As regards his escort it will be a matter for you all, and mine above all others as the chief person among you."

And Odysseus answered, "King Alcinous, if you were to bid me to stay here for a whole twelve months, and then speed me on my way, loaded with your noble gifts, I should obey you gladly and it would redound greatly to my advantage, for I should return fuller-handed to my own people, and should thus be more respected and beloved by all who see me when I get back to Ithaca."

"Odysseus," replied Alcinous, "not one of us who sees you has any idea that you are a charlatan or a swindler. I know there are many people going about who tell such plausible stories that it is very hard to see through them, but there is a style about your language which assures me of your good disposition. Moreover you have told the story of your own misfortunes, and those of the Argives, as though you were a practiced bard; but tell me, and tell me true, whether you saw any of the mighty heroes who went to Troy at the same time with yourself, and perished there. The evenings are still at their longest, and it is not yet bed time—go on, therefore, with your divine story, for I could stay here listening till tomorrow morning, so long as you will continue to tell us of your adventures."

"Alcinous," answered Odysseus, "there is a time for making speeches, and a time for going to bed; nevertheless, since you so desire, I will not refrain from telling you the still sadder tale of those of my comrades who did not fall fighting with the Trojans, but perished on their return, through the treachery of a wicked woman.

"When Persephone had dismissed the female ghosts in all directions, the ghost of Agamemnon son of Atreus came sadly up to me, surrounded by those who had perished with him in the house of Aegisthus. As soon as he had tasted the blood, he knew me, and weeping bitterly stretched out his arms towards me to embrace me; but he had no strength nor substance any more, and I too wept and pitied him as I beheld him. 'How did you come by your death,' said I, 'King Agamemnon? Did Poseidon raise his winds and waves against you when you were at sea, or did your enemies make an end of you on the main land when you were cattle-lifting or sheep-stealing, or while they were fighting in defense of their wives and city?'

"'Odysseus,' he answered, 'noble son of Laertes, I was not lost at sea in any storm of Poseidon's raising, nor did my foes despatch me upon the mainland, but Aegisthus and my wicked wife were the death of me between them. He asked me to his house, feasted me, and then butchered me most miserably as though I were a fat beast in a slaughter house, while all around me my comrades were slain like sheep or pigs for the wedding breakfast, or picnic, or gorgeous banquet of some great nobleman. You must have seen numbers of men killed either in a general engagement, or in single combat, but you never saw anything so truly pitiable as the way in which we fell in that cloister, with the mixing bowl and the loaded tables lying all about, and the ground reeking with our blood. I heard Priam's daughter Cassandra scream as Clytemnestra killed her close beside me. I lay dying upon the earth with the sword in my body, and raised my hands to kill the slut of a murderess, but she slipped away from me; she would not even close my lips nor my eyes when I was dying, for there is nothing in this world so cruel and so shameless as a woman when she has fallen into such guilt as hers was. Fancy murdering her own husband! I thought I was going to be welcomed home by my children and my servants, but her abominable crime has brought disgrace on herself and all women who shall come after—even on the good ones.'

"And I said, 'In truth Zeus has hated the house of Atreus from first to last in the matter of their women's counsels. See how many of us fell for Helen's sake, and now it seems that Clytemnestra hatched mischief against you too during your absence.'

"'Be sure, therefore,' continued Agamemnon, 'and not be too friendly even with your own wife. Do not tell her all that you know perfectly well yourself. Tell her a part only, and keep your own counsel about the rest. Not that your wife, Odysseus, is likely to murder you, for Penelope is a very admirable woman, and has an excellent nature. We left her a young bride with an infant at her breast when we set out for Troy. This child no doubt is now grown up happily to man's estate, and he and his father will have a joyful meeting and embrace one another as it is right they should do, whereas my wicked wife did not even allow me the happiness of looking upon my son, but killed me ere I could do so. Furthermore I say—and lay my saying to your heart—do not tell people when you are bringing your ship to Ithaca, but steal a march upon them, for after all this there is no trusting women.† But now tell me, and tell me true, can you give me any news of my son Orestes? Is he in Orchomenus, or at Pylos, or is he at Sparta with Menelaus—for I presume that he is still living.'

"And I said, 'Agamemnon, why do you ask me? I do not know whether your son is alive or dead, and it is not right to talk when one does not know.'

"As we two sat weeping and talking thus sadly with one another the ghost of Achilles came up to us with Patroclus, Antilochus, and Ajax who was the finest and godliest man of all the Danaans after the son of Peleus. The fleet descendant of Aeacus knew me and spoke piteously, saying, 'Odysseus, noble son of Laertes, what deed of daring will you undertake next, that you venture down to the house of Hades among us silly dead, who are but the ghosts of them that can labor no more?'

"And I said, 'Achilles, son of Peleus, foremost champion of the Achaeans, I came to consult Teiresias, and see if he could advise me about my return home to Ithaca, for I have never yet been able to get near the Achaean land, nor to set foot in my own country, but have been in trouble all the time. As for you, Achilles, no one was ever yet so fortunate as you have been, nor ever will be, for you were adored by all us Argives as long as you were alive, and now that you are here you are a great prince among the dead. Do not, therefore, take it so much to heart even if you are dead.'

"'Say not a word,' he answered, 'in death's favor; I would rather be a paid servant in a poor man's house and be above ground than king of kings among the dead.[†] But give me news about my son; is he gone to the wars and will he be a great soldier, or is this not so? Tell me also if you have heard anything about my father Peleus—does he still rule among the Myrmidons, or do they show him no respect throughout Hellas and Phthia now that he is old and his limbs fail him? Could I but stand by his side, in the light of day, with the same strength that I had when I killed the bravest of our foes upon the plain of Troy—could I but be as I then was and go even for a short time to my father's house, anyone who tried to do him violence or supersede him would soon rue it.'

"'I have heard nothing,' I answered, 'of Peleus, but I can tell you all about your son Neoptolemus, for I took him in my own ship from Scyros with the Achaeans. In our councils of war before Troy he was always first to speak, and his judgement was unerring. Nestor and I were the only two who could surpass him; and when it came to fighting on the plain of Troy, he would never remain with the body of his men, but would dash on far in front, foremost of them all in valor. Many a man did he kill in battle—I cannot name every single one of those whom he slew while fighting on the side of the Argives, but will only say how he killed that valiant hero Eurypylus son of Telephus, who was the handsomest man I ever saw except Memnon; many others also of the Ceteians fell around him by reason of a woman's bribes. Moreover, when all the bravest of the Argives went inside the horse that Epeus had made, and it was left to me to settle when we should either open the door of our ambuscade, or close it, though all the other leaders and chief men among the Danaans were drying their eyes and quaking in every limb, I never once saw him turn pale nor wipe a tear from his cheek; he was all the time urging me to break out from the horse—grasping the handle of his sword and his bronze-shod spear, and breathing fury against the foe. Yet when we had sacked the city of Priam he got his handsome share of the prize money and went on board (such is the fortune of war) without a wound upon him, neither from a thrown spear nor in close combat, for the rage of Ares is a matter of great chance.'[†]

"When I had told him this, the ghost of Achilles strode off across a meadow full of asphodel, exulting over what I had said concerning the prowess of his son.

"The ghosts of other dead men stood near me and told me each his own melancholy tale; but that of Ajax son of Telamon alone held aloof—still angry with me for having won the cause in our dispute about the armor of Achilles. Thetis had offered it as a prize, but the Trojan prisoners and Athena were the judges. Would that I had never gained the day in such a contest, for it cost the life of Ajax, who was foremost of all the Danaans after the son of Peleus, alike in stature and prowess.

"When I saw him I tried to pacify him and said, 'Ajax, will you not forget and forgive even in death, but must the judgement about that hateful armor still rankle with you? It cost us Argives dear enough to lose such a tower of strength as you were to us. We mourned you as much as we mourned Achilles son of Peleus himself, nor can the blame be laid on anything but on the spite which Zeus bore against the Danaans, for it was this that made him counsel your destruction—come hither, therefore, bring your proud spirit into subjection,[†] and hear what I can tell you.'

"He would not answer, but turned away to Erebus and to the other ghosts; nevertheless, I should have made him talk to me in spite of his being so angry, or I should have gone on talking to him, only that there were still others among the dead whom I desired to see.

"Then I saw Minos son of Zeus with his golden sceptre in his hand sitting in judgement on the dead, and the ghosts were gathered sitting and standing round him in the spacious house of Hades, to learn his sentences upon them.

"After him I saw huge Orion in a meadow full of asphodel driving the ghosts of the wild beasts that he had killed upon the mountains, and he had a great bronze club in his hand, unbreakable for ever and ever.

"And I saw Tityus son of Gaia stretched upon the plain and covering some nine acres of ground. Two vultures on either side of him were digging their beaks into his liver, and he kept on trying to beat them off with his hands, but could not; for he had violated Zeus' mistress Leto as she was going through Panopeus on her way to Pytho.

"I saw also the dreadful fate of Tantalus, who stood in a lake that reached his chin; he was dying to quench his thirst, but could never reach the water, for whenever the poor creature stooped to drink, it dried up and vanished, so that there was nothing but dry ground—parched by the spite of heaven. There were tall trees, moreover, that shed their fruit over his head—pears, pomegranates, apples, sweet figs and juicy olives, but whenever the poor creature stretched out his hand to take some, the wind tossed the branches back again to the clouds.

"And I saw Sisyphus at his endless task raising his prodigious stone with both his hands. With hands and feet he tried to roll it up to the top of the hill, but always, just before he could roll it over on to the other side, its weight would be too much for him, and the pitiless stone would come thundering down again on to the plain. Then he would begin trying to push it up hill again, and the sweat ran off him and the steam rose after him.

"After him I saw mighty Heracles, but it was his phantom only, for he is feasting ever with the immortal gods, and has lovely Hebe to wife, who is daughter of Zeus and Hera. The ghosts were screaming round him like scared birds flying everywhere. He looked black as night with his bare bow in his hands and his arrow on the string, glaring around as though ever on the point of taking aim. About his breast there was a wondrous golden belt adorned in the most marvelous fashion with bears, wild boars, and lions with gleaming eyes; there was also war, battle, and death. The man who made that belt, do what he might, would never be able to make another like it. Heracles knew me at once when he saw me, and spoke piteously, saying, 'My poor Odysseus, noble son of Laertes, are you too leading the same sorry kind of life that I did when I was above ground? I was son of Zeus, but I went through an infinity of suffering, for I became bondsman to one who was far beneath me—a low fellow who set me all manner of labors. He once sent me here to fetch the hell-hound—for he did not think he could find anything harder for me than this, but I got the hound out of Hades and brought him to him, for Hermes and Athena helped me.'

"On this Heracles went down again into the house of Hades, but I stayed where I was in case some other of the mighty dead should come to me. And I should have seen still other of them that are gone before, whom I would have liked to see—Theseus and Pirithous—glorious children of the gods, but so many thousands of ghosts came round me and uttered such appalling cries, that I was panic stricken lest Persephone should send up from the house of Hades the head of that awful monster Gorgon. On this I hastened back to my ship and ordered my men to go on board at once and loose the hawsers; so they embarked and took their places, whereon the ship went down the stream of the river Oceanus. We had to row at first, but presently a fair wind sprang up.

The Sirens
Scylla and Charybdis
The cattle of the sun

"AFTER WE WERE clear of the river Oceanus, and had got out into the open sea, we went on till we reached the Aeaean island where there is dawn and sun-rise as in other places. We then drew our ship on to the sands and got out of her on to the shore, where we went to sleep and waited till day should break.

"Then, when the child of morning, rosy-fingered Dawn, appeared, I sent some men to Circe's house to fetch the body of Elpenor. We cut firewood from a wood where the headland jutted out into the sea, and after we had wept over him and lamented him we performed his funeral rites. When his body and armor had been burned to ashes, we raised a cairn, set a stone over it, and at the top of the cairn we fixed the oar that he had been used to row with.

"While we were doing all this, Circe, who knew that we had got back from the house of Hades, dressed herself and came to us as fast as she could; and her maid servants came with her bringing us bread, meat, and wine. Then she stood in the midst of us and said, 'You have done a bold thing in going down alive to the house of Hades, and you will have died twice, to other people's once; now, then, stay here for the rest of the day, feast your fill, and go on with your voyage at daybreak tomorrow morning. In the meantime I will tell Odysseus about your course, and will explain everything to him so as to prevent your suffering from misadventure either by land or sea.'

"We agreed to do as she had said, and feasted through the livelong day to the going down of the sun, but when the sun had set and it came on dark, the men laid themselves down to sleep by the stern cables of the ship. Then Circe took me by the hand and bade me be seated away from the others, while she reclined by my side and asked me all about our adventures.

"'So far so good,' said she, when I had ended my story, 'and now pay attention to what I am about to tell you—heaven itself, indeed, will recall it to your recollection. First you will come to the Sirens who enchant all who come near them. If anyone unwarily draws in too close and hears the singing of the Sirens, his wife and children will never welcome him home again, for they sit in a green field and warble him to death with the sweetness of their song. There is a great heap of dead men's bones lying all around, with the flesh still rotting off them. Therefore pass these Sirens by, and stop your men's ears with wax that none of them may hear; but if you like you can listen yourself, for you may get the men to bind you as you stand upright on a cross piece half way up the mast, and they must lash the rope's ends to the mast itself, that you may have the pleasure of listening. If you beg and pray the men to unloose you, then they must bind you faster.

"'When your crew have taken you past these Sirens, I cannot give you coherent directions as to which of two courses you are to take; I will lay the two alternatives before you, and you must consider them for yourself. On the one hand there are some overhanging rocks against which the deep blue waves of Amphitrite beat with terrific fury; the blessed gods call these rocks the Wanderers. Here not even a bird may pass, no, not even the timid doves that bring ambrosia to Father Zeus, but the sheer rock always carries off one of them, and Father Zeus has to send another to make up their number; no ship that ever yet came to these rocks has got away again, but the waves and whirl-winds of fire are freighted with wreckage and with the bodies of dead men. The only vessel that ever sailed and got through, was the famous Argo on her way from the house of Aetes, and she too would have gone against these great rocks, only that Hera piloted her past them for the love she bore to Jason.[†]

"'Of these two rocks the one reaches heaven and its peak is lost in a dark cloud. This never leaves it, so that the top is never clear not even in summer and early autumn. No man though he had twenty hands and twenty feet could get a foothold on it and climb it, for it runs sheer up, as smooth as though it had been polished. In the middle of it there is a large cavern, looking West and turned towards Erebus; you must take your ship this way, but the cave is so high up that not even the stoutest archer could send an arrow into it. Inside it Scylla sits and yelps with a voice that you might take to be that of a young hound, but in truth she is a dreadful monster and no one—not even a god—could face her without being terror-struck. She has twelve mis-shapen feet, and six necks of the most prodigious length; and at the end of each neck she has a frightful head with three rows of teeth in each, all set very close together, so that they would crunch anyone to death in a moment, and she sits deep within her shady cell thrusting out her heads and peering all round the rock, fishing for dolphins or dogfish or any larger monster that she can catch, of the thousands with which Amphitrite teems. No ship ever yet got past her without losing some men, for she shoots out all her heads at once, and carries off a man in each mouth.

"'You will find the other rock lie lower, but they are so close together that there is not more than a bow-shot between them. A large fig tree in full leaf grows upon it, and under it lies the sucking whirlpool of Charybdis. Three times in the day does she vomit forth her waters, and three times she sucks them down again; see that you be not there when she is sucking, for if you are, Poseidon himself could not save you; you must hug the Scylla side and drive ship by as fast as you can, for you had better lose six men than your whole crew.'†

"'Is there no way,' said I, 'of escaping Charybdis, and at the same time keeping Scylla off when she is trying to harm my men?'

"'You dare devil,' replied the goddess, 'you are always wanting to fight somebody or something; you will not let yourself be beaten even by the immortals. For Scylla is not mortal; moreover she is savage, extreme, rude, cruel and invincible. There is no help for it; your best chance will be to get by her as fast as ever you can, for if you dawdle about her rock while you are putting on your armor, she may catch you with a second cast of her six heads, and snap up another half dozen of your men; so drive your ship past her at full speed, and roar out lustily to Crataiis who is Scylla's dam, bad luck to her; she will then stop her from making a second raid upon you.'

"'You will now come to the Thrinacian island, and here you will see many herds of cattle and flocks of sheep belonging to the sun-god—seven herds of cattle and seven flocks of sheep, with fifty head in each flock. They do not breed, nor do they become fewer in number, and they are tended by the goddesses Phaethusa and Lampetie, who are children of the sun-god Hyperion by Neaera. Their mother when she had borne them and had done suckling them sent them to the Thrinacian island, which was a long way off, to live there and look after their father's flocks and herds. If you leave these flocks unharmed, and think of nothing but getting home, you may yet after much hardship reach Ithaca; but if you harm them, then I forewarn you of the destruction both of your ship and of your comrades; and even though you may yourself escape, you will return late, in bad plight, after losing all your men.'

"Here she ended, and dawn enthroned in gold began to show in heaven, whereon she returned inland. I then went on board and told my men to loose the ship from her moorings; so they at once got into her, took their places, and began to smite the grey sea with their oars. Presently the great and cunning goddess Circe befriended us with a fair wind that blew dead aft, and stayed steadily with us, keeping our sails well filled, so we did whatever wanted doing to the ship's gear, and let her go as wind and helmsman headed her.

"Then, being much troubled in mind, I said to my men, 'My friends, it is not right that one or two of us alone should know the prophecies that Circe has made me, I will therefore tell you about them, so that whether we live or die we may do so with our eyes open. First she said we were to keep clear of the Sirens, who sit and sing most beautifully in a field of flowers; but she said I might hear them myself so long as no one else did. Therefore, take me and bind me to the crosspiece half way up the mast; bind me as I stand upright, with a bond so fast that I cannot possibly break away, and lash the rope's ends to the mast itself. If I beg and pray you to set me free, then bind me more tightly still.'

"I had hardly finished telling everything to the men before we reached the island of the two Sirens, for the wind had been very favorable. Then all of a sudden it fell dead calm; there was not a breath of wind nor a ripple upon the water, so the men furled the sails and stowed them; then taking to their oars they whitened the water with the foam they raised in rowing. Meanwhile I look a large wheel of wax and cut it up small with my sword. Then I kneaded the wax in my strong hands till it became soft, which it soon did between the kneading and the rays of the sun-god son of Hyperion. Then I stopped the ears of all my men, and they bound me hands and feet to the mast as I stood upright on the cross piece; but they went on rowing themselves. When we had got within earshot of the land, and the ship was going at a good rate, the Sirens saw that we were getting in shore and began with their singing.

"'Come here,' they sang, 'renowned Odysseus, honor to the Achaean name, and listen to our two voices. No one ever sailed past us without staying to hear the enchanting sweetness of our song—and he who listens will go on his way not only charmed, but wiser, for we know all the ills that the gods laid upon the Argives and Trojans before Troy, and can tell you everything that is going to happen over the whole world.'

"They sang these words most musically, and as I longed to hear them further I made signs by frowning to my men that they should set me free; but they quickened their stroke, and Eurylochus and Perimedes bound me with still stronger bonds till we had got out of hearing of the Sirens' voices. Then my men took the wax from their ears and unbound me.

"Immediately after we had got past the island I saw a great wave from which spray was rising, and I heard a loud roaring sound. The men were so frightened that they loosed hold of their oars, for the whole sea resounded with the rushing of the waters, but the ship stayed where it was, for the men had left off rowing. I went round, therefore, and exhorted them man by man not to lose heart.

"'My friends,' said I, 'this is not the first time that we have been in danger, and we are in nothing like so bad a case as when the Cyclops shut us up in his cave; nevertheless, my courage and wise counsel saved us then, and we shall live to look back on all this as well. Now, therefore, let us all do as I say, trust in Zeus and row on with might and main. As for you, coxswain, these are your orders; attend to them, for the ship is in your hands; turn her head away from these steaming rapids and hug the rock, or she will give you the slip and be over yonder before you know where you are, and you will be the death of us.'

"So they did as I told them; but I said nothing about the awful monster Scylla, for I knew the men would not go on rowing if I did,[†] but would huddle together in the hold. In one thing only did I disobey Circe's strict instructions—I put on my armor. Then seizing two strong spears I took my stand on the ship's bows, for it was there that I expected first to see the monster of the rock, who was to do my men so much harm; but I could not make her out anywhere, though I strained my eyes with looking the gloomy rock all over and over.

"Then we entered the Straits in great fear of mind, for on the one hand was Scylla, and on the other dread Charybdis kept sucking up the salt water. As she vomited it up, it was like the water in a cauldron when it is boiling over upon a great fire, and the spray reached the top of the rocks on either side. When she began to suck again, we could see the water all inside whirling round and round, and it made a deafening sound as it broke against the rocks. We could see the bottom of the whirlpool all black with sand and mud, and the men were at their wits ends for fear. While we were taken up with this, and were expecting each moment to be our last, Scylla pounced down suddenly upon us and snatched up my six best men. I was looking at once after both ship and men, and in a moment I saw their hands and feet ever so high above me, struggling in the air as Scylla was carrying them off, and I heard them call out my name in one last despairing cry. As a fisherman, seated, spear in hand, upon some jutting rock throws bait into the water to deceive the poor little fishes, and spears them with the ox's horn with which his spear is shod, throwing them gasping on to the land as he catches them one by one—even so did Scylla land these panting creatures on her rock and munch them up at the mouth of her den, while they screamed and stretched out their hands to me in their mortal agony. This was the most sickening sight that I saw throughout all my voyages.[†]

"When we had passed the Wandering rocks, with Scylla and terrible Charybdis, we reached the noble island of the sun-god, where were the goodly cattle and sheep belonging to the sun Hyperion. While still at sea in my ship I could hear the cattle lowing as they came home to the yards, and the sheep bleating. Then I remembered what the blind Theban prophet Teiresias had told me, and how carefully Aeaean Circe had warned me to shun the island of the blessed sun-god. So being much troubled I said to the men, 'My men, I know you are hard pressed, but listen while I tell you the prophecy that Teiresias made me, and how carefully Aeaean Circe warned me to shun the island of the blessed sun-god, for it was here, she said, that our worst danger would lie. Head the ship, therefore, away from the island.'

"The men were in despair at this, and Eurylochus at once gave me an insolent answer. 'Odysseus,' said he, 'you are cruel; you are very strong yourself and never get worn out; you seem to be made of iron, and now, though your men are exhausted with toil and want of sleep, you will not let them land and cook themselves a good supper upon this island, but bid them put out to sea and go faring fruitlessly on through the watches of the flying night. It is by night that the winds blow hardest and do so much damage; how can we escape should one of those sudden squalls spring up from South West or West, which so often wreck a vessel when our lords the gods are unpropitious? Now, therefore, let us obey the behests of night and prepare our supper here hard by the ship; to-morrow morning we will go on board again and put out to sea.'

"Thus spoke Eurylochus, and the men approved his words. I saw that heaven meant us a mischief and said, 'You force me to yield, for you are many against one, but at any rate each one of you must take his solemn oath that if he meet with a herd of cattle or a large flock of sheep, he will not be so mad as to kill a single head of either, but will be satisfied with the food that Circe has given us.'

"They all swore as I bade them, and when they had completed their oath we made the ship fast in a harbor that was near a stream of fresh water, and the men went ashore and cooked their suppers. As soon as they had had enough to eat and drink, they began talking about their poor comrades whom Scylla had snatched up and eaten; this set them weeping and they went on crying till they fell off into a sound sleep.

"In the third watch of the night when the stars had shifted their places, Zeus raised a great gale of wind that flew a hurricane so that land and sea were covered with thick clouds, and night sprang forth out of the heavens. When the child of morning, rosy-fingered Dawn, appeared, we brought the ship to land and drew her into a cave wherein the sea-nymphs hold their courts and dances, and I called the men together in council.

"'My friends,' said I, 'we have meat and drink in the ship, let us mind, therefore, and not touch the cattle, or we shall suffer for it; for these cattle and sheep belong to the mighty sun, who sees and gives ear to everything.' And again they promised that they would obey.

"For a whole month the wind blew steadily from the South, and there was no other wind, but only South and East. As long as corn and wine held out the men did not touch the cattle when they were hungry; when, however, they had eaten all there was in the ship, they were forced to go further afield, with hook and line, catching birds, and taking whatever they could lay their hands on; for they were starving.† One day, therefore, I went up inland that I might pray heaven to show me some means of getting away. When I had gone far enough to be clear of all my men, and had found a place that was well sheltered from the wind, I washed my hands and prayed to all the gods in Olympus till by and by they sent me off into a sweet sleep.

"Meanwhile Eurylochus had been giving evil counsel to the men, 'Listen to me,' said he, 'my poor comrades. All deaths are bad enough but there is none so bad as famine. Why should not we drive in the best of these cows and offer them in sacrifice to the immortal gods? If we ever get back to Ithaca, we can build a fine temple to the sun-god and enrich it with every kind of ornament; if, however, he is determined to sink our ship out of revenge for these homed cattle, and the other gods are of the same mind, I for one would rather drink salt water once for all and have done with it, than be starved to death by inches in such a desert island as this is.'

"Thus spoke Eurylochus, and the men approved his words. Now the cattle, so fair and goodly, were feeding not far from the ship; the men, therefore, drove in the best of them, and they all stood round them saying their prayers, and using young oak-shoots instead of barley-meal, for there was no barley left. When they had done praying they killed the cows and dressed their carcasses; they cut out the thigh bones, wrapped them round in two layers of fat, and set some pieces of raw meat on top of them. They had no wine with which to make drink-offerings over the sacrifice while it was cooking, so they kept pouring on a little water from time to time while the inward meats were being grilled; then, when the thigh bones were burned and they had tasted the inward meats, they cut the rest up small and put the pieces upon the spits.

"By this time my deep sleep had left me, and I turned back to the ship and to the sea shore. As I drew near I began to smell hot roast meat, so I groaned out a prayer to the immortal gods. 'Father Zeus,' I exclaimed, 'and all you other gods who live in everlasting bliss, you have done me a cruel mischief by the sleep into which you have sent me; see what fine work these men of mine have been making in my absence.'

"Meanwhile Lampetie went straight off to the sun and told him we had been killing his cows, whereon he flew into a great rage, and said to the immortals, 'Father Zeus, and all you other gods who live in everlasting bliss, I must have vengeance on the crew of Odysseus' ship: they have had the insolence to kill my cows, which were the one thing I loved to look upon, whether I was going up heaven or down again. If they do not square accounts with me about my cows, I will go down to Hades and shine there among the dead.'

"'Sun,' said Zeus, 'go on shining upon us gods and upon mankind over the fruitful earth. I will shiver their ship into little pieces with a bolt of white lightning as soon as they get out to sea.'

"I was told all this by Calypso, who said she had heard it from the mouth of Hermes.

"As soon as I got down to my ship and to the sea shore I rebuked each one of the men separately, but we could see no way out of it, for the cows were dead already. And indeed the gods began at once to show signs and wonders among us, for the hides of the cattle crawled about, and the joints upon the spits began to low like cows, and the meat, whether cooked or raw, kept on making a noise just as cows do.

"For six days my men kept driving in the best cows and feasting upon them, but when Zeus the son of Cronus had added a seventh day, the fury of the gale abated; we therefore went on board, raised our masts, spread sail, and put out to sea. As soon as we were well away from the island, and could see nothing but sky and sea, the son of Cronus raised a black cloud over our ship, and the sea grew dark beneath it. We did not get on much further, for in another moment we were caught by a terrific squall from the West that snapped the forestays of the mast so that it fell aft, while all the ship's gear tumbled about at the bottom of the vessel. The mast fell upon the head of the helmsman in the ship's stern, so that the bones of his head were crushed to pieces, and he fell overboard as though he were diving, with no more life left in him.

"Then Zeus let fly with his thunderbolts, and the ship went round and round, and was filled with fire and brimstone as the lightning struck it. The men all fell into the sea; they were carried about in the water round the ship, looking like so many sea-gulls, but the god presently deprived them of all chance of getting home again.

"I stuck to the ship till the sea knocked her sides from her keel (which drifted about by itself) and struck the mast out of her in the direction of the keel; but there was a backstay of stout ox-thong still hanging about it, and with this I lashed the mast and keel together, and getting astride of them was carried wherever the winds chose to take me.

"The gale from the West had now spent its force, and the wind got into the South again, which frightened me lest I should be taken back to the terrible whirlpool of Charybdis. This indeed was what actually happened, for I was borne along by the waves all night, and by sunrise had reached the rock of Scylla, and the whirlpool. She was then sucking down the salt sea water, but I was carried aloft toward the fig tree, which I caught hold of and clung on to like a bat. I could not plant my feet anywhere so as to stand securely, for the roots were a long way off and the boughs that overshadowed the whole pool were too high, too vast, and too far apart for me to reach them; so I hung patiently on, waiting till the pool should discharge my mast and raft again— and a very long while it seemed. A jury-man is not more glad to get home to supper, after having been long detained in court by troublesome cases, than

I was to see my raft beginning to work its way out of the whirlpool again. At last I let go with my hands and feet, and fell heavily into the sea, hard by my raft on to which I then got, and began to row with my hands. As for Scylla, the father of gods and men would not let her get further sight of me—otherwise I should have certainly been lost.

"Hence I was carried along for nine days till on the tenth night the gods stranded me on the Ogygian island, where dwells the great and powerful goddess Calypso. She took me in and was kind to me, but I need say no more about this, for I told you and your noble wife all about it yesterday, and I hate saying the same thing over and over again."

B O O K X I I I

Odysseus leaves Scheria and returns to Ithaca.

THUS DID HE speak, and they all held their peace throughout the covered cloister, enthralled by the charm of his story, till presently Alcinous began to speak.

"Odysseus," said he, "now that you have reached my house I doubt not you will get home without further misadventure no matter how much you have suffered in the past. To you others, however, who come here night after night to drink my choicest wine and listen to my bard, I would insist as follows. Our guest has already packed up the clothes, wrought gold, and other valuables which you have brought for his acceptance; let us now, therefore, present him further, each one of us, with a large tripod and a cauldron. We will recoup ourselves by the levy of a general rate; for private individuals cannot be expected to bear the burden of such a handsome present."†

Everyone approved of this, and then they went home to bed each in his own abode. When the child of morning, rosy-fingered Dawn, appeared they hurried down to the ship and brought their cauldrons with them. Alcinous went on board and saw everything so securely stowed under the ship's benches that nothing could break adrift and injure the rowers. Then they went to the house of Alcinous to get dinner, and he sacrificed a bull for them in honor of Zeus who is the lord of all. They set the steaks to grill and made an excellent dinner, after which the inspired bard, Demodocus, who was a favorite with everyone, sang to them; but Odysseus kept on turning his eyes towards the sun, as though to hasten his setting, for he was longing to be on his way. As one who has been all day ploughing a fallow field with a couple of oxen keeps thinking about his supper and is glad when night comes that he may go and get it, for it is all his legs can do to carry him, even so did Odysseus rejoice when the sun went down, and he at once said to the Phaeacians, addressing himself more particularly to King Alcinous:

"Sir, and all of you, farewell. Make your drink-offerings and send me on my way rejoicing, for you have fulfilled my heart's desire by giving me an escort, and making me presents, which heaven grant that I may turn to good account; may I find my admirable wife living in peace among friends, and may you whom I leave behind me give satisfaction to your wives and children; may heaven vouchsafe you every good grace, and may no evil thing come among your people."

Thus did he speak. His hearers all of them approved his saying and agreed that he should have his escort inasmuch as he had spoken reasonably. Alcinous therefore said to his servant, "Pontonous, mix some wine and hand it round to everybody, that we may offer a prayer to father Zeus, and speed our guest upon his way."

Pontonous mixed the wine and handed it to everyone in turn; the others each from his own seat made a drink-offering to the blessed gods that live in heaven, but Odysseus rose and placed the double cup in the hands of queen Arete.

"Farewell, queen," said he, "henceforward and for ever, till age and death, the common lot of mankind, lay their hands upon you. I now take my leave; be happy in this house with your children, your people, and with king Alcinous."

As he spoke he crossed the threshold, and Alcinous sent a man to conduct him to his ship and to the sea shore. Arete also sent some maidservants with him—one with a clean shirt and cloak, another to carry his strong box, and a third with corn and wine. When they got to the waterside the crew took these things and put them on board, with all the meat and drink; but for Odysseus they spread a rug and a linen sheet on deck that he might sleep soundly in the stern of the ship. Then he too went on board and lay down without a word, but the crew took every man his place and loosed the hawser from the pierced stone to which it had been bound. Thereon, when they began rowing out to sea, Odysseus fell into a deep, sweet, and almost deathlike slumber.

The ship bounded forward on her way as a four in hand chariot flies over the course when the horses feel the whip. Her prow curvetted as it were the neck of a stallion, and a great wave of dark blue water seethed in her wake. She held steadily on her course, and even a falcon, swiftest of all birds, could not have kept pace with her. Thus, then, she cut her way through the water, carrying one who was as cunning as the gods, but who was now sleeping peacefully, forgetful of all that he had suffered both on the field of battle and by the waves of the weary sea.

When the bright star that heralds the approach of dawn began to show, the ship drew near to land. Now there is in Ithaca a haven of the old merman Phorcys, which lies between two points that break the line of the sea and shut the harbor in. These shelter it from the storms of wind and sea that rage outside, so that, when once within it, a ship may lie without being even moored. At the head of this harbor there is a large olive tree, and at no great distance a fine overarching cavern sacred to the nymphs who are called Naiads. There are mixing bowls within it and wine-jars of stone, and the bees hive there. Moreover, there are great looms of stone on which the nymphs weave their robes of sea purple—very curious to see—and at all times there is water within it. It has two entrances, one facing North by which mortals can go down into the cave, while the other comes from the South and is more mysterious; mortals cannot possibly get in by it, it is the way taken by the gods.

Into this harbor, then, they took their ship, for they knew the place. She had so much way upon her that she ran half her own length on to the shore; when, however, they had landed, the first thing they did was to lift Odysseus with his rug and linen sheet out of the ship, and lay him down upon the sand still fast asleep. Then they took out the presents which Athena had persuaded the Phaeacians to give him when he was setting out on his voyage homewards. They put these all together by the root of the olive tree, away from the road, for fear some passer by might come and steal them before Odysseus awoke; and then they made the best of their way home again.

But Poseidon did not forget the threats with which he had already threatened Odysseus, so he took counsel with Zeus. "Father Zeus," said he, "I shall no longer be held in any sort of respect among you gods, if mortals like the Phaeacians, who are my own flesh and blood, show such small regard for me. I said I would let Odysseus get home when he had suffered sufficiently. I did not say that he should never get home at all, for I knew you had already nodded your head about it, and promised that he should do so; but now they have brought him in a ship fast asleep and have landed him in Ithaca after loading him with more magnificent presents of bronze, gold, and raiment than he would ever have brought back from Troy, if he had had his share of the spoil and got home without misadventure."†

And Zeus answered, "What, O Lord of the Earthquake, are you talking about? The gods are by no means wanting in respect for you. It would be monstrous were they to insult one so old and honored as you are. As regards mortals, however, if any of them is indulging in insolence and treating you disrespectfully, it will always rest with yourself to deal with him as you may think proper, so do just as you please."

"I should have done so at once," replied Poseidon, "if I were not anxious to avoid anything that might displease you; now, therefore, I should like to wreck the Phaeacian ship as it is returning from its escort. This will stop them from escorting people in future; and I should also like to bury their city under a huge mountain."

"My good friend," answered Zeus, "I should recommend you at the very moment when the people from the city are watching the ship on her way, to turn it into a rock near the land and looking like a ship. This will astonish everybody, and you can then bury their city under the mountain."

When earth-encircling Poseidon heard this he went to Scheria where the Phaeacians live, and stayed there till the ship, which was making rapid way, had got close in. Then he went up to it, turned it into stone, and drove it down with the flat of his hand so as to root it in the ground. After this he went away.

The Phaeacians then began talking among themselves, and one would turn towards his neighbor, saying, "Bless my heart, who is it that can have rooted the ship in the sea just as she was getting into port? We could see the whole of her only a moment ago."

This was how they talked, but they knew nothing about it; and Alcinous said, "I remember now the old prophecy of my father. He said that Poseidon would be angry with us for taking everyone so safely over the sea, and would one day wreck a Phaeacian ship as it was returning from an escort, and bury our city under a high mountain. This was what my old father used to say, and now it is all coming true. Now therefore let us all do as I say; in the first place we must leave off giving people escorts when they come here, and in the next let us sacrifice twelve picked bulls to Poseidon that he may have mercy upon us, and not bury our city under the high mountain." When the people heard this they were afraid and got ready the bulls.

Thus did the chiefs and rulers of the Phaeacians pray to king Poseidon, standing round his altar; and at the same time Odysseus woke up once more upon his own soil. He had been so long away that he did not know it again; moreover, Zeus' daughter Athena had made it a foggy day, so that people might not know of his having come,[†] and that she might tell him everything without either his wife or his fellow citizens and friends recognising him until he had taken his revenge upon the wicked suitors. Everything, therefore, seemed quite different to him—the long straight tracks, the harbors, the precipices, and the goodly trees, appeared all changed as he started up and looked upon his native land. So he smote his thighs with the flat of his hands and cried aloud despairingly.

"Alas," he exclaimed, "among what manner of people am I fallen? Are they savage and uncivilized or hospitable and humane? Where shall I put all this treasure, and which way shall I go? I wish I had staid over there with the Phaeacians; or I could have gone to some other great chief who would have been good to me and given me an escort. As it is I do not know where to put my treasure, and I cannot leave it here for fear somebody else should get hold of it. In good truth the chiefs and rulers of the Phaeacians have not been dealing fairly by me, and have left me in the wrong country; they said they would take me back to Ithaca and they have not done so: may Zeus the protector of suppliants chastise them, for he watches over everybody and punishes those who do wrong. Still, I suppose I must count my goods and see if the crew have gone off with any of them."

He counted his goodly coppers and cauldrons, his gold and all his clothes, but there was nothing missing; still he kept grieving about not being in his own country, and wandered up and down by the shore of the sounding sea bewailing his hard fate. Then Athena came up to him disguised as a young shepherd of delicate and princely mien, with a good cloak folded double about her shoulders; she had sandals on her comely feet and held a javelin in her hand. Odysseus was glad when he saw her, and went straight up to her.[†]

"My friend," said he, "you are the first person whom I have met with in this country; I salute you, therefore, and beg you to be well disposed towards me. Protect these my goods, and myself too, for I embrace your knees and pray to you as though you were a god. Tell me, then, and tell me truly, what land and country is this? Who are its inhabitants? Am I on an island, or is this the sea board of some continent?"

Athena answered, "Stranger, you must be very simple, or must have come from somewhere a long way off, not to know what country this is. It is a very celebrated place, and everybody knows it East and West. It is rugged and not a good driving country, but it is by no means a bad island for what there is of it. It grows any quantity of corn and also wine, for it is watered both by rain and dew; it breeds cattle also and goats; all kinds of timber grow here, and there are watering places where the water never runs dry; so, sir, the name of Ithaca is known even as far as Troy, which I understand to be a long way off from this Achaean country."

Odysseus was glad at finding himself, as Athena told him, in his own country, and he began to answer, but he did not speak the truth, and made up a lying story in the instinctive wiliness of his heart.[†]

"I heard of Ithaca," said he, "when I was in Crete beyond the seas, and now it seems I have reached it with all these treasures. I have left as much more behind me for my children, but am flying because I killed Orsilochus son of Idomeneus, the fleetest runner in Crete. I killed him because he wanted to rob me of the spoils I had got from Troy with so much trouble and danger both on the field of battle and by the waves of the weary sea; he said I had not served his father loyally at Troy as vassal, but had set myself up as an independent ruler, so I lay in wait for him with one of my followers by the road side, and speared him as he was coming into town from the country. It was a very dark night and nobody saw us; it was not known, therefore, that I had killed him, but as soon as I had done so I went to a ship and besought the owners, who were Phoenicians, to take me on board and set me in Pylos or in Elis where the Epeans rule, giving them as much spoil as satisfied them. They meant no guile, but the wind drove them off their course, and we sailed on till we came hither by night. It was all we could do to get inside the harbor, and none of us said a word about supper though we wanted it badly, but we all went on shore and lay down just as we were. I was very tired and fell asleep directly, so they took my goods out of the ship, and placed them beside me where I was lying upon the sand. Then they sailed away to Sidonia, and I was left here in great distress of mind."

Such was his story, but Athena smiled and caressed him with her hand. Then she took the form of a woman, fair, stately, and wise, "He must be indeed a shifty lying fellow," said she, "who could surpass you in all manner of craft even though you had a god for your antagonist. Dare devil that you are, full of guile, unwearying in deceit, can you not drop your tricks and your instinctive falsehood, even now that you are in your own country again? We will say no more, however, about this, for we can both of us deceive upon occasion—you are the most accomplished counsellor and orator among all mankind, while I for diplomacy and subtlety have no equal among the gods. Did you not know Zeus' daughter Athena—me, who have been ever with you, who kept watch over you in all your troubles, and who made the Phaeacians take so great a liking to you? And now, again, I am come here to talk things over with you, and help you to hide the treasure I made the Phaeacians give you; I want to tell you about the troubles that await you in your own house; you have got to face them, but tell no one, neither man nor woman, that you have come home again. Bear everything, and put up with every man's insolence, without a word."

And Odysseus answered, "A man, goddess, may know a great deal, but you are so constantly changing your appearance that when he meets you it is a hard matter for him to know whether it is you or not. This much, however, I know exceedingly well; you were very kind to me as long as we Achaeans were fighting before Troy, but from the day on which we went on board ship after having sacked the city of Priam, and heaven dispersed us—from that day, Athena, I saw no more of you, and cannot ever remember your coming to my ship to help me in a difficulty; I had to wander on sick and sorry till the gods delivered me from evil and I reached the city of the Phaeacians, where you encouraged me and took me into the town. And now, I beseech you in your father's name, tell me the truth, for I do not believe I am really back in Ithaca. I am in some other country and you are mocking me and deceiving me in all you have been saying. Tell me then truly, have I really got back to my own country?"

"You are always taking something of that sort in your head," replied Athena, "and that is why I cannot desert you in your afflictions; you are so plausible, shrewd and shifty. Anyone but yourself on returning from so long a voyage would at once have gone home to see his wife and children, but you do not seem to care about asking after them or hearing any news about them till you have exploited your wife, who remains at home vainly grieving for you, and having no peace night or day for the tears she sheds on your behalf. As for my not coming near you, I was never uneasy about you, for I was certain you would get back safely though you would lose all your men, and I did not wish to quarrel with my uncle Poseidon, who never forgave you for having blinded his son. I will now, however, point out to you the lie of the land, and you will then perhaps believe me. This is the haven of the old merman Phorcys, and here is the olive tree that grows at the head of it; near it is the cave sacred to the Naiads; here too is the overarching cavern in which you have offered many an acceptable hecatomb to the nymphs, and this is the wooded mountain Neritum."

As she spoke the goddess dispersed the mist and the land appeared. Then Odysseus rejoiced at finding himself again in his own land, and kissed the bounteous soil; he lifted up his hands and prayed to the nymphs, saying, "Naiad nymphs, daughters of Zeus, I made sure that I was never again to see you, now therefore I greet you with all loving salutations, and I will bring you offerings as in the old days, if Zeus' redoubtable daughter will grant me life, and bring my son to manhood."

"Take heart, and do not trouble yourself about that," rejoined Athena, "let us rather set about stowing your things at once in the cave, where they will be quite safe. Let us see how we can best manage it all."

Therewith she went down into the cave to look for the safest hiding places, while Odysseus brought up all the treasure of gold, bronze, and good clothing which the Phaeacians had given him. They stowed everything carefully away, and Athena set a stone against the door of the cave. Then the two sat down by the root of the great olive, and consulted how to carry out the destruction of the wicked suitors.

"Odysseus," said Athena, "noble son of Laertes, think how you can lay hands on these disreputable people who have been lording it in your house these three years, courting your wife and making wedding presents to her, while she does nothing but lament your absence, giving hope and sending encouraging messages to everyone of them, but meaning the very opposite of all she says."

And Odysseus answered, "In good truth, goddess, it seems I should have come to much the same bad end in my own house as Agamemnon did, if you had not given me such timely information. Advise me how I shall best avenge myself. Stand by my side and put your courage into my heart as on the day when we loosed Troy's fair diadem from her brow. Help me now as you did then, and I will fight three hundred men, if you, goddess, will be with me."

"Trust me for that," said she, "I will not lose sight of you when once we set about it, and I imagine that some of those who are devouring your substance will then bespatter the pavement with their blood and brains. I will begin by disguising you so that no human being shall know you; I will cover your body with wrinkles; you shall lose all your yellow hair; I will clothe you in a garment that shall fill all who see it with loathing; I will blear your fine eyes for you, and make you an unseemly object in the sight of the suitors, of your wife, and of the son whom you left behind you.[†] Then go at once to the swineherd who is in charge of your pigs; he has been always well affected towards you, and is devoted to Penelope and your son; you will find him feeding his pigs near the rock that is called Raven by the fountain Arethusa, where they are fattening on beechmast and spring water after their manner. Stay with him and find out how things are going, while I proceed to Sparta and see your son, who is with Menelaus at Lacedaemon, where he has gone to try and find out whether you are still alive."

"But why," said Odysseus, "did you not tell him, for you knew all about it? Did you want him too to go sailing about amid all kinds of hardship while others are eating up his estate?"

Athena answered, "Never mind about him, I sent him that he might be well spoken of for having gone. He is in no sort of difficulty, but is staying quite comfortably with Menelaus, and is surrounded with abundance of every kind. The suitors have put out to sea and are lying in wait for him, for they mean to kill him before he can get home. I do not much think they will succeed, but rather that some of those who are now eating up your estate will first find a grave themselves."

As she spoke Athena touched him with her wand and covered him with wrinkles, took away all his yellow hair, and withered the flesh over his whole body; she bleared his eyes, which were naturally very fine ones; she changed his clothes and threw an old rag of a wrap about him, and a tunic, tattered, filthy, and begrimed with smoke; she also gave him an undressed deer skin as an outer garment, and furnished him with a staff and a wallet all in holes, with a twisted thong for him to sling it over his shoulder.

When the pair had thus laid their plans they parted, and the goddess went straight to Lacedaemon to fetch Telemachus.

B O O K X I V

Odysseus in the hut with Eumaeus

ODYSSEUS NOW LEFT the haven, and took the rough track up through the wooded country and over the crest of the mountain till he reached the place where Athena had said that he would find the swineherd, who was the most thrifty servant he had. He found him sitting in front of his hut, which was by the yards that he had built on a site which could be seen from far. He had made them spacious and fair to see, with a free run for the pigs all round them; he had built them during his master's absence, of stones which he had gathered out of the ground, without saying anything to Penelope or Laertes, and he had fenced them on top with thorn bushes. Outside the yard he had run a strong fence of oaken posts, split, and set pretty close together, while inside he had built twelve styes near one another for the sows to lie in. There were fifty pigs wallowing in each sty, all of them breeding sows; but the boars slept outside and were much fewer in number, for the suitors kept on eating them, and the swineherd had to send them the best he had continually. There were three hundred and sixty boar pigs, and the herdsman's four hounds, which were as fierce as wolves, slept always with them.† The swineherd was at that moment cutting out a pair of sandals from a good stout oxhide. Three of his men were out herding the pigs in one place or another, and he had sent the fourth to town with a boar that he had been forced to send the suitors that they might sacrifice it and have their fill of meat.

When the hounds saw Odysseus they set up a furious barking and flew at him, but Odysseus was cunning enough to sit down and loose his hold of the stick that he had in his hand: still, he would have been torn by them in his own homestead had not the swineherd dropped his oxhide, rushed full speed through the gate of the yard and driven the dogs off by shouting and throwing stones at them. Then he said to Odysseus, "Old man, the dogs were likely to have made short work of you, and then you would have got me into trouble. The gods have given me quite enough worries without that, for I have lost the best of masters, and am in continual grief on his account. I have to attend swine for other people to eat, while he, if he yet lives to see the light of day, is starving in some distant land. But come inside, and when you have had your fill of bread and wine, tell me where you come from, and all about your misfortunes."[†]

On this the swineherd led the way into the hut and bade him sit down. He strewed a good thick bed of rushes upon the floor, and on the top of this he threw the shaggy chamois skin—a great thick one—on which he used to sleep by night. Odysseus was pleased at being made thus welcome, and said "May Zeus, sir, and the rest of the gods grant you your heart's desire in return for the kind way in which you have received me."

To this you answered, O swineherd Eumaeus, "Stranger, though a still poorer man should come here, it would not be right for me to insult him, for all strangers and beggars are from Zeus. You must take what you can get and be thankful, for servants live in fear when they have young lords for their masters; and this is my misfortune now, for heaven has hindered the return of him who would have been always good to me and given me something of my own—a house, a piece of land, a good looking wife, and all else that a liberal master allows a servant who has worked hard for him, and whose labor the gods have prospered as they have mine in the situation which I hold. If my master had grown old here he would have done great things by me, but he is gone, and I wish that Helen's whole race were utterly destroyed, for she has been the death of many a good man.[†] It was this matter that took my master to Ilius, the land of noble steeds, to fight the Trojans in the cause of king Agamemnon."

As he spoke he bound his girdle round him and went to the styes where the young sucking pigs were penned. He picked out two which he brought back with him and sacrificed. He singed them, cut them up, and spitted them; when the meat was cooked he brought it all in and set it before Odysseus, hot and still on the spit, whereon Odysseus sprinkled it over with white barley meal. The swineherd then mixed wine in a bowl of ivy-wood, and taking a seat opposite Odysseus told him to begin.

"Fall to, stranger," said he, "on a dish of servant's pork. The fat pigs have to go to the suitors, who eat them up without shame or scruple; but the blessed gods love not such shameful doings, and respect those who do what is lawful and right. Even the fierce freebooters who go raiding on other people's land, and Zeus gives them their spoil—even they, when they have filled their ships and got home again live conscience-stricken, and look fearfully for judgement; but some god seems to have told these people that Odysseus is dead and gone; they will not, therefore, go back to their own homes and make their offers of marriage in the usual way, but waste his estate by force, without fear or stint. Not a day or night comes out of heaven, but they sacrifice not one victim nor two only, and they take the run of his wine, for he was exceedingly rich. No other great man either in Ithaca or on the mainland is as rich as he was; he had as much as twenty men put together. I will tell you what he had. There are twelve herds of cattle upon the main land, and as many flocks of sheep, there are also twelve droves of pigs, while his own men and hired strangers feed him twelve widely spreading herds of goats. Here in Ithaca he runs even large flocks of goats on the far end of the island, and they are in the charge of excellent goat herds. Each one of these sends the suitors the best goat in the flock every day. As for myself, I am in charge of the pigs that you see here, and I have to keep picking out the best I have and sending it to them."

This was his story, but Odysseus went on eating and drinking ravenously without a word, brooding his revenge. When he had eaten enough and was satisfied, the swineherd took the bowl from which he usually drank, filled it with wine, and gave it to Odysseus, who was pleased, and said as he took it in his hands, "My friend, who was this master of yours that bought you and paid for you, so rich and so powerful as you tell me? You say he perished in the cause of King Agamemnon; tell me who he was, in case I may have met with such a person. Zeus and the other gods know, but I may be able to give you news of him, for I have traveled much."

Eumaeus answered, "Old man, no traveler who comes here with news will get Odysseus' wife and son to believe his story. Nevertheless, tramps in want of a lodging keep coming with their mouths full of lies, and not a word of truth; everyone who finds his way to Ithaca goes to my mistress and tells her falsehoods, whereon she takes them in, makes much of them, and asks them all manner of questions, crying all the time as women will when they have lost their husbands.[†] And you too, old man, for a shirt and a cloak would doubtless make up a very pretty story. But the wolves and birds of prey have long since torn Odysseus to pieces, or the fishes of the sea have eaten him, and his bones are lying buried deep in sand upon some foreign shore; he is dead and gone, and a bad business it is for all his friends—for me especially; go where I may I shall never find so good a master, not even if I were to go home to my mother and father where I was bred and born. I do not so much care, however, about my parents now, though I should dearly like to see them again in my own country; it is the loss of Odysseus that grieves me most; I cannot speak of him without reverence though he is here no longer, for he was very fond of me, and took such care of me that wherever he may be I shall always honor his memory."

"My friend," replied Odysseus, "you are very positive, and very hard of belief about your master's coming home again, nevertheless I will not merely say, but will swear, that he is coming. Do not give me anything for my news till he has actually come, you may then give me a shirt and cloak of good wear if you will. I am in great want, but I will not take anything at all till then, for I hate a man, even as I hate hell fire, who lets his poverty tempt him into lying. I swear by king Zeus, by the rites of hospitality, and by that hearth of Odysseus to which I have now come, that all will surely happen as I have said it will. Odysseus will return in this self same year; with the end of this moon and the beginning of the next he will be here to do vengeance on all those who are ill treating his wife and son."

To this you answered, O swineherd Eumaeus,[†] "Old man, you will neither get paid for bringing good news, nor will Odysseus ever come home; drink your wine in peace, and let us talk about something else. Do not keep on reminding me of all this; it always pains me when anyone speaks about my honored master. As for your oath we will let it alone, but I only wish he may come, as do Penelope, his old father Laertes, and his son Telemachus. I am terribly unhappy too about this same boy of his; he was running up fast into manhood, and bade fare to be no worse man, face and figure, than his father, but someone, either god or man, has been unsettling his mind, so he has gone off to Pylos to try and get news of his father, and the suitors are lying in wait for him as he is coming home, in the hope of leaving the house of Arceisius[†] without a name in Ithaca. But let us say no more about him, and leave him to be taken, or else to escape if the son of Cronus holds his hand over him to protect him. And now, old man, tell me your own story; tell me also, for I want to know, who you are and where you come from. Tell me of your town and parents, what manner of ship you came in, how crew brought you to Ithaca, and from what country they professed to come—for you cannot have come by land."

And Odysseus answered, "I will tell you all about it. If there were meat and wine enough, and we could stay here in the hut with nothing to do but to eat and drink while the others go to their work, I could easily talk on for a whole twelve months without ever finishing the story of the sorrows with which it has pleased heaven to visit me.

"I am by birth a Cretan; my father was a well to do man, who had many sons born in marriage, whereas I was the son of a slave whom he had purchased for a concubine; nevertheless, my father Castor son of Hylax (whose lineage I claim, and who was held in the highest honor among the Cretans for his wealth, prosperity, and the valor of his sons) put me on the same level with my brothers who had been born in wedlock. When, however, death took him to the house of Hades, his sons divided his estate and cast lots for their shares, but to me they gave a holding and little else; nevertheless, my valor enabled me to marry into a rich family, for I was not given to bragging, or shirking on the field of battle. It is all over now; still, if you look at the straw you can see what the ear was, for I have had trouble enough and to spare. Ares and Athena made me doughty in war; when I had picked my men to surprise the enemy with an ambuscade I never gave death so much as a thought, but was the first to leap forward and spear all whom I could overtake. Such was I in battle, but I did not care about farm work, nor the frugal home life of those who would bring up children. My delight was in ships, fighting, javelins, and arrows—things that most men shudder to think of; but one man likes one thing and another another, and this was what I was most naturally inclined to. Before the Achaeans went to Troy, nine times was I in command of men and ships on foreign service, and I amassed much wealth. I had my pick of the spoil in the first instance, and much more was allotted to me later on.

"My house grew apace and I became a great man among the Cretans, but when Zeus counselled that terrible expedition, in which so many perished, the people required me and Idomeneus to lead their ships to Troy, and there was no way out of it, for they insisted on our doing so. There we fought for nine whole years, but in the tenth we sacked the city of Priam and sailed home again as heaven dispersed us. Then it was that Zeus devised evil against me. I spent but one month happily with my children, wife, and property, and then I conceived the idea of making a descent on Egypt, so I fitted out a fine fleet and manned it. I had nine ships, and the people flocked to fill them. For six days I and my men made feast, and I found them many victims both for sacrifice to the gods and for themselves, but on the seventh day we went on board and set sail from Crete with a fair North wind behind us though we were going down a river. Nothing went ill with any of our ships, and we had no sickness on board, but sat where we were and let the ships go as the wind and steersmen took them. On the fifth day we reached the river Aegyptus; there I stationed my ships in the river, bidding my men stay by them and keep guard over them while I sent out scouts to reconnoitre from every point of vantage.

"But the men disobeyed my orders, took to their own devices, and ravaged the land of the Egyptians, killing the men, and taking their wives and children captive. The alarm was soon carried to the city, and when they heard the war cry, the people came out at daybreak till the plain was filled with horsemen and foot soldiers and with the gleam of armor. Then Zeus spread panic among my men, and they would no longer face the enemy, for they found themselves surrounded. The Egyptians killed many of us, and took the rest alive to do forced labor for them.[†] Zeus, however, put it in my mind to do thus—and I wish I had died then and there in Egypt instead, for there was much sorrow in store for me—I took off my helmet and shield and dropped my spear from my hand; then I went straight up to the king's chariot, clasped his knees and kissed them, whereon he spared my life, bade me get into his chariot, and took me weeping to his own home. Many made at me with their ashen spears and tried to kill me in their fury, but the king protected me, for he feared the wrath of Zeus the protector of strangers, who punishes those who do evil.

"I stayed there for seven years and got together much money among the Egyptians, for they all gave me something; but when it was now going on for eight years there came a certain Phoenician, a cunning rascal, who had already committed all sorts of villainy, and this man talked me over into going with him to Phoenicia, where his house and his possessions lay. I stayed there for a whole twelve months, but at the end of that time when months and days had gone by till the same season had come round again, he set me on board a ship bound for Libya, on a pretense that I was to take a cargo along with him to that place, but really that he might sell me as a slave and take the money I fetched. I suspected his intention, but went on board with him, for I could not help it.

"The ship ran before a fresh North wind till we had reached the sea that lies between Crete and Libya; there, however, Zeus counselled their destruction, for as soon as we were well out from Crete and could see nothing but sea and sky, he raised a black cloud over our ship and the sea grew dark beneath it. Then Zeus let fly with his thunderbolts and the ship went round and round and was filled with fire and brimstone as the lightning struck it. The men fell all into the sea; they were carried about in the water round the ship looking like so many sea-gulls, but the god presently deprived them of all chance of getting home again. I was all dismayed. Zeus, however, sent the ship's mast within my reach, which saved my life, for I clung to it, and drifted before the fury of the gale. Nine days did I drift but in the darkness of the tenth night a great wave bore me on to the Thesprotian coast. There Pheidon king of the Thesprotians entertained me hospitably without charging me anything at all—for his son found me when I was nearly dead with cold and fatigue, whereon he raised me by the hand, took me to his father's house and gave me clothes to wear.

"There it was that I heard news of Odysseus, for the king told me he had entertained him, and shown him much hospitality while he was on his homeward journey. He showed me also the treasure of gold, and wrought iron that Odysseus had got together. There was enough to keep his family for ten generations, so much had he left in the house of king Pheidon. But the king said Odysseus had gone to Dodona that he might learn Zeus' mind from the god's high oak tree, and know whether after so long an absence he should return to Ithaca openly, or in secret. Moreover the king swore in my presence, making drink-offerings in his own house as he did so, that the ship was by the water-side, and the crew found, that should take him to his own country. He sent me off however before Odysseus returned, for there happened to be a Thesprotian ship sailing for the wheat-growing island of Dulichium, and he told those in charge of her to be sure and take me safely to King Acastus.

"These men hatched a plot against me that would have reduced me to the very extreme of misery, for when the ship had got some way out from land they resolved on selling me as a slave. They stripped me of the shirt and cloak that I was wearing, and gave me instead the tattered old clouts in which you now see me; then, towards nightfall, they reached the tilled lands of Ithaca, and there they bound me with a strong rope fast in the ship, while they went on shore to get supper by the sea side. But the gods soon undid my bonds for me, and having drawn my rags over my head I slid down the rudder into the sea, where I struck out and swam till I was well clear of them, and came ashore near a thick wood in which I lay concealed. They were very angry at my having escaped and went searching about for me, till at last they thought it was no further use and went back to their ship. The gods, having hidden me thus easily, then took me to a good man's door—for it seems that I am not to die yet awhile."

To this you answered, O swineherd Eumaeus, "Poor unhappy stranger, I have found the story of your misfortunes extremely interesting, but that part about Odysseus is not right; and you will never get me to believe it. Why should a man like you go about telling lies in this way? I know all about the return of my master. The gods one and all of them detest him, or they would have taken him before Troy, or let him die with friends around him when the days of his fighting were done; for then the Achaeans would have built a mound over his ashes and his son would have been heir to his renown, but now the storm winds have spirited him away we know not whither.

"As for me I live out of the way here with the pigs, and never go to the town unless when Penelope sends for me on the arrival of some news about Odysseus. Then they all sit round and ask questions, both those who grieve over the king's absence, and those who rejoice at it because they can eat up his property without paying for it. For my own part I have never cared about asking anyone else since the time when I was taken in by an Aetolian, who had killed a man and come a long way till at last he reached my station, and I was very kind to him. He said he had seen Odysseus with Idomeneus among the Cretans, refitting his ships which had been damaged in a gale. He said Odysseus would return in the following summer or autumn with his men, and that he would bring back much wealth. And now you, you unfortunate old man, since fate has brought you to my door, do not try to flatter me in this way with vain hopes. It is not for any such reason that I shall treat you kindly, but only out of respect for Zeus the god of hospitality, as fearing him and pitying you."

Odysseus answered, "I see that you are of an unbelieving mind; I have given you my oath, and yet you will not credit me; let us then make a bargain, and call all the gods in heaven to witness it. If your master comes home, give me a cloak and shirt of good wear, and send me to Dulichium where I want to go; but if he does not come as I say he will, set your men on to me, and tell them to throw me from yonder precipice, as a warning to tramps not to go about the country telling lies."

"And a pretty figure I should cut then," replied Eumaeus, "both now and hereafter, if I were to kill you after receiving you into my hut and showing you hospitality. I should have to say my prayers in good earnest if I did; but it is just supper time and I hope my men will come in directly, that we may cook something savory for supper."

Thus did they converse, and presently the swineherds came up with the pigs, which were then shut up for the night in their styes, and a tremendous squealing they made as they were being driven into them. But Eumaeus called to his men and said, "Bring in the best pig you have, that I may sacrifice him for this stranger, and we will take toll of him ourselves. We have had trouble enough this long time feeding pigs, while others reap the fruit of our labor."

On this he began chopping firewood, while the others brought in a fine fat five year old boar pig, and set it at the altar. Eumaeus did not forget the gods, for he was a man of good principles, so the first thing he did was to cut bristles from the pig's face and throw them into the fire, praying to all the gods as he did so that Odysseus might return home again. Then he clubbed the pig with a billet of oak which he had kept back when he was chopping the firewood, and stunned it, while the others slaughtered and singed it. Then they cut it up, and Eumaeus began by putting raw pieces from each joint on to some of the fat; these he sprinkled with barley meal, and laid upon the embers; they cut the rest of the meat up small, put the pieces upon the spits and roasted them till they were done; when they had taken them off the spits they threw them on to the dresser in a heap. The swineherd, who was a most equitable man, then stood up to give everyone his share. He made seven portions; one of these he set apart for Hermes the son of Maia and the nymphs, praying to them as he did so; the others he dealt out to the men man by man. He gave Odysseus some slices cut lengthways down the loin as a mark of especial honor, and Odysseus was much pleased. "I hope, Eumaeus," said he, "that Zeus will be as well disposed towards you as I am, for the respect you are showing to an outcast like myself."

To this you answered, O swineherd Eumaeus, "Eat, my good fellow, and enjoy your supper, such as it is. God grants this, and withholds that, just as he thinks right, for he can do whatever he chooses."

As he spoke he cut off the first piece and offered it as a burnt sacrifice to the immortal gods; then he made them a drink-offering, put the cup in the hands of Odysseus, and sat down to his own portion. Mesaulius brought them their bread; the swineherd had brought this man on his own account from among the Taphians during his master's absence, and had paid for him with his own money without saying anything either to his mistress or Laertes. They then laid their hands upon the good things that were before them, and when they had had enough to eat and drink, Mesaulius took away what was left of the bread, and they all went to bed after having made a hearty supper.

Now the night came on stormy and very dark, for there was no moon. It poured without ceasing, and the wind blew strong from the West, which is a wet quarter, so Odysseus thought he would see whether Eumaeus, in the excellent care he took of him, would take off his own cloak and give it him, or make one of his men give him one. "Listen to me," said he, "Eumaeus and the rest of you; when I have said a prayer I will tell you something. It is the wine that makes me talk in this way; wine will make even a wise man fall to singing; it will make him chuckle and dance and say many a word that he had better leave unspoken; still, as I have begun, I will go on. Would that I were still young and strong as when we got up an ambuscade before Troy. Menelaus and Odysseus were the leaders, but I was in command also, for the other two would have it so. When we had come up to the wall of the city we crouched down beneath our armor and lay there under cover of the reeds and thick brushwood that grew about the swamp. It came on to freeze with a North wind blowing; the snow fell small and fine like hoar frost, and our shields were coated thick with rime. The others had all got cloaks and shirts, and slept comfortably enough with their shields about their shoulders, but I had carelessly left my cloak behind me, not thinking that I should be too cold, and had gone off in nothing but my shirt and shield. When the night was two-thirds through and the stars had shifted their places, I nudged Odysseus who was close to me with my elbow, and he at once gave me his ear.

"'Odysseus,' said I, 'this cold will be the death of me, for I have no cloak; some god fooled me into setting off with nothing on but my shirt, and I do not know what to do.'

"Odysseus, who was as crafty as he was valiant, hit upon the following plan:

"'Keep still,' said he in a low voice, 'or the others will hear you.' Then he raised his head on his elbow.

"'My friends,' said he, 'I have had a dream from heaven in my sleep. We are a long way from the ships; I wish some one would go down and tell Agamemnon to send us up more men at once.'

"On this Thoas son of Andraemon threw off his cloak and set out running to the ships, whereon I took the cloak and lay in it comfortably enough till morning. Would that I were still young and strong as I was in those days, for then some one of you swineherds would give me a cloak both out of good will and for the respect due to a brave soldier; but now people look down upon me because my clothes are shabby."

And Eumaeus answered, "Old man, you have told us an excellent story, and have said nothing so far but what is quite satisfactory; for the present, therefore, you shall want neither clothing nor anything else that a stranger in distress may reasonably expect, but to-morrow morning you have to shake your own old rags about your body again, for we have not many spare cloaks nor shirts up here, but every man has only one. When Odysseus' son comes home again he will give you both cloak and shirt, and send you wherever you may want to go."

With this he got up and made a bed for Odysseus by throwing some goatskins and sheepskins on the ground in front of the fire. Here Odysseus lay down, and Eumaeus covered him over with a great heavy cloak that he kept for a change in case of extraordinarily bad weather.

Thus did Odysseus sleep, and the young men slept beside him. But the swineherd did not like sleeping away from his pigs, so he got ready to go outside, and Odysseus was glad to see that he looked after his property during his master's absence. First he slung his sword over his brawny shoulders and put on a thick cloak to keep out the wind. He also took the skin of a large and well fed goat, and a javelin in case of attack from men or dogs. Thus equipped he went to his rest where the pigs were camping under an overhanging rock that gave them shelter from the North wind.

B O O K XV

Athena summons
Telemachus home from Lacedaemon
He meets with Theoclymenus at pylos and brings him to Ithaca
On landing he goes to the hut of Eumaeus

BUT ATHENA WENT to the fair city of Lacedaemon to tell Odysseus' son that he was to return at once. She found him and Pisistratus sleeping in the forecourt of Menelaus' house; Pisistratus was fast asleep, but Telemachus could get no rest all night for thinking of his unhappy father, so Athena went close up to him and said:

"Telemachus, you should not remain so far away from home any longer, nor leave your property with such dangerous people in your house; they will eat up everything you have among them, and you will have been on a fool's errand. Ask Menelaus to send you home at once if you wish to find your excellent mother still there when you get back. Her father and brothers are already urging her to marry Eurymachus, who has given her more than any of the others, and has been greatly increasing his wedding presents. I hope nothing valuable may have been taken from the house in spite of you, but you know what women are—they always want to do the best they can for the man who marries them, and never give another thought to the children of their first husband, nor to their father either when he is dead and done with.† Go home, therefore, and put everything in charge of the most respectable woman servant that you have, until it shall please heaven to send you a wife of your own. Let me tell you also of another matter which you had better attend to. The chief men among the suitors are lying in wait for you in the Strait between Ithaca and Samos, and they mean to kill you before you can reach home. I do not much think they will succeed; it is more likely that some of those who are now eating up your property will find a grave themselves. Sail night and day, and keep your ship well away from the islands; the god who watches over you and protects you will send you a fair wind. As soon as you get to Ithaca send your ship and men on to the town, but yourself go straight to the swineherd who has charge of your pigs; he is well disposed towards you, stay with him, therefore, for the night, and then send him to Penelope to tell her that you have got back safe from Pylos."

Then she went back to Olympus; but Telemachus stirred Pisistratus with his heel to rouse him, and said, "Wake up Pisistratus, and yoke the horses to the chariot, for we must set off home."

But Pisistratus said, "No matter what hurry we are in we cannot drive in the dark. It will be morning soon; wait till Menelaus has brought his presents and put them in the chariot for us; and let him say good bye to us in the usual way. So long as he lives a guest should never forget a host who has shown him kindness."

As he spoke day began to break, and Menelaus, who had already risen, leaving Helen in bed, came towards them. When Telemachus saw him he put on his shirt as fast as he could, threw a great cloak over his shoulders, and went out to meet him. "Menelaus," said he, "let me go back now to my own country, for I want to get home."

And Menelaus answered, "Telemachus, if you insist on going I will not detain you. I do not like to see a host either too fond of his guest or too rude to him. Moderation is best in all things, and not letting a man go when he wants to do so is as bad as telling him to go if he would like to stay. One should treat a guest well as long as he is in the house and speed him when he wants to leave it. Wait, then, till I can get your beautiful presents into your chariot, and till you have yourself seen them. I will tell the women to prepare a sufficient dinner for you of what there may be in the house; it will be at once more proper and cheaper for you to get your dinner before setting out on such a long journey. If, moreover, you have a fancy for making a tour in Hellas or in the Peloponnese, I will yoke my horses, and will conduct you myself through all our principal cities. No one will send us away empty handed; everyone will give us something—a bronze tripod, a couple of mules, or a gold cup."

"Menelaus," replied Telemachus, "I want to go home at once, for when I came away I left my property without protection, and fear that while looking for my father I shall come to ruin myself, or find that something valuable has been stolen during my absence."

When Menelaus heard this he immediately told his wife and servants to prepare a sufficient dinner from what there might be in the house. At this moment Eteoneus joined him, for he lived close by and had just got up; so

Menelaus told him to light the fire and cook some meat, which he at once did. Then Menelaus went down into his fragrant store room, not alone, but Helen went too, with Megapenthes. When he reached the place where the treasures of his house were kept, he selected a double cup, and told his son Megapenthes to bring also a silver mixing bowl. Meanwhile Helen went to the chest where she kept the lovely dresses which she had made with her own hands, and took out one that was largest and most beautifully enriched with embroidery; it glittered like a star, and lay at the very bottom of the chest. Then they all came back through the house again till they got to Telemachus, and Menelaus said, "Telemachus, may Zeus, the mighty husband of Hera, bring you safely home according to your desire. I will now present you with the finest and most precious piece of plate in all my house. It is a mixing bowl of pure silver, except the rim, which is inlaid with gold, and it is the work of Hephaestus. Phaedimus king of the Sidonians made me a present of it in the course of a visit that I paid him while I was on my return home. I should like to give it to you."

With these words he placed the double cup in the hands of Telemachus, while Megapenthes brought the beautiful mixing bowl and set it before him. Hard by stood lovely Helen with the robe ready in her hand.

"I too, my son," said she, "have something for you as a keepsake from the hand of Helen; it is for your bride to wear upon her wedding day. Till then, get your dear mother to keep it for you; thus may you go back rejoicing to your own country and to your home."

So saying she gave the robe over to him and he received it gladly. Then Pisistratus put the presents into the chariot, and admired them all as he did so. Presently Menelaus took Telemachus and Pisistratus into the house, and they both of them sat down to table. A maid servant brought them water in a beautiful golden ewer, and poured it into a silver basin for them to wash their hands, and she drew a clean table beside them; an upper servant brought them bread and offered them many good things of what there was in the house. Eteoneus carved the meat and gave them each their portions, while Megapenthes poured out the wine. Then they laid their hands upon the good things that were before them, but as soon as they had had enough to eat and drink Telemachus and Pisistratus yoked the horses, and took their places in the chariot. They drove out through the inner gateway and under the echoing gatehouse of the outer court, and Menelaus came after them with a golden goblet of wine in his right hand that they might make a drink-offering before they set out. He stood in front of the horses and pledged them, saying, "Farewell to both of you; see that you tell Nestor how I have treated you, for he was as kind to me as any father could be while we Achaeans were fighting before Troy."

"We will be sure, sir," answered Telemachus, "to tell him everything as soon as we see him. I wish I were as certain of finding Odysseus returned when I get back to Ithaca, that I might tell him of the very great kindness you have shown me and of the many beautiful presents I am taking with me."

As he was thus speaking a bird flew on his right hand—an eagle with a great white goose in its talons which it had carried off from the farm yard—and all the men and women were running after it and shouting. It came quite close up to them and flew away on their right hands in front of the horses. When they saw it they were glad, and their hearts took comfort within them, whereon Pisistratus said, "Tell me, Menelaus, has heaven sent this omen for us or for you?"

Menelaus was thinking what would be the most proper answer for him to make, but Helen was too quick for him and said, "I will read this matter as heaven has put it in my heart, and as I doubt not that it will come to pass. The eagle came from the mountain where it was bred and has its nest, and in like manner Odysseus, after having traveled far and suffered much, will return to take his revenge—if indeed he is not back already and hatching mischief for the suitors."

"May Zeus so grant it," replied Telemachus, "if it should prove to be so, I will make vows to you as though you were a god, even when I am at home."

As he spoke he lashed his horses and they started off at full speed through the town towards the open country. They swayed the yoke upon their necks and traveled the whole day long till the sun set and darkness was over all the land. Then they reached Pherae, where Diocles lived who was son of Ortilochus, the son of Alpheus. There they passed the night and were treated hospitably. When the child of morning, rosy-fingered Dawn, appeared, they again yoked their horses and their places in the chariot. They drove out through the inner gateway and under the echoing gatehouse of the outer court. Then Pisistratus lashed his horses on and they flew forward nothing loath; ere long they came to Pylos, and then Telemachus said:

"Pisistratus, I hope you will promise to do what I am going to ask you. You know our fathers were old friends before us; moreover, we are both of an age, and this journey has brought us together still more closely; do not, therefore, take me past my ship, but leave me there, for if I go to your father's house he will try to keep me in the warmth of his good will towards me, and I must go home at once."

Pisistratus thought how he should do as he was asked, and in the end he deemed it best to turn his horses towards the ship, and put Menelaus' beautiful presents of gold and raiment in the stern of the vessel. Then he said, "Go on board at once and tell your men to do so also before I can reach home to tell my father. I know how obstinate he is, and am sure he will not let you go; he will come down here to fetch you, and he will not go back without you. But he will be very angry."†

With this he drove his goodly steeds back to the city of the Pylians and soon reached his home, but Telemachus called the men together and gave his orders. "Now, my men," said he, "get everything in order on board the ship, and let us set out home."

Thus did he speak, and they went on board even as he had said. But as Telemachus was thus busied, praying also and sacrificing to Athena in the ship's stern, there came to him a man from a distant country, a seer, who was flying from Argos because he had killed a man. He was descended from Melampus, who used to live in Pylos, the land of sheep; he was rich and owned a great house, but he was driven into exile by the great and powerful king Neleus. Neleus seized his goods and held them for a whole year, during which he was a close prisoner in the house of king Phylacus, and in much distress of mind both on account of the daughter of Neleus and because he was haunted by a great sorrow that dread Erinys had laid upon him. In the end, however, he escaped with his life, drove the cattle from Phylace to Pylos, avenged the wrong that had been done him, and gave the daughter of Neleus to his brother. Then he left the country and went to Argos, where it was ordained that he should reign over much people. There he married, established himself, and had two famous sons Antiphates and Mantius. Antiphates became father of Oicleus, and Oicleus of Amphiaraus, who was dearly loved both by Zeus and by Apollo, but he did not live to old age, for he was killed in Thebes by reason of a woman's gifts. His sons were Alcmaeon and Amphilochus. Mantius, the other son of Melampus, was father to Polypheides and Cleitus. Aurora, throned in gold, carried off Cleitus for his beauty's sake, that he might dwell among the immortals, but Apollo made Polypheides the greatest seer in the whole world now that Amphiaraus was dead. He quarrelled with his father and went to live in Hyperesia, where he remained and prophesied for all men.

His son, Theoclymenus, it was who now came up to Telemachus as he was making drink-offerings and praying in his ship. "Friend," said he, "now that I find you sacrificing in this place, I beseech you by your sacrifices themselves, and by the god to whom you make them, I pray you also by your own head and by those of your followers tell me the truth and nothing but the truth. Who and whence are you? Tell me also of your town and parents."

Telemachus said, "I will answer you quite truly. I am from Ithaca, and my father is Odysseus, as surely as that he ever lived. But he has come to some miserable end. Therefore I have taken this ship and got my crew together to see if I can hear any news of him, for he has been away a long time."

"I too," answered Theoclymenus, "am an exile, for I have killed a man of my own race. He has many brothers and kinsmen in Argos, and they have great power among the Argives. I am flying to escape death at their hands, and am thus doomed to be a wanderer on the face of the earth. I am your suppliant; take me, therefore, on board your ship that they may not kill me, for I know they are in pursuit."

"I will not refuse you," replied Telemachus, "if you wish to join us. Come, therefore, and in Ithaca we will treat you hospitably according to what we have."

On this he received Theoclymenus' spear and laid it down on the deck of the ship. He went on board and sat in the stern, bidding Theoclymenus sit beside him; then the men let go the hawsers. Telemachus told them to catch hold of the ropes, and they made all haste to do so. They set the mast in its socket in the cross plank, raised it and made it fast with the forestays, and they hoisted their white sails with sheets of twisted oxhide. Athena sent them a fair wind that blew fresh and strong to take the ship on her course as fast as possible. Thus then they passed by Crouni and Chalcis.

Presently the sun set and darkness was over all the land. The vessel made a quick passage to Pheae and thence on to Elis, where the Epeans rule. Telemachus then headed her for the flying islands, wondering within himself whether he should escape death or should be taken prisoner.

Meanwhile Odysseus and the swineherd were eating their supper in the hut, and the men supped with them. As soon as they had had to eat and drink, Odysseus began trying to prove the swineherd and see whether he would continue to treat him kindly, and ask him to stay on at the station or pack him off to the city; so he said:

"Eumaeus, and all of you, to-morrow I want to go away and begin begging about the town, so as to be no more trouble to you or to your men. Give me your advice therefore, and let me have a good guide to go with me and show me the way. I will go the round of the city begging as I needs must, to see if anyone will give me a drink and a piece of bread. I should like also to go to the house of Odysseus and bring news of her husband to Queen Penelope. I could then go about among the suitors and see if out of all their abundance they will give me a dinner. I should soon make them an excellent servant in all sorts of ways. Listen and believe when I tell you that by the blessing of Hermes who gives grace and good name to the works of all men, there is no one living who would make a more handy servant than I should—to put fresh wood on the fire, chop fuel, carve, cook, pour out wine, and do all those services that poor men have to do for their betters."

The swineherd was very much disturbed when he heard this. "Heaven help me," he exclaimed, "what ever can have put such a notion as that into your head? If you go near the suitors you will be undone to a certainty, for their pride and insolence reach the very heavens. They would never think of taking a man like you for a servant. Their servants are all young men, well dressed, wearing good cloaks and shirts, with well looking faces and their hair always tidy, the tables are kept quite clean and are loaded with bread, meat, and wine. Stay where you are, then; you are not in anybody's way; I do not mind your being here, no more do any of the others, and when Telemachus comes home he will give you a shirt and cloak and will send you wherever you want to go."

Odysseus answered, "I hope you may be as dear to the gods as you are to me, for having saved me from going about and getting into trouble; there is nothing worse than being always on the tramp; still, when men have once got low down in the world they will go through a great deal on behalf of their miserable bellies. Since, however, you press me to stay here and await the return of Telemachus, tell me about Odysseus' mother, and his father whom he left on the threshold of old age when he set out for Troy. Are they still living or are they already dead and in the house of Hades?"

"I will tell you all about them," replied Eumaeus, "Laertes is still living and prays heaven to let him depart peacefully in his own house, for he is terribly distressed about the absence of his son, and also about the death of his wife, which grieved him greatly and aged him more than anything else did. She came to an unhappy end through sorrow for her son: may no friend or neighbor who has dealt kindly by me come to such an end as she did. As long as she was still living, though she was always grieving, I used to like seeing her and asking her how she did, for she brought me up along with her daughter Ctimene, the youngest of her children; we were boy and girl together, and she made little difference between us. When, however, we both grew up, they sent Ctimene to Same and received a splendid dowry for her. As for me, my mistress gave me a good shirt and cloak with a pair of sandals for my feet, and sent me off into the country, but she was just as fond of me as ever. This is all over now. Still it has pleased heaven to prosper my work in the situation which I now hold. I have enough to eat and drink, and can find something for any respectable stranger who comes here; but there is no getting a kind word or deed out of my mistress, for the house has fallen into the hands of wicked people. Servants want sometimes to see their mistress and have a talk with her; they like to have something to eat and drink at the house, and something too to take back with them into the country. This is what will keep servants in a good humor."†

Odysseus answered, "Then you must have been a very little fellow, Eumaeus, when you were taken so far away from your home and parents. Tell me, and tell me true, was the city in which your father and mother lived sacked and pillaged, or did some enemies carry you off when you were alone tending sheep or cattle, ship you off here, and sell you for whatever your master gave them?"

"Stranger," replied Eumaeus, "as regards your question: sit still, make yourself comfortable, drink your wine, and listen to me. The nights are now at their longest; there is time both for sleeping and sitting up talking together;

you ought not to go to bed till bed time, too much sleep is as bad as too little; if any one of the others wishes to go to bed let him leave us and do so; he can then take my master's pigs out when he has done breakfast in the morning. We too will sit here eating and drinking in the hut, and telling one another stories about our misfortunes; for when a man has suffered much, and been buffeted about in the world, he takes pleasure in recalling the memory of sorrows that have long gone by. As regards your question, then, my tale is as follows:

"You may have heard of an island called Syra that lies over above Ortygia, where the land begins to turn round and look in another direction. It is not very thickly peopled, but the soil is good, with much pasture fit for cattle and sheep, and it abounds with wine and wheat. Dearth never comes there, nor are the people plagued by any sickness, but when they grow old Apollo comes with Artemis and kills them with his painless shafts. It contains two communities, and the whole country is divided between these two. My father Ctesius son of Ormenus, a man comparable to the gods, reigned over both.

"Now to this place there came some cunning traders from Phoenicia (for the Phoenicians are great mariners) in a ship which they had freighted with gewgaws of all kinds. There happened to be a Phoenician woman in my father's house, very tall and comely, and an excellent servant; these scoundrels got hold of her one day when she was washing near their ship, seduced her, and cajoled her in ways that no woman can resist, no matter how good she may be by nature. The man who had seduced her asked her who she was and where she came from, and on this she told him her father's name. 'I come from Sidon,' said she, 'and am daughter to Arybas, a man rolling in wealth. One day as I was coming into the town from the country, some Taphian pirates seized me and took me here over the sea, where they sold me to the man who owns this house, and he gave them their price for me.'

"The man who had seduced her then said, 'Would you like to come along with us to see the house of your parents and your parents themselves? They are both alive and are said to be well off.'

"'I will do so gladly,' answered she, 'if you men will first swear me a solemn oath that you will do me no harm by the way.'

"They all swore as she told them, and when they had completed their oath the woman said, 'Hush; and if any of your men meets me in the street or at the well, do not let him speak to me, for fear someone should go and tell my master, in which case he would suspect something. He would put me in prison, and would have all of you murdered; keep your own counsel therefore; buy your merchandise as fast as you can, and send me word when you have done loading. I will bring as much gold as I can lay my hands on, and there is something else also that I can do towards paying my fare. I am nurse to the son of the good man of the house, a funny little fellow just able to run about. I will carry him off in your ship, and you will get a great deal of money for him if you take him and sell him in foreign parts.'

"On this she went back to the house. The Phoenicians stayed a whole year till they had loaded their ship with much precious merchandise, and then, when they had got freight enough, they sent to tell the woman. Their messenger, a very cunning fellow, came to my father's house bringing a necklace of gold with amber beads strung among it; and while my mother and the servants had it in their hands admiring it and bargaining about it, he made a sign quietly to the woman and then went back to the ship, whereon she took me by the hand and led me out of the house. In the fore part of the house she saw the tables set with the cups of guests who had been feasting with my father, as being in attendance on him; these were now all gone to a meeting of the public assembly, so she snatched up three cups and carried them off in the bosom of her dress, while I followed her, for I knew no better. The sun was now set, and darkness was over all the land, so we hurried on as fast as we could till we reached the harbor, where the Phoenician ship was lying. When they had got on board they sailed their ways over the sea, taking us with them, and Zeus sent then a fair wind; six days did we sail both night and day, but on the seventh day Artemis struck the woman and she fell heavily down into the ship's hold as though she were a sea gull alighting on the water; so they threw her overboard to the seals and fishes, and I was left all sorrowful and alone. Presently the winds and waves took the ship to Ithaca, where Laertes gave sundry of his chattels for me, and thus it was that ever I came to set eyes upon this country."

Odysseus answered, "Eumaeus, I have heard the story of your misfortunes with the most lively interest and pity, but Zeus has given you good as well as evil, for in spite of everything you have a good master, who sees that you always have enough to eat and drink; and you lead a good life, whereas I am still going about begging my way from city to city."

Thus did they converse, and they had only a very little time left for sleep, for it was soon daybreak. In the mean time Telemachus and his crew were nearing land, so they loosed the sails, took down the mast, and rowed the ship into the harbor. They cast out their mooring stones and made fast the hawsers; they then got out upon the sea shore, mixed their wine, and got dinner ready. As soon as they had had enough to eat and drink Telemachus said, "Take the ship on to the town, but leave me here, for I want to look after the herdsmen on one of my farms. In the evening, when I have seen all I want, I will come down to the city, and to-morrow morning in return for your trouble I will give you all a good dinner with meat and wine."

Then Theoclymenus said, 'And what, my dear young friend, is to become of me? To whose house, among all your chief men, am I to repair? or shall I go straight to your own house and to your mother?"

"At any other time," replied Telemachus, "I should have bidden you go to my own house, for you would find no want of hospitality; at the present moment, however, you would not be comfortable there, for I shall be away, and my mother will not see you; she does not often show herself even to the suitors, but sits at her loom weaving in an upper chamber, out of their way; but I can tell you a man whose house you can go to—I mean Eurymachus the son of Polybus, who is held in the highest estimation by everyone in Ithaca. He is much the best man and the most persistent wooer, of all those who are paying court to my mother and trying to take Odysseus' place. Zeus, however, in heaven alone knows whether or no they will come to a bad end before the marriage takes place."

As he was speaking a bird flew by upon his right hand—a hawk, Apollo's messenger. It held a dove in its talons, and the feathers, as it tore them off, fell to the ground midway between Telemachus and the ship. On this Theoclymenus called him apart and caught him by the hand. "Telemachus," said he, "that bird did not fly on your right hand without having been sent there by some god. As soon as I saw it I knew it was an omen; it means that you will remain powerful and that there will be no house in Ithaca more royal than your own."[†]

"I wish it may prove so," answered Telemachus. "If it does, I will show you so much good will and give you so many presents that all who meet you will congratulate you."

Then he said to his friend Piraeus, "Piraeus, son of Clytius, you have throughout shown yourself the most willing to serve me of all those who have accompanied me to Pylos; I wish you would take this stranger to your own house and entertain him hospitably till I can come for him."

And Piraeus answered, "Telemachus, you may stay away as long as you please, but I will look after him for you, and he shall find no lack of hospitality."

As he spoke he went on board, and bade the others do so also and loose the hawsers, so they took their places in the ship. But Telemachus bound on his sandals, and took a long and doughty spear with a head of sharpened bronze from the deck of the ship. Then they loosed the hawsers, thrust the ship off from land, and made on towards the city as they had been told to do, while Telemachus strode on as fast as he could, till he reached the homestead where his countless herds of swine were feeding, and where dwelt the excellent swineherd, who was so devoted a servant to his master.

B O O K XVI

Odysseus reveals himself to Telemachus

MEANWHILE ODYSSEUS AND the swineherd had lit a fire in the hut and were were getting breakfast ready at daybreak, for they had sent the men out with the pigs. When Telemachus came up, the dogs did not bark but fawned upon him, so Odysseus, hearing the sound of feet and noticing that the dogs did not bark, said to Eumaeus:

"Eumaeus, I hear footsteps; I suppose one of your men or some one of your acquaintance is coming here, for the dogs are fawning upon him and not barking."

The words were hardly out of his mouth before his son stood at the door. Eumaeus sprang to his feet, and the bowls in which he was mixing wine fell from his hands, as he made towards his master. He kissed his head and both his beautiful eyes, and wept for joy. A father could not be more delighted at the return of an only son, the child of his old age, after ten years' absence in a foreign country and after having gone through much hardship. He embraced him, kissed him all over as though he had come back from the dead, and spoke fondly to him saying:

"So you are come, Telemachus, light of my eyes that you are. When I heard you had gone to Pylos I made sure I was never going to see you any more. Come in, my dear child, and sit down, that I may have a good look at you now you are home again; it is not very often you come into the country to see us herdsmen; you stick pretty close to the town generally. I suppose you think it better to keep an eye on what the suitors are doing."

"So be it, old friend," answered Telemachus, "but I am come now because

I want to see you, and to learn whether my mother is still at her old home or whether someone else has married her, so that the bed of Odysseus is without bedding and covered with cobwebs."†

"She is still at the house," replied Eumaeus, "grieving and breaking her heart, and doing nothing but weep, both night and day continually."

As he spoke he took Telemachus' spear, whereon he crossed the stone threshold and came inside. Odysseus rose from his seat to give him place as he entered, but Telemachus checked him; "Sit down, stranger," said he, "I can easily find another seat, and there is one here who will lay it for me."

Odysseus went back to his own place, and Eumaeus strewed some green brushwood on the floor and threw a sheepskin on top of it for Telemachus to sit upon. Then the swineherd brought them platters of cold meat, the remains from what they had eaten the day before, and he filled the bread baskets with bread as fast as he could. He mixed wine also in bowls of ivy-wood, and took his seat facing Odysseus. Then they laid their hands on the good things that were before them, and as soon as they had had enough to eat and drink Telemachus said to Eumaeus, "Old friend, where does this stranger come from? How did his crew bring him to Ithaca, and who were they?—for assuredly he did not come here by land."

To this you answered, O swineherd Eumaeus, "My son, I will tell you the real truth. He says he is a Cretan, and that he has been a great traveler. At this moment he is running away from a Thesprotian ship, and has taken refuge at my station, so I will put him into your hands. Do whatever you like with him, only remember that he is your suppliant."

"I am very much distressed," said Telemachus, "by what you have just told me. How can I take this stranger into my house? I am as yet young, and am not strong enough to hold my own if any man attacks me.† My mother cannot make up her mind whether to stay where she is and look after the house out of respect for public opinion and the memory of her husband, or whether the time is now come for her to take the best man of those who are wooing her, and the one who will make her the most advantageous offer; still, as the stranger has come to your station I will find him a cloak and shirt of good wear, with a sword and sandals, and will send him wherever he wants to go. Or if you like you can keep him here at the station, and I will send him clothes and food that he may be no burden on you and on your men; but I will not have him go near the suitors, for they are very insolent, and are sure to ill treat him in a way that would greatly grieve me; no matter how valiant a man may be he can do nothing against numbers, for they will be too strong for him."

Then Odysseus said, "Sir, it is right that I should say something myself. I am much shocked about what you have said about the insolent way in which the suitors are behaving in despite of such a man as you are. Tell me, do you submit to such treatment tamely, or has some god set your people against you?

May you not complain of your brothers—for it is to these that a man may look for support, however great his quarrel may be? I wish I were as young as you are and in my present mind; if I were son to Odysseus, or, indeed, Odysseus himself, I would rather someone came and cut my head off, but I would go to the house and be the bane of everyone of these men. If they were too many for me—I being single-handed—I would rather die fighting in my own house than see such disgraceful sights day after day, strangers grossly maltreated, and men dragging the women servants about the house in an unseemly way, wine drawn recklessly, and bread wasted all to no purpose for an end that shall never be accomplished."†

And Telemachus answered, "I will tell you truly everything. There is no enmity between me and my people, nor can I complain of brothers, to whom a man may look for support however great his quarrel may be. Zeus has made us a race of only sons. Laertes was the only son of Arceisius, and Odysseus only son of Laertes. I am myself the only son of Odysseus who left me behind him when he went away, so that I have never been of any use to him. Hence it comes that my house is in the hands of numberless marauders; for the chiefs from all the neighboring islands, Dulichium, Same, Zacynthus, as also all the principal men of Ithaca itself, are eating up my house under the pretext of paying court to my mother, who will neither say directly that she will not marry, nor yet bring matters to an end, so they are making havoc of my estate, and before long will do so with myself into the bargain. The issue, however, rests with heaven. But do you, old friend Eumaeus, go at once and tell Penelope that I am safe and have returned from Pylos. Tell it to herself alone, and then come back here without letting anyone else know, for there are many who are plotting mischief against me."

"I understand and heed you," replied Eumaeus; "you need instruct me no further, only as I am going that way say whether I had not better let poor Laertes know that you are returned. He used to superintend the work on his farm in spite of his bitter sorrow about Odysseus, and he would eat and drink at will along with his servants; but they tell me that from the day on which you set out for Pylos he has neither eaten nor drunk as he ought to do, nor does he look after his farm, but sits weeping and wasting the flesh from off his bones."

"More's the pity," answered Telemachus, "I am sorry for him, but we must leave him to himself just now. If people could have everything their own way, the first thing I should choose would be the return of my father; but go, and give your message; then make haste back again, and do not turn out of your way to tell Laertes.† Tell my mother to send one of her women secretly with the news at once, and let him hear it from her."

Thus did he urge the swineherd; Eumaeus, therefore, took his sandals, bound them to his feet, and started for the town. Athena watched him well off the station, and then came up to it in the form of a woman—fair, stately, and wise. She stood against the side of the entry, and revealed herself to Odysseus, but Telemachus could not see her, and knew not that she was there, for the gods do not let themselves be seen by everybody. Odysseus saw her, and so did the dogs, for they did not bark, but went scared and whining off to the other side of the yards. She nodded her head and motioned to Odysseus with her eyebrows; whereon he left the hut and stood before her outside the main wall of the yards. Then she said to him:

"Odysseus, noble son of Laertes, it is now time for you to tell your son: do not keep him in the dark any longer, but lay your plans for the destruction of the suitors, and then make for the town. I will not be long in joining you, for I too am eager for the fray."

As she spoke she touched him with her golden wand. First she threw a fair clean shirt and cloak about his shoulders; then she made him younger and of more imposing presence; she gave him back his color, filled out his cheeks, and let his beard become dark again. Then she went away and Odysseus came back inside the hut. His son was astounded when he saw him, and turned his eyes away for fear he might be looking upon a god.

"Stranger," said he, "how suddenly you have changed from what you were a moment or two ago. You are dressed differently and your color is not the same. Are you some one or other of the gods that live in heaven? If so, be propitious to me till I can make you due sacrifice and offerings of wrought gold. Have mercy upon me."†

And Odysseus said, "I am no god, why should you take me for one? I am your father, on whose account you grieve and suffer so much at the hands of lawless men."

As he spoke he kissed his son, and a tear fell from his cheek on to the ground, for he had restrained all tears till now. But Telemachus could not yet believe that it was his father, and said:

"You are not my father, but some god is flattering me with vain hopes that I may grieve the more hereafter; no mortal man could of himself contrive to do as you have been doing, and make yourself old and young at a moment's notice, unless a god were with him. A second ago you were old and all in rags, and now you are like some god come down from heaven."

Odysseus answered, "Telemachus, you ought not to be so immeasurably astonished at my being really here. There is no other Odysseus who will come hereafter. Such as I am, it is I, who after long wandering and much hardship have got home in the twentieth year to my own country. What you wonder at is the work of the redoubtable goddess Athena, who does with me whatever she will, for she can do what she pleases. At one moment she makes me like a beggar, and the next I am a young man with good clothes on my back; it is an easy matter for the gods who live in heaven to make any man look either rich or poor."

As he spoke he sat down, and Telemachus threw his arms about his father and wept. They were both so much moved that they cried aloud like eagles or vultures with crooked talons that have been robbed of their half fledged young by peasants. Thus piteously did they weep, and the sun would have gone down upon their mourning if Telemachus had not suddenly said, "In what ship, my dear father, did your crew bring you to Ithaca? Of what nation did they declare themselves to be—for you cannot have come by land?"

"I will tell you the truth, my son," replied Odysseus. "It was the Phaeacians who brought me here. They are great sailors, and are in the habit of giving escorts to any one who reaches their coasts. They took me over the sea while I was fast asleep, and landed me in Ithaca, after giving me many presents in bronze, gold, and raiment. These things by heaven's mercy are lying concealed in a cave, and I am now come here on the suggestion of Athena that we may consult about killing our enemies. First, therefore, give me a list of the suitors, with their number, that I may learn who, and how many, they are. I can then turn the matter over in my mind, and see whether we two can fight the whole body of them ourselves, or whether we must find others to help us."

To this Telemachus answered, "Father, I have always heard of your renown both in the field and in council, but the task you talk of is a very great one: I am awed at the mere thought of it; two men cannot stand against many and brave ones. There are not ten suitors only, nor twice ten, but ten many times over; you shall learn their number at once. There are fifty-two chosen youths from Dulichium, and they have six servants; from Same there are twenty-four; twenty young Achaeans from Zacynthus, and twelve from Ithaca itself, all of them well born. They have with them a servant Medon, a bard, and two men who can carve at table. If we face such numbers as this, you may have bitter cause to rue your coming, and your revenge. See whether you cannot think of someone who would be willing to come and help us."

"Listen to me," replied Odysseus, "and think whether Athena and her father Zeus may seem sufficient, or whether I am to try and find someone else as well."

"Those whom you have named," answered Telemachus, "are a couple of good allies, for though they dwell high up among the clouds they have power over both gods and men."

"These two," continued Odysseus, "will not keep long out of the fray, when the suitors and we join fight in my house. Now, therefore, return home early to-morrow morning, and go about among the suitors as before. Later on the swineherd will bring me to the city disguised as a miserable old beggar. If you see them ill treating me, steel your heart against my sufferings; even though they drag me feet foremost out of the house, or throw things at me, look on and do nothing beyond gently trying to make them behave more reasonably; but they will not listen to you, for the day of their reckoning is at hand. Furthermore I say, and lay my saying to your heart; when Athena shall put it in my mind, I will nod my head to you, and on seeing me do this you must collect all the armor that is in the house and hide it in the strong store room. Make some excuse when the suitors ask you why you are removing it; say that you have taken it to be out of the way of the smoke, inasmuch as it is no longer what it was when Odysseus went away, but has become soiled and begrimed with soot. Add to this more particularly that you are afraid Zeus may set them on to quarrel over their wine, and that they may do each other some harm which may disgrace both banquet and wooing, for the sight of arms sometimes tempts people to use them. But leave a sword and a spear apiece for yourself and me, and a couple of oxhide shields so that we can snatch them up at any moment; Zeus and Athena will then soon quiet these people. There is also another matter; if you are indeed my son and my blood runs in your veins, let no one know that Odysseus is within the house—neither Laertes, nor yet the swineherd, nor any of the servants, nor even Penelope herself. Let you and me exploit the women alone, and let us also make trial of some other of the men servants, to see who is on our side and whose hand is against us."

"Father," replied Telemachus, "you will come to know me by and by, and when you do you will find that I can keep your counsel. I do not think, however, the plan you propose will turn out well for either of us. Think it over. It will take us a long time to go the round of the farms and exploit the men, and all the time the suitors will be wasting your estate with impunity and without compunction. Prove the women by all means, to see who are disloyal and who guiltless, but I am not in favor of going round and trying the men. We can attend to that later on, if you really have some sign from Zeus that he will support you."

Thus did they converse, and meanwhile the ship which had brought Telemachus and his crew from Pylos had reached the town of Ithaca. When they had come inside the harbor they drew the ship on to the land; their servants came and took their armor from them, and they left all the presents at the house of Clytius. Then they sent a servant to tell Penelope that Telemachus had gone into the country, but had sent the ship to the town to prevent her from being alarmed and made unhappy. This servant and Eumaeus happened to meet when they were both on the same errand of going to tell Penelope. When they reached the House, the servant stood up and said to the queen in the presence of the waiting women, "Your son, Madam, is now returned from Pylos"; but Eumaeus went close up to Penelope, and said privately all that her son had bidden him tell her. When he had given his message he left the house with its outbuildings and went back to his pigs again.

The suitors were surprised and angry at what had happened, so they went outside the great wall that ran round the outer court, and held a council near the main entrance.[†] Eurymachus, son of Polybus, was the first to speak.

"My friends," said he, "this voyage of Telemachus' is a very serious matter; we had made sure that it would come to nothing. Now, however, let us draw a ship into the water, and get a crew together to send after the others and tell them to come back as fast as they can."

He had hardly done speaking when Amphinomus turned in his place and saw the ship inside the harbor, with the crew lowering her sails, and putting by their oars; so he laughed, and said to the others, "We need not send them any message, for they are here. Some god must have told them, or else they saw the ship go by, and could not overtake her."

On this they rose and went to the waterside. The crew then drew the ship on shore; their servants took their armor from them, and they went up in a body to the place of assembly, but they would not let anyone old or young sit along with them, and Antinous, son of Eupeithes, spoke first.

"Good heavens," said he, "see how the gods have saved this man from destruction. We kept a succession of scouts upon the headlands all day long, and when the sun was down we never went on shore to sleep, but waited in the ship all night till morning in the hope of capturing and killing him; but some god has conveyed him home in spite of us. Let us consider how we can make an end of him. He must not escape us; our affair is never likely to come off while he is alive, for he is very shrewd, and public feeling is by no means all on our side. We must make haste before he can call the Achaeans in assembly; he will lose no time in doing so, for he will be furious with us, and will tell all the world how we plotted to kill him, but failed to take him. The people will not like this when they come to know of it; we must see that they do us no hurt, nor drive us from our own country into exile. Let us try and lay hold of him either on his farm away from the town, or on the road hither. Then we can divide up his property amongst us, and let his mother and the man who marries her have the house. If this does not please you, and you wish Telemachus to live on and hold his father's property, then we must not gather here and eat up his goods in this way, but must make our offers to Penelope each from his own house, and she can marry the man who will give the most for her, and whose lot it is to win her."

They all held their peace until Amphinomus rose to speak. He was the son of Nisus, who was son to king Aretias, and he was foremost among all the suitors from the wheat-growing and well grassed island of Dulichium; his conversation, moreover, was more agreeable to Penelope than that of any of the other suitors, for he was a man of good natural disposition.[†] "My friends," said he, speaking to them plainly and in all honestly, "I am not in favor of killing

Telemachus. It is a heinous thing to kill one who is of noble blood. Let us first take counsel of the gods, and if the oracles of Zeus advise it, I will both help to kill him myself, and will urge everyone else to do so; but if they dissuade us, I would have you hold your hands."

Thus did he speak, and his words pleased them well, so they rose forthwith and went to the house of Odysseus, where they took their accustomed seats.

Then Penelope resolved that she would show herself to the suitors. She knew of the plot against Telemachus, for the servant Medon had overheard their counsels and had told her; she went down therefore to the court attended by her maidens, and when she reached the suitors she stood by one of the bearing-posts supporting the roof of the cloister holding a veil before her face, and rebuked Antinous saying:

"Antinous, insolent and wicked schemer, they say you are the best speaker and counsellor of any man your own age in Ithaca, but you are nothing of the kind. Madman, why should you try to compass the death of Telemachus, and take no heed of suppliants, whose witness is Zeus himself? It is not right for you to plot thus against one another. Do you not remember how your father fled to this house in fear of the people, who were enraged against him for having gone with some Taphian pirates and plundered the Thesprotians who were at peace with us? They wanted to tear him in pieces and eat up everything he had, but Odysseus stayed their hands although they were infuriated, and now you devour his property without paying for it, and break my heart by wooing his wife and trying to kill his son. Leave off doing so, and stop the others also."

To this Eurymachus son of Polybus answered, "Take heart, Queen Penelope daughter of Icarius, and do not trouble yourself about these matters. The man is not yet born, nor never will be, who shall lay hands upon your son Telemachus, while I yet live to look upon the face of the earth. I say—and it shall surely be—that my spear shall be reddened with his blood; for many a time has Odysseus taken me on his knees, held wine up to my lips to drink, and put pieces of meat into my hands. Therefore Telemachus is much the dearest friend I have, and has nothing to fear from the hands of us suitors. Of course, if death comes to him from the gods, he cannot escape it."† He said this to quiet her, but in reality he was plotting against Telemachus.

Then Penelope went upstairs again and mourned her husband till Athena shed sleep over her eyes. In the evening Eumaeus got back to Odysseus and his son, who had just sacrificed a young pig of a year old and were helping one another to get supper ready; Athena therefore came up to Odysseus, turned him into an old man with a stroke of her wand, and clad him in his old clothes again, for fear that the swineherd might recognize him and not keep the secret, but go and tell Penelope.

Telemachus was the first to speak. "So you have got back, Eumaeus," said he. "What is the news of the town? Have the suitors returned, or are they still waiting over yonder, to take me on my way home?"

"I did not think of asking about that," replied Eumaeus, "when I was in the town. I thought I would give my message and come back as soon as I could. I met a man sent by those who had gone with you to Pylos, and he was the first to tell the news to your mother, but I can say what I saw with my own eyes; I had just got on to the crest of the hill of Hermes above the town when I saw a ship coming into harbor with a number of men in her. They had many shields and spears, and I thought it was the suitors, but I cannot be sure."

On hearing this Telemachus smiled to his father, but so that Eumaeus could not see him.

Then, when they had finished their work and the meal was ready, they ate it, and every man had his full share so that all were satisfied. As soon as they had had enough to eat and drink, they laid down to rest and enjoyed the boon of sleep.

basin for them to wash their hands; and she drew a clean table beside them. An upper servant brought them bread and offered them many good things of what there was in the house. Opposite them sat Penelope, reclining on a couch by one of the bearing-posts of the cloister, and spinning. Then they laid their hands on the good things that were before them, and as soon as they had had enough to eat and drink Penelope said:

"Telemachus, I shall go upstairs and lie down on that sad couch, which I have not ceased to water with my tears, from the day Odysseus set out for Troy with the sons of Atreus. You failed, however, to make it clear to me before the suitors came back to the house, whether or no you had been able to hear anything about the return of your father."

"I will tell you then truth," replied her son. "We went to Pylos and saw Nestor, who took me to his house and treated me as hospitably as though I were a son of his own who had just returned after a long absence; so also did his sons; but he said he had not heard a word from any human being about Odysseus, whether he was alive or dead. He sent me, therefore, with a chariot and horses to Menelaus. There I saw Helen, for whose sake so many, both Argives and Trojans, were in heaven's wisdom doomed to suffer. Menelaus asked me what it was that had brought me to Lacedaemon, and I told him the whole truth, whereon he said, 'So, then, these cowards would usurp a brave man's bed? A hind might as well lay her new-born young in the lair of a lion, and then go off to feed in the forest or in some grassy dell. The lion, when he comes back to his lair, will make short work with the pair of them, and so will Odysseus with these suitors. By father Zeus, Athena, and Apollo, if Odysseus is still the man that he was when he wrestled with Philomeleides in Lesbos, and threw him so heavily that all the Greeks cheered him—if he is still such, and were to come near these suitors, they would have a short shrift and a sorry wedding. As regards your question, however, I will not prevaricate nor deceive you, but what the old man of the sea told me, so much will I tell you in full. He said he could see Odysseus on an island sorrowing bitterly in the house of the nymph Calypso, who was keeping him prisoner, and he could not reach his home, for he had no ships nor sailors to take him over the sea.' This was what Menelaus told me, and when I had heard his story I came away; the gods then gave me a fair wind and soon brought me safe home again."

With these words he moved the heart of Penelope. Then Theoclymenus said to her:

"Madam, wife of Odysseus, Telemachus does not understand these things; listen therefore to me, for I can divine them surely, and will hide nothing from you. May Zeus the king of heaven be my witness, and the rites of hospitality, with that hearth of Odysseus to which I now come, that Odysseus himself is even now in Ithaca, and, either going about the country or staying in one place, is enquiring into all these evil deeds and preparing a day of reckoning for the suitors. I saw an omen when I was on the ship which meant this, and I told Telemachus about it."

"May it be even so," answered Penelope; "if your words come true, you shall have such gifts and such good will from me that all who see you shall congratulate you."

Thus did they converse. Meanwhile the suitors were throwing discs, or aiming with spears at a mark on the levelled ground in front of the house, and behaving with all their old insolence.† But when it was now time for dinner, and the flock of sheep and goats had come into the town from all the country round, with their shepherds as usual, then Medon, who was their favorite servant, and who waited upon them at table, said, "Now then, my young masters, you have had enough sport, so come inside that we may get dinner ready. Dinner is not a bad thing, at dinner time."

They left their sports as he told them, and when they were within the house, they laid their cloaks on the benches and seats inside, and then sacrificed some sheep, goats, pigs, and a heifer, all of them fat and well grown. Thus they made ready for their meal. In the meantime Odysseus and the swineherd were about starting for the town, and the swineherd said, "Stranger, I suppose you still want to go to town to-day, as my master said you were to do; for my own part I should have liked you to stay here as a station hand, but I must do as my master tells me, or he will scold me later on, and a scolding from one's master is a very serious thing. Let us then be off, for it is now broad day; it will be night again directly and then you will find it colder."

"I know, and understand you," replied Odysseus; "you need say no more. Let us be going, but if you have a stick ready cut, let me have it to walk with, for you say the road is a very rough one."

As he spoke he threw his shabby old tattered wallet over his shoulders, by the cord from which it hung, and Eumaeus gave him a stick to his liking. The two then started, leaving the station in charge of the dogs and herdsmen who remained behind; the swineherd led the way and his master followed after, looking like some broken down old tramp as he leaned upon his staff, and his clothes were all in rags. When they had got over the rough steep ground and were nearing the city, they reached the fountain from which the citizens drew their water. This had been made by Ithacus, Neritus, and Polyctor. There was a grove of water-loving poplars planted in a circle all round it, and the clear cold water came down to it from a rock high up, while above the fountain there was an altar to the nymphs, at which all wayfarers used to sacrifice. Here Melanthius son of Dolius overtook them as he was driving down some goats, the best in his flock, for the suitors' dinner, and there were two shepherds with him. When he saw Eumaeus and Odysseus he reviled them with outrageous and unseemly language, which made Odysseus very angry.

"There you go," cried he, "and a precious pair you are. See how heaven brings birds of the same feather to one another. Where, pray, master swine-herd, are you taking this poor miserable object? It would make anyone sick to see such a creature at table. A fellow like this never won a prize for anything in his life, but will go about rubbing his shoulders against every man's door post, and begging, not for swords and cauldrons like a man, but only for a few scraps not worth begging for. If you would give him to me for a hand on my station, he might do to clean out the folds, or bring a bit of sweet feed to the kids, and he could fatten his thighs as much as he pleased on whey; but he has taken to bad ways and will not go about any kind of work; he will do nothing but beg victuals all the town over, to feed his insatiable belly. I say, therefore—and it shall surely be—if he goes near Odysseus' house he will get his head broken by the stools they will fling at him, till they turn him out."

On this, as he passed, he gave Odysseus a kick on the hip out of pure wantonness, but Odysseus stood firm, and did not budge from the path. For a moment he considred whether or not to fly at Melanthius and kill him with his staff, or fling him to the ground and beat his brains out; he resolved, however, to endure it and keep himself in check, but the swineherd looked straight at Melanthius and rebuked him, lifting up his hands and praying to heaven as he did so.

"Fountain nymphs," he cried, "children of Zeus, if ever Odysseus burned you thigh bones covered with fat whether of lambs or kids, grant my prayer that heaven may send him home. He would soon put an end to the swaggering threats with which such men as you go about insulting people—gadding all over the town while your flocks are going to ruin through bad shepherding."

Then Melanthius the goatherd answered, "You ill conditioned cur, what are you talking about? Some day or other I will put you on board ship and take you to a foreign country, where I can sell you and pocket the money you will fetch. I wish I were as sure that Apollo would strike Telemachus dead this very day, or that the suitors would kill him, as I am that Odysseus will never come home again."†

With this he left them to come on at their leisure, while he went quickly forward and soon reached the house of his master. When he got there he went in and took his seat among the suitors opposite Eurymachus, who liked him better than any of the others. The servants brought him a portion of meat, and an upper woman servant set bread before him that he might eat. Presently Odysseus and the swineherd came up to the house and stood by it, amid a sound of music, for Phemius was just beginning to sing to the suitors. Then Odysseus took hold of the swineherd's hand, and said:

"Eumaeus, this house of Odysseus is a very fine place. No matter how far you go, you will find few like it. One building keeps following on after another. The outer court has a wall with battlements all round it; the doors are double folding, and of good workmanship; it would be a hard matter to take it by force of arms. I perceive, too, that there are many people banqueting within it, for there is a smell of roast meat, and I hear a sound of music, which the gods have made to go along with feasting."

Then Eumaeus said, "You have perceived aright, as indeed you generally do; but let us think what will be our best course. Will you go inside first and join the suitors, leaving me here behind you, or will you wait here and let me go in first? But do not wait long, or someone may see you loitering about outside, and throw something at you. Consider this matter I pray you."

And Odysseus answered, "I understand and heed. Go in first and leave me here where I am. I am quite used to being beaten and having things thrown at me. I have been so much buffeted about in war and by sea that I am case-hardened, and this too may go with the rest. But a man cannot hide away the cravings of a hungry belly; this is an enemy which gives much trouble to all men; it is because of this that ships are fitted out to sail the seas, and to make war upon other people."

As they were thus talking, a dog that had been lying asleep raised his head and pricked up his ears. This was Argos, whom Odysseus had bred before setting out for Troy, but he had never had any work out of him. In the old days he used to be taken out by the young men when they went hunting wild goats, or deer, or hares, but now that his master was gone he was lying neglected on the heaps of mule and cow dung that lay in front of the stable doors till the men should come and draw it away to manure the great close; and he was full of fleas. As soon as he saw Odysseus standing there, he dropped his ears and wagged his tail, but he could not get close up to his master. When Odysseus saw the dog on the other side of the yard, he dashed a tear from his eyes without Eumaeus seeing it, and said:

"Eumaeus, what a noble hound that is over yonder on the manure heap: his build is splendid; is he as fine a fellow as he looks, or is he only one of those dogs that come begging about a table, and are kept merely for show?"

"This hound," answered Eumaeus, "belonged to him who has died in a far country. If he were what he was when Odysseus left for Troy, he would soon show you what he could do. There was not a wild beast in the forest that could get away from him when he was once on its tracks. But now he has fallen on evil times, for his master is dead and gone, and the women take no care of him. Servants never do their work when their master's hand is no longer over them, for Zeus takes half the goodness out of a man when he makes a slave of him."

As he spoke he went inside the buildings to the cloister where the suitors were, but Argos died as soon as he had recognized his master.

Telemachus saw Eumaeus long before anyone else did, and beckoned him to come and sit beside him; so he looked about and saw a seat lying near where the carver sat serving out their portions to the suitors; he picked it up, brought it to Telemachus' table, and sat down opposite him. Then the servant brought him his portion, and gave him bread from the bread-basket.

Immediately afterwards Odysseus came inside, looking like a poor miserable old beggar, leaning on his staff and with his clothes all in rags. He sat down upon the threshold of ash-wood just inside the doors leading from the outer to the inner court, and against a bearing-post of cypress-wood which the carpenter had skilfully planed, and had made to join truly with rule and line. Telemachus took a whole loaf from the bread-basket, with as much meat as he could hold in his two hands, and said to Eumaeus, "Take this to the stranger, and tell him to go the round of the suitors, and beg from them; a beggar must not be shamefaced."

So Eumaeus went up to him and said, "Stranger, Telemachus sends you this, and says you are to go the round of the suitors begging, for beggars must not be shamefaced."

Odysseus answered, "May King Zeus grant all happiness to Telemachus, and fulfil the desire of his heart."

Then with both hands he took what Telemachus had sent him, and laid it on the dirty old wallet at his feet. He went on eating it while the bard was singing, and had just finished his dinner as he left off. The suitors applauded the bard, whereupon Athena went up to Odysseus and prompted him to beg pieces of bread from each one of the suitors, that he might see what kind of people they were, and tell the good from the bad; but come what might she was not going to save a single one of them.[†] Odysseus, therefore, went on his round, going from left to right, and stretched out his hands to beg as though he were a real beggar. Some of them pitied him, and were curious about him, asking one another who he was and where he came from; whereon the goatherd Melanthius said, "Suitors of my noble mistress, I can tell you something about him, for I have seen him before. The swineherd brought him here, but I know nothing about the man himself, nor where he comes from."

On this Antinous began to abuse the swineherd. "You precious idiot," he cried, "what have you brought this man to town for? Have we not tramps and beggars enough already to pester us as we sit at meat? Do you think it a small thing that such people gather here to waste your master's property—and must you needs bring this man as well?"

And Eumaeus answered, "Antinous, your birth is good but your words evil. It was no doing of mine that he came here. Who is likely to invite a stranger from a foreign country, unless it be one of those who can do public service as a seer, a healer of hurts, a carpenter, or a bard who can charm us with his singing? Such men are welcome all the world over, but no one is likely to ask a beggar who will only worry him. You are always harder on Odysseus' servants than any of the other suitors are, and above all on me, but I do not care so long as Telemachus and Penelope are alive and here."

But Telemachus said, "Hush, do not answer him; Antinous has the bitterest tongue of all the suitors, and he makes the others worse."

Then turning to Antinous he said, "Antinous, you take as much care of my interests as though I were your son. Why should you want to see this stranger turned out of the house? Heaven forbid; take something and give it him yourself; I do not grudge it; I bid you take it. Never mind my mother, nor any of the other servants in the house; but I know you will not do what I say, for you are more fond of eating things yourself than of giving them to other people."

"What do you mean, Telemachus," replied Antinous, "by this swaggering talk? If all the suitors were to give him as much as I will, he would not come here again for another three months."

As he spoke he drew the stool on which he rested his dainty feet from under the table, and made as though he would throw it at Odysseus, but the other suitors all gave him something, and filled his wallet with bread and meat; he was about, therefore, to go back to the threshold and eat what the suitors had given him, but he first went up to Antinous and said:

"Sir, give me something; you are not, surely, the poorest man here; you seem to be a chief, foremost among them all; therefore you should be the better giver, and I will tell far and wide of your bounty. I too was a rich man once, and had a fine house of my own; in those days I gave to many a tramp such as I now am, no matter who he might be nor what he wanted. I had any number of servants, and all the other things which people have who live well and are accounted wealthy, but it pleased Zeus to take all away from me. He sent me with a band of roving robbers to Egypt; it was a long voyage and I was undone by it. I stationed my ships in the river Aegyptus, and bade my men stay by them and keep guard over them, while I sent out scouts to reconnoitre from every point of vantage.

"But the men disobeyed my orders, took to their own devices, and ravaged the land of the Egyptians, killing the men, and taking their wives and children captives. The alarm was soon carried to the city, and when they heard the war-cry, the people came out at daybreak till the plain was filled with soldiers horse and foot, and with the gleam of armor. Then Zeus spread panic among my men, and they would no longer face the enemy, for they found themselves surrounded. The Egyptians killed many of us, and took the rest alive to do forced labor for them; as for myself, they gave me to a friend who met them, to take to Cyprus, Dmetor by name, son of Iasus, who was a great man in Cyprus. Thence I am come hither in a state of great misery."

Then Antinous said, "What god can have sent such a pestilence to plague us during our dinner? Get out, into the open part of the court, or I will give you Egypt and Cyprus over again for your insolence and importunity; you have begged of all the others, and they have given you lavishly, for they have abundance round them, and it is easy to be free with other people's property when there is plenty of it."

On this Odysseus began to move off, and said, "Your looks, my fine sir, are better than your breeding; if you were in your own house you would not spare a poor man so much as a pinch of salt, for though you are in another man's, and surrounded with abundance, you cannot find it in you to give him even a piece of bread."

This made Antinous very angry, and he scowled at him saying, "You shall pay for this before you get clear of the court." With these words he threw a footstool at him, and hit him on the right shoulder blade near the top of his back. Odysseus stood firm as a rock and the blow did not even stagger him, but he shook his head in silence as he brooded on his revenge. Then he went back to the threshold and sat down there, laying his well filled wallet at his feet.

"Listen to me," he cried, "you suitors of Queen Penelope, that I may speak even as I am minded. A man knows neither ache nor pain if he gets hit while fighting for his money, or for his sheep or his cattle; and even so Antinous has hit me while in the service of my miserable belly, which is always getting people into trouble. Still, if the poor have gods and avenging deities at all, I pray them that Antinous may come to a bad end before his marriage."

"Sit where you are, and eat your victuals in silence, or be off elsewhere," shouted Antinous. "If you say more I will have you dragged hand and foot through the courts, and the servants shall flay you alive."

The other suitors were much displeased at this, and one of the young men said, "Antinous, you did ill in striking that poor wretch of a tramp: it will be worse for you if he should turn out to be some god—and we know the gods go about disguised in all sorts of ways as people from foreign countries, and travel about the world to see who do amiss and who righteously."†

Thus said the suitors, but Antinous paid them no heed. Meanwhile Telemachus was furious about the blow that had been given to his father, and though no tear fell from him, he shook his head in silence and brooded on his revenge.

Now when Penelope heard that the beggar had been struck in the ban-queting-cloister, she said before her maids, "Would that Apollo would so strike you, Antinous," and her waiting woman Eurynome answered, "If our prayers were answered not one of the suitors would ever again see the sun rise." Then Penelope said, "Nurse, I hate every single one of them, for they mean nothing but mischief, but I hate Antinous like the darkness of death itself. A poor unfortunate tramp has come begging about the house for sheer want. Everyone else has given him something to put in his wallet, but Antinous has hit him on the right shoulder-blade with a footstool."

Thus did she talk with her maids as she sat in her own room, and in the meantime Odysseus was getting his dinner. Then she called for the swineherd and said, "Eumaeus, go and tell the stranger to come here, I want to see him and ask him some questions. He seems to have traveled much, and he may have seen or heard something of my unhappy husband."

To this you answered, O swineherd Eumaeus, "If these Achaeans, Madam, would only keep quiet, you would be charmed with the history of his adventures. I had him three days and three nights with me in my hut, which was the first place he reached after running away from his ship, and he has not yet completed the story of his misfortunes. If he had been the most heaventaught minstrel in the whole world, on whose lips all hearers hang entranced, I could not have been more charmed as I sat in my hut and listened to him. He says there is an old friendship between his house and that of Odysseus, and that he comes from Crete where the descendants of Minos live, after having been driven hither and thither by every kind of misfortune; he also declares that he has heard of Odysseus as being alive and near at hand among the Thesprotians, and that he is bringing great wealth home with him."

"Call him here, then," said Penelope, "that I too may hear his story. As for the suitors, let them take their pleasure indoors or out as they will, for they have nothing to fret about. Their corn and wine remain unwasted in their houses with none but servants to consume them, while they keep hanging about our house day after day sacrificing our oxen, sheep, and fat goats for their banquets, and never giving so much as a thought to the quantity of wine they drink. No estate can stand such recklessness, for we have now no Odysseus to protect us. If he were to come again, he and his son would soon have their revenge."

As she spoke Telemachus sneezed so loudly that the whole house resounded with it. Penelope laughed when she heard this, and said to Eumaeus, "Go and call the stranger; did you not hear how my son sneezed just as I was speaking? This can only mean that all the suitors are going to be killed, and that not one of them shall escape.† Furthermore I say, and lay my saying to your heart: if I am satisfied that the stranger is speaking the truth I shall give him a shirt and cloak of good wear."

When Eumaeus heard this he went straight to Odysseus and said, "Father stranger, my mistress Penelope, mother of Telemachus, has sent for you; she is in great grief, but she wishes to hear anything you can tell her about her husband, and if she is satisfied that you are speaking the truth, she will give you a shirt and cloak, which are the very things that you are most in want of. As for bread, you can get enough of that to fill your belly, by begging about the town, and letting those give that will."

"I will tell Penelope," answered Odysseus, "nothing but what is strictly true. I know all about her husband, and have been partner with him in affliction, but I am afraid of passing through this crowd of cruel suitors, for their pride and insolence reach heaven. Just now, moreover, as I was going about the house without doing any harm, a man gave me a blow that hurt me very much, but neither Telemachus nor anyone else defended me. Tell Penelope, therefore, to be patient and wait till sundown. Let her give me a seat close up to the fire, for my clothes are worn very thin—you know they are, for you have seen them ever since I first asked you to help me—she can then ask me about the return of her husband."

The swineherd went back when he heard this, and Penelope said as she saw him cross the threshold, "Why do you not bring him here, Eumaeus? Is he afraid that someone will ill-treat him, or is he shy of coming inside the house at all? Beggars should not be shamefaced."

To this you answered, O swineherd Eumaeus, "The stranger is quite reasonable. He is avoiding the suitors, and is only doing what anyone else would do. He asks you to wait till sundown, and it will be much better, madam, that you should have him all to yourself, when you can hear him and talk to him as you will."

"The man is no fool," answered Penelope, "it would very likely be as he says, for there are no such abominable people in the whole world as these men are."

When she had done speaking Eumaeus went back to the suitors, for he had explained everything. Then he went up to Telemachus and said in his ear so that none could overhear him, "My dear sir, I will now go back to the pigs, to see after your property and my own business. You will look to what is going on here, but above all be careful to keep out of danger, for there are many who bear you ill will. May Zeus bring them to a bad end before they do us a mischief."

"Very well," replied Telemachus, "go home when you have had your dinner, and in the morning come here with the victims we are to sacrifice for the day. Leave the rest to heaven and me."

On this Eumaeus took his seat again, and when he had finished his dinner he left the courts and the cloister with the men at table, and went back to his pigs. As for the suitors, they presently began to amuse themselves with singing and dancing, for it was now getting on towards evening.

B O O K X V I I I

The fight with Irus
Odysseus warns Amphinomus
Penelope gets presents from the suitors
The Braziers
Odysseus rebukes Eurymachus

NOW THERE CAME a certain common tramp who used to go begging all over the city of Ithaca, and was notorious as an incorrigible glutton and drunkard. This man had no strength nor stay in him, but he was a great hulking fellow to look at; his real name, the one his mother gave him, was Arnaeus, but the young men of the place called him Irus, because he used to run errands for anyone who would send him. As soon as he came he began to insult Odysseus, and to try and drive him out of his own house.

"Be off, old man," he cried, "from the doorway, or you shall be dragged out neck and heels. Do you not see that they are all giving me the wink, and wanting me to turn you out by force, only I do not like to do so? Get up then, and go of yourself, or we shall come to blows."

Odysseus frowned on him and said, "My friend, I do you no manner of harm; people give you a great deal, but I am not jealous. There is room enough in this doorway for the pair of us, and you need not grudge me things that are not yours to give. You seem to be just such another tramp as myself, but perhaps the gods will give us better luck by and by. Do not, however, talk too much about fighting or you will incense me, and old though I am, I shall cover your mouth and chest with blood. I shall have more peace tomorrow if I do, for you will not come to the house of Odysseus any more."

Irus was very angry and answered, "You filthy glutton, you run on trippingly like an old fishtail. I have a good mind to lay both hands about you, and knock your teeth out of your head like so many boar's tusks. Get ready, therefore, and let these people here stand by and look on. You will never be able to fight one who is so much younger than yourself."

Thus roundly did they rate one another on the smooth pavement in front of the doorway, and when Antinous saw what was going on he laughed heartily and said to the others, "This is the finest sport that you ever saw; heaven never yet sent anything like it into this house. The stranger and Irus have quarreled and are going to fight, let us set them on to do so at once."

The suitors all came up laughing, and gathered round the two ragged tramps. "Listen to me," said Antinous, "there are some goats' paunches down at the fire, which we have filled with blood and fat, and set aside for supper; he who is victorious and proves himself to be the better man shall have his pick of the lot; he shall be free of our table and we will not allow any other beggar about the house at all."

The others all agreed, but Odysseus, to throw them off the scent,[†] said, "Sirs, an old man like myself, worn out with suffering, cannot hold his own against a young one; but my irrepressible belly urges me on, though I know it can only end in my getting a drubbing. You must swear, however that none of you will give me a foul blow to favor Irus and secure him the victory."

They swore as he told them, and when they had completed their oath Telemachus put in a word and said, "Stranger, if you have a mind to settle with this fellow, you need not be afraid of anyone here. Whoever strikes you will have to fight more than one. I am host, and the other chiefs, Antinous and Eurymachus, both of them men of understanding, are of the same mind as I am."

Everyone assented, and Odysseus girded his old rags about his loins, thus baring his stalwart thighs, his broad chest and shoulders, and his mighty arms; but Athena came up to him and made his limbs even stronger still. The suitors were beyond measure astonished, and one would turn towards his neighbor saying, "The stranger has brought such a thigh out of his old rags that there will soon be nothing left of Irus."

Irus began to be very uneasy as he heard them, but the servants girded him by force, and brought him into the open part of the court in such a fright that his limbs were all of a tremble. Antinous scolded him and said, "You swaggering bully, you ought never to have been born at all if you are afraid of such an old broken down creature as this tramp is. I say, therefore—and it shall surely be—if he beats you and proves himself the better man, I shall pack you off on board ship to the mainland and send you to king Echetus, who kills everyone that comes near him. He will cut off your nose and ears, and draw out your entrails for the dogs to eat."

This frightened Irus still more, but they brought him into the middle of the court, and the two men raised their hands to fight. Then Odysseus considered whether he should let drive so hard at him as to make an end of him then and there, or whether he should give him a lighter blow that should only knock him down; in the end he deemed it best to give the lighter blow for fear the Achaeans should begin to suspect who he was. Then they began to fight, and Irus hit Odysseus on the right shoulder; but Odysseus gave Irus a blow on the neck under the ear that broke in the bones of his skull, and the blood came gushing out of his mouth; he fell groaning in the dust, gnashing his teeth and kicking on the ground, but the suitors threw up their hands and nearly died of laughter, as Odysseus caught hold of him by the foot and dragged him into the outer court as far as the gate-house. There he propped him up against the wall and put his staff in his hands. "Sit here," said he, "and keep the dogs and pigs off; you are a pitiful creature, and if you try to make yourself king of the beggars any more you shall fare still worse."

Then he threw his dirty old wallet, all tattered and torn over his shoulder with the cord by which it hung, and went back to sit down upon the threshold; but the suitors went within the cloisters, laughing and saluting him, "May Zeus, and all the other gods," said they, "grant you whatever you want for having put an end to the importunity of this insatiable tramp. We will take him over to the mainland presently, to king Echetus, who kills everyone that comes near him."

Odysseus hailed this as of good omen, and Antinous set a great goat's paunch before him filled with blood and fat. Amphinomus took two loaves out of the bread-basket and brought them to him, pledging him as he did so in a golden goblet of wine. "Good luck to you," he said, "father stranger, you are very badly off at present, but I hope you will have better times by and by."

To this Odysseus answered, "Amphinomus, you seem to be a man of good understanding, as indeed you may well be, seeing whose son you are. I have heard your father well spoken of; he is Nisus of Dulichium, a man both brave and wealthy. They tell me you are his son, and you appear to be a considerable person; listen, therefore, and take heed to what I am saying. Man is the vainest of all creatures that have their being upon earth. As long as heaven vouchsafes him health and strength, he thinks that he shall come to no harm hereafter, and even when the blessed gods bring sorrow upon him, he bears it as he needs must, and makes the best of it; for God almighty gives men their daily minds day by day. I know all about it, for I was a rich man once, and did much wrong in the stubbornness of my pride, and in the confidence that my father and my brothers would support me; therefore let a man fear God in all things always, and take the good that heaven may see fit to send him without vain glory. Consider the infamy of what these suitors are doing; see how they are wasting the estate, and doing dishonor to the wife, of one who is certain to return some day, and that, too, not long hence. Nay, he will be here soon; may heaven send you home quietly first that you may not meet with him in the day of his coming, for once he is here the suitors and he will not part bloodlessly."

With these words he made a drink-offering, and when he had drunk he put the gold cup again into the hands of Amphinomus, who walked away serious and bowing his head, for he foreboded evil. But even so he did not escape destruction, for Athena had doomed him to fall by the hand of Telemachus.[†] So he took his seat again at the place from which he had come.

Then Athena put it into the mind of Penelope to show herself to the suitors, that she might make them still more enamoured of her, and win still further honor from her son and husband. So she feigned a mocking laugh and said, "Eurynome, I have changed my mind, and have a fancy to show myself to the suitors although I detest them. I should like also to give my son a hint that he had better not have anything more to do with them. They speak fairly enough but they mean mischief."

"My dear child," answered Eurynome, "all that you have said is true, go and tell your son about it, but first wash yourself and anoint your face. Do not go about with your cheeks all covered with tears; it is not right that you should grieve so incessantly; for Telemachus, whom you always prayed that you might live to see with a beard, is already grown up."

"I know, Eurynome," replied Penelope, "that you mean well, but do not try and persuade me to wash and to anoint myself, for heaven robbed me of all my beauty on the day my husband sailed; nevertheless, tell Autonoe and Hippodamia that I want them. They must be with me when I am in the cloister; I am not going among the men alone; it would not be proper for me to do so."

On this the old woman went out of the room to bid the maids go to their mistress. In the meantime Athena thought her another matter, and sent Penelope off into a sweet slumber; so she lay down on her couch and her limbs became heavy with sleep. Then the goddess shed grace and beauty over her that all the Achaeans might admire her. She washed her face with the ambrosial loveliness that Aphrodite wears when she goes dancing with the Graces; she made her taller and of a more commanding figure, while as for her complexion it was whiter than sawn ivory. When Athena had done all this she went away, whereon the maids came in from the women's room and woke Penelope with the sound of their talking.

"What an exquisitely delicious sleep I have been having," said she, as she passed her hands over her face, "in spite of all my misery. I wish Artemis would let me die so sweetly now at this very moment, that I might no longer waste in despair for the loss of my dear husband, who possessed every kind of good quality and was the most distinguished man among the Achaeans."

With these words she came down from her upper room, not alone but attended by two of her maidens, and when she reached the suitors she stood by one of the bearing-posts supporting the roof of the cloister, holding a veil before her face, and with a staid maid servant on either side of her. As they beheld her the suitors were so overpowered and became so desperately enamoured of her, that each one prayed he might win her for his own bedfellow.

"Telemachus," said she, addressing her son, "I fear you are no longer so discreet and well conducted as you used to be. When you were younger you had a greater sense of propriety; now, however, that you are grown up, though a stranger to look at you would take you for the son of a well to do father as far as size and good looks go, your conduct is by no means what it should be. What is all this disturbance that has been going on, and how came you to allow a stranger to be so disgracefully ill-treated? What would have happened if he had suffered serious injury while a suppliant in our house? Surely this would have been very discreditable to you."

"I am not surprised, my dear mother, at your displeasure," replied Telemachus, "I understand all about it and know when things are not as they should be, which I could not do when I was younger; I cannot, however, behave with perfect propriety at all times. First one and then another of these wicked people here keeps driving me out of my mind, and I have no one to stand by me. After all, however, this fight between Irus and the stranger did not turn out as the suitors meant it to do, for the stranger got the best of it. I wish Father Zeus, Athena, and Apollo would break the neck of every one of these wooers of yours, some inside the house and some out; and I wish they might all be as limp as Irus is over yonder in the gate of the outer court. See how he nods his head like a drunken man; he has had such a thrashing that he cannot stand on his feet nor get back to his home, wherever that may be, for he has no strength left in him."

Thus did they converse. Eurymachus then came up and said, "Queen Penelope, daughter of Icarius, if all the Achaeans in Iasian Argos could see you at this moment, you would have still more suitors in your house by tomorrow morning, for you are the most admirable woman in the whole world both as regards personal beauty and strength of understanding."

To this Penelope replied, "Eurymachus, heaven robbed me of all my beauty whether of face or figure when the Argives set sail for Troy and my dear husband with them. If he were to return and look after my affairs, I should both be more respected and show a better presence to the world. As it is, I am oppressed with care, and with the afflictions which heaven has seen fit to heap upon me. My husband foresaw it all, and when he was leaving home he took my right wrist in his hand—'Wife,' he said, 'we shall not all of us come safe home from Troy, for the Trojans fight well both with bow and spear. They are excellent also at fighting from chariots, and nothing decides the issue of a fight sooner than this.[†] I know not, therefore, whether heaven will send me back to you, or whether I may not fall over there at Troy. In the meantime do you look after things here. Take care of my father and mother as at present, and even more so during my absence, but when you see our son growing a beard, then marry whom you will, and leave this your present home.' This is what he said and now it is all coming true. A night will come when I shall have to yield myself to a marriage which I detest, for Zeus has taken from me all hope of happiness. This further grief, moreover, cuts me to the very heart. You suitors are not wooing me after the custom of my country. When men are courting a woman who they think will be a good wife to them and who is of noble birth, and when they are each trying to win her for himself, they usually bring oxen and sheep to feast the friends of the lady, and they make her magnificent presents, instead of eating up other people's property without paying for it."

This was what she said, and Odysseus was glad when he heard her trying to get presents out of the suitors, and flattering them with fair words which he knew she did not mean.[†]

Then Antinous said, "Queen Penelope, daughter of Icarius, take as many presents as you please from anyone who will give them to you; it is not well to refuse a present; but we will not go about our business nor stir from where we are, till you have married the best man among us whoever he may be."

The others applauded what Antinous had said, and each one sent his servant to bring his present. Antinous' man returned with a large and lovely dress most exquisitely embroidered. It had twelve beautifully made brooch pins of pure gold with which to fasten it. Eurymachus immediately brought her a magnificent chain of gold and amber beads that gleamed like sunlight. Eurydamas' two men returned with some earrings fashioned into three brilliant pendants which glistened most beautifully; while king Pisander son of Polyctor gave her a necklace of the rarest workmanship, and everyone else brought her a beautiful present of some kind.

Then the queen went back to her room upstairs, and her maids brought the presents after her. Meanwhile the suitors took to singing and dancing, and stayed till evening came. They danced and sang till it grew dark; they then brought in three braziers to give light, and piled them up with chopped firewood very old and dry, and they lit torches from them, which the maids held up turn and turn about. Then Odysseus said:

"Maids, servants of Odysseus who has so long been absent, go to the queen inside the house; sit with her and amuse her, or spin, and pick wool. I will hold the light for all these people. They may stay till morning, but shall not beat me, for I can stand a great deal."

The maids looked at one another and laughed, while pretty Melantho began to gibe at him contemptuously. She was daughter to Dolius, but had been brought up by Penelope, who used to give her toys to play with, and looked after her when she was a child; but in spite of all this she showed no consideration for the sorrows of her mistress, and used to misconduct herself with Eurymachus, with whom she was in love.

"Poor wretch," said she, "are you gone clean out of your mind? Go and sleep in some smithy, or place of public gossips, instead of chattering here. Are you not ashamed of opening your mouth before your betters—so many of them too? Has the wine been getting into your head, or do you always babble in this way? You seem to have lost your wits because you beat the tramp Irus; take care that a better man than he does not come and cudgel you about the head till he pack you bleeding out of the house."

"Vixen," replied Odysseus, scowling at her, "I will go and tell Telemachus what you have been saying, and he will have you torn limb from limb."

With these words he scared the women, and they went off into the body of the house. They trembled all over, for they thought he would do as he said. But Odysseus took his stand near the burning braziers, holding up torches and looking at the people—brooding the while on things that should surely come to pass.

But Athena would not let the suitors for one moment cease their insolence, for she wanted Odysseus to become even more bitter against them; she therefore set Eurymachus son of Polybus on to gibe at him, which made the others laugh. "Listen to me," said he, "you suitors of Queen Penelope, that I may speak even as I am minded. It is not for nothing that this man has come to the house of Odysseus; I believe the light has not been coming from the torches, but from his own head—for his hair is all gone, every bit of it."

Then turning to Odysseus he said, "Stranger, will you work as a servant, if I send you to the wolds and see that you are well paid? Can you build a stone fence, or plant trees? I will have you fed all the year round, and will find you in shoes and clothing. Will you go, then? Not you; for you have got into bad ways, and do not want to work; you had rather fill your belly by going round the country begging."

"Eurymachus," answered Odysseus, "if you and I were to work one against the other in early summer when the days are at their longest—give me a good scythe, and take another yourself, and let us see which will last the longer or mow the stronger, from dawn till dark when the mowing grass is about. Or if you will plough against me, let us each take a yoke of tawny oxen, well-mated and of great strength and endurance: turn me into a four acre field, and see whether you or I can drive the straighter furrow. If, again, war were to break out this day, give me a shield, a couple of spears and a helmet fitting well upon my temples—you would find me foremost in the fray, and would cease your gibes about my belly. You are insolent and cruel, and think yourself a great man because you live in a little world,[†] and that a bad one. If Odysseus comes to his own again, the doors of his house are wide, but you will find them narrow when you try to fly through them."

Eurymachus was furious at all this. He scowled at him and cried, "You wretch, I will soon pay you out for daring to say such things to me, and in public too. Has the wine been getting into your head or do you always babble in this way? You seem to have lost your wits because you beat the tramp Irus." With this he caught hold of a footstool, but Odysseus sought protection at the knees of Amphinomus of Dulichium, for he was afraid. The stool hit the cupbearer on his right hand and knocked him down: the man fell with a cry flat on his back, and his wine-jug fell ringing to the ground. The suitors in the covered cloister were now in an uproar, and one would turn towards his neighbor, saying, "I wish the stranger had gone somewhere else, bad luck to him, for all the trouble he gives us. We cannot permit such disturbance about a beggar; if such ill counsels are to prevail we shall have no more pleasure at our banquet."

On this Telemachus came forward and said, "Sirs, are you mad? Can you not carry your meat and your liquor decently? Some evil spirit has possessed you. I do not wish to drive any of you away, but you have had your suppers, and the sooner you all go home to bed the better."

The suitors bit their lips and marveled at the boldness of his speech; but Amphinomus the son of Nisus, who was son to Aretias, said, "Do not let us take offense; it is reasonable, so let us make no answer. Neither let us do violence to the stranger nor to any of Odysseus' servants. Let the cupbearer go round with the drink-offerings, that we may make them and go home to our rest. As for the stranger, let us leave Telemachus to deal with him, for it is to his house that he has come."

Thus did he speak, and his saying pleased them well, so Mulius of Dulichium, servant to Amphinomus, mixed them a bowl of wine and water and handed it round to each of them man by man, whereon they made their drink-offerings to the blessed gods: Then, when they had made their drink-offerings and had drunk each one as he was minded, they took their several ways each of them to his own abode.

B O O K X I X

Telemachus and Odysseus remove the armor
Odysseus interviews Penelope
Euryclea washes his feet and recognizes the scar on his leg
Penelope tells her dream to Odysseus

ODYSSEUS WAS LEFT in the cloister, pondering on the means whereby with Athena's help he might be able to kill the suitors. Presently he said to Telemachus, "Telemachus, we must get the armor together and take it down inside. Make some excuse when the suitors ask you why you have removed it. Say that you have taken it to be out of the way of the smoke, inasmuch as it is no longer what it was when Odysseus went away, but has become soiled and begrimed with soot. Add to this more particularly that you are afraid Zeus may set them on to quarrel over their wine, and that they may do each other some harm which may disgrace both banquet and wooing, for the sight of arms sometimes tempts people to use them."

Telemachus approved of what his father had said, so he called nurse Euryclea and said, "Nurse, shut the women up in their room, while I take the armor that my father left behind him down into the store room. No one looks after it now my father is gone, and it has got all smirched with soot during my own boyhood. I want to take it down where the smoke cannot reach it."

"I wish, child," answered Euryclea, "that you would take the management of the house into your own hands altogether, and look after all the property yourself. But who is to go with you and light you to the store-room? The maids would have done so, but you would not let them."

"The stranger," said Telemachus, "shall show me a light; when people eat my bread they must earn it, no matter where they come from."

Euryclea did as she was told, and bolted the women inside their room. Then Odysseus and his son made all haste to take the helmets, shields, and spears inside; and Athena went before them with a gold lamp in her hand that shed a soft and brilliant radiance, whereon Telemachus said, "Father, my eyes behold a great marvel: the walls, with the rafters, crossbeams, and the supports on which they rest are all aglow as with a flaming fire. Surely there is some god here who has come down from heaven."

"Hush," answered Odysseus, "hold your peace and ask no questions, for this is the manner of the gods. Get you to your bed, and leave me here to talk with your mother and the maids. Your mother in her grief will ask me all sorts of questions."

On this Telemachus went by torch-light to the other side of the inner court, to the room in which he always slept. There he lay in his bed till morning, while Odysseus was left in the cloister pondering on the means whereby with Athena's help he might be able to kill the suitors.

Then Penelope came down from her room looking like Aphrodite or Artemis, and they set her a seat inlaid with scrolls of silver and ivory near the fire in her accustomed place. It had been made by Icmalius and had a footstool all in one piece with the seat itself; and it was covered with a thick fleece: on this she now sat, and the maids came from the women's room to join her. They set about removing the tables at which the wicked suitors had been dining, and took away the bread that was left, with the cups from which they had drunk. They emptied the embers out of the braziers, and heaped much wood upon them to give both light and heat; but Melantho began to rail at Odysseus a second time and said, "Stranger, do you mean to plague us by hanging about the house all night and spying upon the women? Be off, you wretch, outside, and eat your supper there, or you shall be driven out with a firebrand."

Odysseus scowled at her and answered, "My good woman, why should you be so angry with me? Is it because I am not clean, and my clothes are all in rags, and because I am obliged to go begging about after the manner of tramps and beggars generally? I too was a rich man once, and had a fine house of my own; in those days I gave to many a tramp such as I now am, no matter who he might be nor what he wanted. I had any number of servants, and all the other things which people have who live well and are accounted wealthy, but it pleased Zeus to take all away from me; therefore, woman, beware lest you too come to lose that pride and place in which you now wanton above your fellows; have a care lest you get out of favor with your mistress, and lest Odysseus should come home, for there is still a chance that he may do so. Moreover, though he be dead as you think he is, yet by Apollo's will he has left a son behind him, Telemachus, who will note anything done amiss by the maids in the house, for he is now no longer in his boyhood."

Penelope heard what he was saying and scolded the maid, "Impudent baggage," said she, "I see how abominably you are behaving, and you shall smart for it. You knew perfectly well, for I told you myself, that I was going to see the stranger and ask him about my husband, for whose sake I am in such continual sorrow."

Then she said to her head waiting woman Eurynome, "Bring a seat with a fleece upon it, for the stranger to sit upon while he tells his story, and listens to what I have to say. I wish to ask him some questions."

Eurynome brought the seat at once and set a fleece upon it, and as soon as Odysseus had sat down Penelope began by saying, "Stranger, I shall first ask you who and whence are you? Tell me of your town and parents."

"Madam," answered Odysseus, "who on the face of the whole earth can dare to chide with you? Your fame reaches the firmament of heaven itself; you are like some blameless king, who upholds righteousness, as the monarch over a great and valiant nation: the earth yields its wheat and barley, the trees are loaded with fruit, the ewes bring forth lambs, and the sea abounds with fish by reason of his virtues, and his people do good deeds under him. Nevertheless, as I sit here in your house, ask me some other question and do not seek to know my race and family, or you will recall memories that will yet more increase my sorrow. I am full of heaviness, but I ought not to sit weeping and wailing in another person's house, nor is it well to be thus grieving continually. I shall have one of the servants or even yourself complaining of me, and saying that my eyes swim with tears because I am heavy with wine."

Then Penelope answered, "Stranger, heaven robbed me of all beauty, whether of face or figure, when the Argives set sail for Troy and my dear husband with them. If he were to return and look after my affairs I should be both more respected and should show a better presence to the world. As it is, I am oppressed with care, and with the afflictions which heaven has seen fit to heap upon me. The chiefs from all our islands—Dulichium, Same, and Zacynthus, as also from Ithaca itself, are wooing me against my will and are wasting my estate. I can therefore show no attention to strangers, nor suppliants, nor to people who say that they are skilled artisans, but am all the time broken-hearted about Odysseus. They want me to marry again at once, and I have to invent stratagems in order to deceive them. In the first place heaven put it in my mind to set up a great tambour-frame in my room, and to begin working upon an enormous piece of fine needlework. Then I said to them, 'Sweethearts, Odysseus is indeed dead, still, do not press me to marry again immediately; wait—for I would not have my skill in needlework perish unrecorded—till I have finished making a pall for the hero Laertes, to be ready against the time when death shall take him. He is very rich, and the women of the place will talk if he is laid out without a pall.' This was what I said, and they assented; whereon I used to keep working at my great web all day long, but at night I would unpick the stitches again by torch light. I fooled them in this way for three years without their finding it out, but as time wore on and I was now in my fourth year, in the waning of moons, and many days had been accomplished, those good for nothing hussies my maids betrayed me to the suitors, who broke in upon me and caught me; they were very angry with me, so I was forced to finish my work whether I would or no. And now I do not see how I can find any further shift for getting out of this marriage. My parents are putting great pressure upon me, and my son chafes at the ravages the suitors are making upon his estate, for he is now old enough to understand all about it and is perfectly able to look after his own affairs, for heaven has blessed him with an excellent disposition. Still, notwithstanding all this, tell me who you are and where you come from—for you must have had father and mother of some sort; you cannot be the son of an oak or of a rock."

Then Odysseus answered, "Madam, wife of Odysseus, since you persist in asking me about my family, I will answer, no matter what it costs me: people must expect to be pained when they have been exiles as long as I have, and suffered as much among as many peoples. Nevertheless, as regards your question I will tell you all you ask. There is a fair and fruitful island in mid-ocean called Crete; it is thickly peopled and there are ninety cities in it: the people speak many different languages which overlap one another, for there are Achaeans, brave Eteocretans, Dorians of three-fold race, and noble Pelasgi. There is a great town there, Cnossus, where Minos reigned who every nine years had a conference with Zeus himself. Minos was father to Deucalion, whose son I am, for Deucalion had two sons Idomeneus and myself. Idomeneus sailed for Troy, and I, who am the younger, am called Aethon; my brother, however, was at once the older and the more valiant of the two; hence it was in Crete that I saw Odysseus and showed him hospitality, for the winds took him there as he was on his way to Troy, carrying him out of his course from cape Malea and leaving him in Amnisus off the cave of Ilithuia, where the harbors are difficult to enter and he could hardly find shelter from the winds that were then raging. As soon as he got there he went into the town and asked for Idomeneus, claiming to be his old and valued friend, but Idomeneus had already set sail for Troy some ten or twelve days earlier, so I took him to my own house and showed him every kind of hospitality, for I had abundance of everything. Moreover, I fed the men who were with him with barley meal from the public store, and got subscriptions of wine and oxen for them to sacrifice to their heart's content. They stayed with me twelve days, for there was a gale blowing from the North so strong that one could hardly keep one's feet on land. I suppose some unfriendly god had raised it for them, but on the thirteenth day the wind dropped, and they got away."

Many a plausible tale did Odysseus further tell her, and Penelope wept as she listened, for her heart was melted. As the snow wastes upon the mountain tops when the winds from South East and West have breathed upon it and thawed it till the rivers run bank full with water, even so did her cheeks overflow with tears for the husband who was all the time sitting by her side. Odysseus felt for her and was sorry for her, but he kept his eyes as hard as horn or iron without letting them so much as quiver, so cunningly did he restrain his tears.† Then, when she had relieved herself by weeping, she turned to him again and said: "Now, stranger, I shall put you to the test and see whether or no you really did entertain my husband and his men, as you say you did. Tell me, then, how he was dressed, what kind of a man he was to look at, and so also with his companions."†

"Madam," answered Odysseus, "it is such a long time ago that I can hardly say. Twenty years are come and gone since he left my home, and went elsewhither; but I will tell you as well as I can recollect. Odysseus wore a mantle of purple wool, double lined, and it was fastened by a gold brooch with two catches for the pin. On the face of this there was a device that showed a dog holding a spotted fawn between his fore paws, and watching it as it lay panting upon the ground. Everyone marveled at the way in which these things had been done in gold, the dog looking at the fawn, and strangling it, while the fawn was struggling convulsively to escape. As for the shirt that he wore next his skin, it was so soft that it fitted him like the skin of an onion, and glistened in the sunlight to the admiration of all the women who beheld it. Furthermore I say, and lay my saying to your heart, that I do not know whether Odysseus wore these clothes when he left home, or whether one of his companions had given them to him while he was on his voyage; or possibly someone at whose house he was staying made him a present of them, for he was a man of many friends and had few equals among the Achaeans. I myself gave him a sword of bronze and a beautiful purple mantle, double lined, with a shirt that went down to his feet, and I sent him on board his ship with every mark of honor. He had a servant with him, a little older than himself, and I can tell you what he was like; his shoulders were hunched, he was dark, and he had thick curly hair. His name was Eurybates, and Odysseus treated him with greater familiarity than he did any of the others, as being the most like-minded with himself."

Penelope was moved still more deeply as she heard the indisputable proofs that Odysseus laid before her; and when she had again found relief in tears she said to him, "Stranger, I was already disposed to pity you, but henceforth you shall be honored and made welcome in my house. It was I who gave Odysseus the clothes you speak of. I took them out of the store room and folded them up myself, and I gave him also the gold brooch to wear as an ornament. Alas! I shall never welcome him home again. It was by an ill fate that he ever set out for that detested city whose very name I cannot bring myself even to mention."

Then Odysseus answered, "Madam, wife of Odysseus, do not disfigure yourself further by grieving thus bitterly for your loss, though I can hardly blame you for doing so. A woman who has loved her husband and borne him children, would naturally be grieved at losing him, even though he were a worse man than Odysseus, who they say was like a god. Still, cease your tears and listen to what I can tell you. I will hide nothing from you, and can say with perfect truth that I have lately heard of Odysseus as being alive and on his way home; he is among the Thesprotians, and is bringing back much valuable treasure that he has begged from one and another of them; but his ship and all his crew were lost as they were leaving the Thrinacian island, for Zeus and the sun-god were angry with him because his men had slaughtered the sun-god's cattle, and they were all drowned to a man. But Odysseus stuck to the keel of the ship and was drifted on to the land of the Phaeacians, who are near of kin to the immortals, and who treated him as though he had been a god, giving him many presents, and wishing to escort him home safe and sound. In fact Odysseus would have been here long ago, had he not thought better to go from land to land gathering wealth; for there is no man living who is so wily as he is; there is no one can compare with him. Pheidon king of the Thesprotians told me all this, and he swore to me—making drink-offerings in his house as he did so—that the ship was by the waterside and the crew found who would take Odysseus to his own country. He sent me off first, for there happened to be a Thesprotian ship sailing for the wheat-growing island of Dulichium, but he showed me all the treasure Odysseus had got together, and he had enough lying in the house of king Pheidon to keep his family for ten generations; but the king said Odysseus had gone to Dodona that he might learn Zeus' mind from the high oak tree, and know whether after so long an absence he should return to Ithaca openly or in secret. So you may know he is safe and will be here shortly; he is close at hand and cannot remain away from home much longer; nevertheless I will confirm my words with an oath, and call Zeus who is the first and mightiest of all gods to witness, as also that hearth of Odysseus to which I have now come, that all I have spoken shall surely come to pass. Odysseus will return in this self same year; with the end of this moon and the beginning of the next he will be here."

"May it be even so," answered Penelope; "if your words come true you shall have such gifts and such good will from me that all who see you shall congratulate you; but I know very well how it will be. Odysseus will not return, neither will you get your escort hence, for so surely as that Odysseus ever was, there are now no longer any such masters in the house as he was, to receive honorable strangers or to further them on their way home. And now, you maids, wash his feet for him, and make him a bed on a couch with rugs and blankets, that he may be warm and quiet till morning. Then, at daybreak wash him and anoint him again, that he may sit in the cloister and take his meals with Telemachus. It shall be the worse for any one of these hateful people who is uncivil to him; like it or not, he shall have no more to do in this house. For how, sir, shall you be able to learn whether or no I am superior to others of my sex both in goodness of heart and understanding, if I let you dine in my cloisters squalid and ill clad? Men live but for a little season; if they are hard, and deal hardly, people wish them ill so long as they are alive, and speak contemptuously of them when they are dead, but he that is righteous and deals righteously, the people tell of his praise among all lands, and many shall call him blessed."[†]

Odysseus answered, "Madam, I have foresworn rugs and blankets from the day that I left the snowy ranges of Crete to go on shipboard. I will lie as I have lain on many a sleepless night hitherto. Night after night have I passed in any rough sleeping place, and waited for morning. Nor, again, do I like having my feet washed; I shall not let any of the young hussies about your house touch my feet; but, if you have any old and respectable woman who has gone through as much trouble as I have, I will allow her to wash them."

To this Penelope said, "My dear sir, of all the guests who ever yet came to my house there never was one who spoke in all things with such admirable propriety as you do. There happens to be in the house a most respectable old woman—the same who received my poor dear husband in her arms the night he was born, and nursed him in infancy. She is very feeble now, but she shall wash your feet." "Come here," said she, "Euryclea, and wash your master's age-mate; I suppose Odysseus' hands and feet are very much the same now as his are, for trouble ages all of us dreadfully fast."

On these words the old woman covered her face with her hands; she began to weep and made lamentation saying, "My dear child, I cannot think whatever I am to do with you. I am certain no one was ever more god-fearing than yourself, and yet Zeus hates you.[†] No one in the whole world ever burned him more thigh bones, nor gave him finer hecatombs when you prayed you might come to a green old age yourself and see your son grow up to take after you: yet see how he has prevented you alone from ever getting back to your own home. I have no doubt the women in some foreign palace which Odysseus has got to are gibing at him as all these sluts here have been gibing at you. I do not wonder at your not choosing to let them wash you after the manner in which they have insulted you; I will wash your feet myself gladly enough, as Penelope has said that I am to do so; I will wash them both for Penelope's sake and for your own, for you have raised the most lively feelings of compassion in my mind; and let me say this moreover, which pray attend to; we have had all kinds of strangers in distress come here before now, but I make bold to say that no one ever yet came who was so like Odysseus in figure, voice, and feet as you are."

"Those who have seen us both," answered Odysseus, "have always said we were wonderfully like each other, and now you have noticed it too."

Then the old woman took the cauldron in which she was going to wash his feet, and poured a great deal of cold water into it, adding hot till the bath was warm enough. Odysseus sat by the fire, but before long he turned away from the light, for it occurred to him that when the old woman had hold of his leg she would recognize a certain scar which it bore, whereon the whole truth would come out. And indeed as soon as she began washing her master, she at once knew the scar as one that had been given him by a wild boar when he was hunting on Mt. Parnassus with his excellent grandfather Autolycus—who was the most accomplished thief and perjurer in the whole world†—and with the sons of Autolycus. Hermes himself had endowed him with this gift, for he used to burn the thigh bones of goats and kids to him, so he took pleasure in his companionship. It happened once that Autolycus had gone to Ithaca and had found the child of his daughter just born. As soon as he had done supper Euryclea set the infant upon his knees and said, "Autolycus, you must find a name for your grandson; you greatly wished that you might have one."

"Son-in-law and daughter," replied Autolycus, "call the child thus: I am highly displeased with a large number of people in one place and another, both men and women; so name the child 'Odysseus,' or the child of anger. When he grows up and comes to visit his mother's family on Mt. Parnassus, where my possessions lie, I will make him a present and will send him on his way rejoicing."

Odysseus, therefore, went to Parnassus to get the presents from Autolycus, who with his sons shook hands with him and gave him welcome. His grandmother Amphithea threw her arms about him, and kissed his head, and both his beautiful eyes, while Autolycus desired his sons to get dinner ready, and they did as he told them. They brought in a five year old bull, flayed it, made it ready and divided it into joints; these they then cut carefully up into smaller pieces and spitted them; they roasted them sufficiently and served the portions round. Thus through the livelong day to the going down of the sun they feasted, and every man had his full share so that all were satisfied; but when the sun set and it came on dark, they went to bed and enjoyed the boon of sleep.

When the child of morning, rosy-fingered Dawn, appeared, the sons of Autolycus went out with their hounds hunting, and Odysseus went too. They climbed the wooded slopes of Parnassus and soon reached its breezy upland valleys; but as the sun was beginning to beat upon the fields, fresh-risen from the slow still currents of Oceanus, they came to a mountain dell. The dogs were in front searching for the tracks of the beast they were chasing, and after them came the sons of Autolycus, among whom was Odysseus, close behind the dogs, and he had a long spear in his hand. Here was the lair of a huge boar among some thick brushwood, so dense that the wind and rain could not get through it, nor could the sun's rays pierce it, and the ground underneath lay thick with fallen leaves. The boar heard the noise of the men's feet, and the hounds baying on every side as the huntsmen came up to him, so he rushed from his lair, raised the bristles on his neck, and stood at bay with fire flashing from his eyes. Odysseus was the first to raise his spear and try to drive it into the brute, but the boar was too quick for him, and charged him sideways, ripping him above the knee with a gash that tore deep though it did not reach the bone. As for the boar, Odysseus hit him on the right shoulder, and the point of the spear went right through him, so that he fell groaning in the dust until the life went out of him. The sons of Autolycus busied themselves with the carcass of the boar, and bound Odysseus' wound; then, after saying a spell to stop the bleeding, they went home as fast as they could. But when Autolycus and his sons had thoroughly healed Odysseus, they made him some splendid presents, and sent him back to Ithaca with much mutual good will. When he got back, his father and mother were rejoiced to see him, and asked him all about it, and how he had hurt himself to get the scar; so he told them how the boar had ripped him when he was out hunting with Autolycus and his sons on Mt. Parnassus.

As soon as Euryclea had got the scarred limb in her hands and had well hold of it, she recognized it and dropped the foot at once. The leg fell into the bath, which rang out and was overturned, so that all the water was spilt on the ground; Euryclea's eyes between her joy and her grief filled with tears, and she could not speak, but she caught Odysseus by the beard and said, "My dear child, I am sure you must be Odysseus himself, only I did not know you till I had actually touched and handled you."

As she spoke she looked towards Penelope, as though wanting to tell her that her dear husband was in the house, but Penelope was unable to look in that direction and observe what was going on, for Athena had diverted her attention; so Odysseus caught Euryclea by the throat with his right hand and with his left drew her close to him, and said, "Nurse, do you wish to be the ruin of me, you who nursed me at your own breast, now that after twenty years of wandering I am at last come to my own home again? Since it has been borne in upon you by heaven to recognize me, hold your tongue, and do not say a word about it to anyone else in the house, for if you do I tell you—and it shall surely be—that if heaven grants me to take the lives of these suitors, I will not spare you, though you are my own nurse, when I am killing the other women."

"My child," answered Euryclea, "what are you talking about? You know very well that nothing can either bend or break me. I will hold my tongue like a stone or a piece of iron; furthermore let me say, and lay my saying to your heart, when heaven has delivered the suitors into your hand, I will give you a list of the women in the house who have been ill-behaved, and of those who are guiltless."

And Odysseus answered, "Nurse, you ought not to speak in that way; I am well able to form my own opinion about one and all of them; hold your tongue and leave everything to heaven."

As he said this Euryclea left the cloister to fetch some more water, for the first had been all spilt; and when she had washed him and anointed him with oil, Odysseus drew his seat nearer to the fire to warm himself, and hid the scar under his rags. Then Penelope began talking to him and said:

"Stranger, I should like to speak with you briefly about another matter. It is indeed nearly bed time—for those, at least, who can sleep in spite of sorrow. As for myself, heaven has given me a life of such unmeasurable woe, that even by day when I am attending to my duties and looking after the servants, I am still weeping and lamenting during the whole time; then, when night comes, and we all of us go to bed, I lie awake thinking, and my heart becomes a prey to the most incessant and cruel tortures. As the dun nightingale, daughter of Pandareus, sings in the early spring from her seat in shadiest covert hid, and with many a plaintive trill pours out the tale how by mishap she killed her own child Itylus, son of king Zethus, even so does my mind toss and turn in its uncertainty whether I ought to stay with my son here, and safeguard my substance, my bondsmen, and the greatness of my house, out of regard to public opinion and the memory of my late husband, or whether it is not now time for me to go with the best of these suitors who are wooing me and making me such magnificent presents. As long as my son was still young, and unable to understand, he would not hear of my leaving my husband's house, but now that he is full grown he begs and prays me to do so, being incensed at the way in which the suitors are eating up his property. Listen, then, to a dream that I have had and interpret it for me if you can. I have twenty geese about the house that eat mash out of a trough, and of which I am exceedingly fond. I dreamed that a great eagle came swooping down from a mountain, and dug his curved beak into the neck of each of them till he had killed them all. Presently he soared off into the sky, and left them lying dead about the yard; whereon I wept in my dream till all my maids gathered round me, so piteously was I grieving because the eagle had killed my geese.† Then he came back again, and perching on a projecting rafter spoke to me with human voice, and told me to leave off crying. 'Be of good courage,' he said, 'daughter of Icarius; this is no dream, but a vision of good omen that shall surely come to pass. The geese are the suitors, and I am no longer an eagle, but your own husband, who am come back to you, and who will bring these suitors to a disgraceful end.'

On this I woke, and when I looked out I saw my geese at the trough eating their mash as usual."

"This dream, Madam," replied Odysseus, "can admit but of one interpretation, for had not Odysseus himself told you how it shall be fulfilled? The death of the suitors is portended, and not one single one of them will escape."

And Penelope answered, "Stranger, dreams are very curious and unaccountable things, and they do not by any means invariably come true. There are two gates through which these unsubstantial fancies proceed; the one is of horn, and the other ivory. Those that come through the gate of ivory are fatuous, but those from the gate of horn mean something to those that see them. I do not think, however, that my own dream came through the gate of horn, though I and my son should be most thankful if it proves to have done so. Furthermore I say—and lay my saying to your heart—the coming dawn will usher in the ill-omened day that is to sever me from the house of Odysseus, for I am about to hold a tournament of axes. My husband used to set up twelve axes in the court, one in front of the other, like the stays upon which a ship is built; he would then go back from them and shoot an arrow through the whole twelve. I shall make the suitors try to do the same thing, and whichever of them can string the bow most easily, and send his arrow through all the twelve axes, him will I follow, and quit this house of my lawful husband, so goodly and so abounding in wealth. But even so, I doubt not that I shall remember it in my dreams."

Then Odysseus answered, "Madam, wife of Odysseus, you need not defer your tournament, for Odysseus will return ere ever they can string the bow, handle it how they will, and send their arrows through the iron."

To this Penelope said, "As long, sir, as you will sit here and talk to me, I can have no desire to go to bed. Still, people cannot do permanently without sleep, and heaven has appointed us dwellers on earth a time for all things. I will therefore go upstairs and recline upon that couch which I have never ceased to flood with my tears from the day Odysseus set out for the city with a hateful name."

She then went upstairs to her own room, not alone, but attended by her maidens, and when there, she lamented her dear husband till Athena shed sweet sleep over her eyelids.

BOOK XX

Odysseus cannot sleep
Penelope's prayer to Artemis
The two signs from Heaven
Eumaeus and Philoetius arrive
The suitors dine
Ctesippus throws an ox's foot at Odysseus
Theoclymenus foretells disaster and leaves the house

ODYSSEUS SLEPT IN the cloister upon an undressed bullock's hide, on the top of which he threw several skins of the sheep the suitors had eaten, and Eurynome threw a cloak over him after he had laid himself down. There, then, Odysseus lay wakefully brooding upon the way in which he should kill the suitors; and by and by, the women who had been in the habit of misconducting themselves with them, left the house giggling and laughing with one another. This made Odysseus very angry, and he doubted whether to get up and kill every single one of them then and there, or to let them sleep one more and last time with the suitors. His heart growled within him, and as a bitch with puppies growls and shows her teeth when she sees a stranger, so did his heart growl with anger at the evil deeds that were being done: but he beat his breast and said, "Heart, be still, you had worse than this to bear on the day when the terrible Cyclops ate your brave companions; yet you bore it in silence till your cunning got you safe out of the cave, though you made sure of being killed."

Thus he chided with his heart, and checked it into endurance, but he tossed about as one who turns a paunch full of blood and fat in front of a hot fire, doing it first on one side and then on the other, that he may get it cooked as soon as possible, even so did he turn himself about from side to side, thinking all the time how, single handed as he was, he should contrive to kill so large a body of men as the wicked suitors. But by and by Athena came down from heaven in the likeness of a woman, and hovered over his head saying, "My poor unhappy man, why do you lie awake in this way? This is your house: your wife is safe inside it, and so is your son who is just such a young man as any father may be proud of."

"Goddess," answered Odysseus, "all that you have said is true, but I am in some doubt as to how I shall be able to kill these wicked suitors single handed, seeing what a number of them there always are. And there is this further difficulty, which is still more considerable. Supposing that with Zeus' and your assistance I succeed in killing them, I must ask you to consider where I am to escape for safety when it is all over."†

"For shame," replied Athena, "why, anyone else would trust a worse ally than myself, even though that ally were only a mortal and less wise than I am. Am I not a goddess, and have I not protected you throughout in all your troubles? I tell you plainly that even though there were fifty bands of men surrounding us and eager to kill us, you should take all their sheep and cattle, and drive them away with you. But go to sleep; it is a very bad thing to lie awake all night, and you shall be out of your troubles before long."

As she spoke she shed sleep over his eyes, and then went back to Olympus.

While Odysseus was thus yielding himself to a very deep slumber that eased the burden of his sorrows, his admirable wife awoke, and sitting up in her bed began to cry. When she had relieved herself by weeping she prayed to Artemis saying, "Great Goddess Artemis, daughter of Zeus, drive an arrow into my heart and slay me; or let some whirlwind snatch me up and bear me through paths of darkness till it drop me into the mouths of over-flowing Oceanus, as it did the daughters of Pandareus. The daughters of Pandareus lost their father and mother, for the gods killed them, so they were left orphans. But Aphrodite took care of them, and fed them on cheese, honey, and sweet wine. Hera taught them to excel all women in beauty of form and understanding; Artemis gave them an imposing presence, and Athena endowed them with every kind of accomplishment; but one day when Aphrodite had gone up to Olympus to see Zeus about getting them married (for well does he know both what shall happen and what not happen to everyone) the storm winds came and spirited them away to become handmaids to the dread Erinyes. Even so I wish that the gods who live in heaven would hide me from mortal sight, or that fair Artemis might strike me, for I would fain go even beneath the sad earth if I might do so still looking towards Odysseus only, and without having to yield myself to a worse man than he was. Besides, no matter how much people may grieve by day, they can put up with it so long as they can sleep at night, for when the eyes are closed in slumber people forget good and ill alike; whereas my misery haunts me even in my dreams. This very night methought there was one lying by my side who was like Odysseus as he was when he went away with his host, and I rejoiced, for I believed that it was no dream, but the very truth itself."

On this the day broke, but Odysseus heard the sound of her weeping, and it puzzled him, for it seemed as though she already knew him and was by his side. Then he gathered up the cloak and the fleeces on which he had lain, and set them on a seat in the cloister, but he took the bullock's hide out into the open. He lifted up his hands to heaven, and prayed, saying "Father Zeus, since you have seen fit to bring me over land and sea to my own home after all the afflictions you have laid upon me, give me a sign out of the mouth of some one or other of those who are now waking within the house, and let me have another sign of some kind from outside."

Thus did he pray. Zeus heard his prayer and forthwith thundered high up among the clouds from the splendor of Olympus, and Odysseus was glad when he heard it. At the same time within the house, a miller-woman from hard by in the mill room lifted up her voice and gave him another sign. There were twelve miller-women whose business it was to grind wheat and barley which are the staff of life. The others had ground their task and had gone to take their rest, but this one had not yet finished, for she was not so strong as they were, and when she heard the thunder she stopped grinding and gave the sign to her master. "Father Zeus," said she, "you, who rule over heaven and earth, you have thundered from a clear sky without so much as a cloud in it, and this means something for somebody; grant the prayer, then, of me your poor servant who calls upon you, and let this be the very last day that the suitors dine in the house of Odysseus.† They have worn me out with labor of grinding meal for them, and I hope they may never have another dinner anywhere at all."

Odysseus was glad when he heard the omens conveyed to him by the woman's speech, and by the thunder, for he knew they meant that he should avenge himself on the suitors.

Then the other maids in the house rose and lit the fire on the hearth; Telemachus also rose and put on his clothes. He girded his sword about his shoulder, bound his sandals on to his comely feet, and took a doughty spear with a point of sharpened bronze; then he went to the threshold of the cloister and said to Euryclea, "Nurse, did you make the stranger comfortable both as regards bed and board, or did you let him shift for himself?—for my mother, good woman though she is, has a way of paying great attention to second-rate people, and of neglecting others who are in reality much better men."

"Do not find fault child," said Euryclea, "when there is no one to find fault with. The stranger sat and drank his wine as long as he liked: your mother did ask him if he would take any more bread and he said he would not. When he wanted to go to bed she told the servants to make one for him, but he said he was such a wretched outcast that he would not sleep on a bed and under blankets; he insisted on having an undressed bullock's hide and some sheepskins put for him in the cloister and I threw a cloak over him myself."

Then Telemachus went out of the court to the place where the Achaeans were meeting in assembly; he had his spear in his hand, and he was not alone, for his two dogs went with him. But Euryclea called the maids and said, "Come, wake up; set about sweeping the cloisters and sprinkling them with water to lay the dust; put the covers on the seats; wipe down the tables, some of you, with a wet sponge; clean out the mixing-jugs and the cups, and go for water from the fountain at once; the suitors will be here directly; they will be here early, for it is a feast day."

Thus did she speak, and they did even as she had said: twenty of them went to the fountain for water, and the others set themselves busily to work about the house. The men who were in attendance on the suitors also came up and began chopping firewood. By and by the women returned from the fountain, and the swineherd came after them with the three best pigs he could pick out. These he let feed about the premises, and then he said good-humoredly to Odysseus, "Stranger, are the suitors treating you any better now, or are they as insolent as ever?"

"May heaven," answered Odysseus, "requite to them the wickedness with which they deal high-handedly in another man's house without any sense of shame."

Thus did they converse; meanwhile Melanthius the goatherd came up, for he too was bringing in his best goats for the suitors' dinner; and he had two shepherds with him. They tied the goats up under the gatehouse, and then Melanthius began gibing at Odysseus. "Are you still here, stranger," said he, "to pester people by begging about the house? Why can you not go elsewhere? You and I shall not come to an understanding before we have given each other a taste of our fists. You beg without any sense of decency: are there not feasts elsewhere among the Achaeans, as well as here?"

Odysseus made no answer, but bowed his head and brooded. Then a third man, Philoetius, joined them, who was bringing in a barren heifer and some goats. These were brought over by the boatmen who are there to take people over when any one comes to them. So Philoetius made his heifer and his goats secure under the gatehouse, and then went up to the swineherd. "Who, Swineherd," said he, "is this stranger that is lately come here? Is he one of your men? What is his family? Where does he come from? Poor fellow, he looks as if he had been some great man, but the gods give sorrow to whom they will—even to kings if it so pleases them."

As he spoke he went up to Odysseus and saluted him with his right hand; "Good day to you, father stranger," said he, "you seem to be very poorly off now, but I hope you will have better times by and by. Father Zeus, of all gods you are the most malicious. We are your own children, yet you show us no mercy in all our misery and afflictions. A sweat came over me when I saw this man, and my eyes filled with tears, for he reminds me of Odysseus, who I fear is going about in just such rags as this man's are, if indeed he is still among the living. If he is already dead and in the house of Hades, then, alas! for my good master, who made me his stockman when I was quite young among the Cephallenians, and now his cattle are countless; no one could have done better with them than I have, for they have bred like ears of corn; nevertheless I have to keep bringing them in for others to eat, who take no heed to his son though he is in the house, and fear not the wrath of heaven, but are already eager to divide Odysseus' property among them because he has been away so long. I have often thought—only it would not be right while his son is living—of going off with the cattle to some foreign country; bad as this would be, it is still harder to stay here and be ill-treated about other people's herds. My position is intolerable, and I should long since have run away and put myself under the protection of some other chief, only that I believe my poor master will yet return, and send all these suitors flying out of the house."

"Stockman," answered Odysseus, "you seem to be a very well-disposed person, and I can see that you are a man of sense. Therefore I will tell you, and will confirm my words with an oath. By Zeus, the chief of all gods, and by that hearth of Odysseus to which I am now come, Odysseus shall return before you leave this place, and if you are so minded you shall see him killing the suitors who are now masters here."

"If Zeus were to bring this to pass," replied the stockman, "you should see how I would do my very utmost to help him."

And in like manner Eumaeus prayed that Odysseus might return home.

Thus did they converse. Meanwhile the suitors were hatching a plot to murder Telemachus: but a bird flew near them on their left hand—an eagle with a dove in its talons. On this Amphinomus said, "My friends, this plot of ours to murder Telemachus will not succeed; let us go to dinner instead."†

The others assented, so they went inside and laid their cloaks on the benches and seats. They sacrificed the sheep, goats, pigs, and the heifer, and when the inward meats were cooked they served them round. They mixed the wine in the mixing-bowls, and the swineherd gave every man his cup, while Philoetius handed round the bread in the bread baskets, and Melanthius poured them out their wine. Then they laid their hands upon the good things that were before them.

Telemachus purposely made Odysseus sit in the part of the cloister that was paved with stone; he gave him a shabby looking seat at a little table to himself, and had his portion of the inward meats brought to him, with his wine in a gold cup. "Sit there," said he, "and drink your wine among the great people. I will put a stop to the gibes and blows of the suitors, for this is no public house, but belongs to Odysseus, and has passed from him to me. Therefore, suitors, keep your hands and your tongues to yourselves, or there will be mischief."

The suitors bit their lips, and marveled at the boldness of his speech; then Antinous said, "We do not like such language but we will put up with it, for Telemachus is threatening us in good earnest.† If Zeus had let us we should have put a stop to his brave talk ere now."

Thus spoke Antinous, but Telemachus heeded him not. Meanwhile the heralds were bringing the holy hecatomb through the city, and the Achaeans gathered under the shady grove of Apollo.

Then they roasted the outer meat, drew it off the spits, gave every man his portion, and feasted to their heart's content; those who waited at table gave Odysseus exactly the same portion as the others had, for Telemachus had told them to do so.

But Athena would not let the suitors for one moment drop their insolence, for she wanted Odysseus to become still more bitter against them. Now there happened to be among them a ribald fellow, whose name was Ctesippus, and who came from Same. This man, confident in his great wealth, was paying court to the wife of Odysseus, and said to the suitors, "Hear what I have to say. The stranger has already had as large a portion as anyone else; this is well, for it is not right nor reasonable to ill-treat any guest of Telemachus who comes here. I will, however, make him a present on my own account, that he may have something to give to the bath-woman, or to some other of Odysseus' servants."

As he spoke he picked up a heifer's foot from the meat-basket in which it lay, and threw it at Odysseus, but Odysseus turned his head a little aside, and avoided it, smiling grimly Sardinian fashion† as he did so, and it hit the wall, not him. On this Telemachus spoke fiercely to Ctesippus, "It is a good thing for you," said he, "that the stranger turned his head so that you missed him. If you had hit him I should have run you through with my spear, and your father would have had to see about getting you buried rather than married in this house. So let me have no more unseemly behavior from any of you, for I am grown up now to the knowledge of good and evil and understand what is going on, instead of being the child that I have been heretofore. I have long seen you killing my sheep and making free with my corn and wine: I have put up with this, for one man is no match for many, but do me no further violence. Still, if you wish to kill me, kill me; I would far rather die than see such disgraceful scenes day after day—guests insulted, and men dragging the women servants about the house in an unseemly way."

They all held their peace till at last Agelaus son of Damastor said, "No one should take offense at what has just been said, nor gainsay it, for it is quite reasonable. Leave off, therefore, ill-treating the stranger, or anyone else of the servants who are about the house; I would say, however, a friendly word to Telemachus and his mother, which I trust may commend itself to both. 'As long,' I would say, 'as you had ground for hoping that Odysseus would one day come home, no one could complain of your waiting and suffering the suitors to be in your house. It would have been better that he should have returned, but it is now sufficiently clear that he will never do so; therefore talk all this quietly over with your mother, and tell her to marry the best man, and the one who makes her the most advantageous offer. Thus you will yourself be able to manage your own inheritance, and to eat and drink in peace, while your mother will look after some other man's house, not yours.'"

To this Telemachus answered, "By Zeus, Agelaus, and by the sorrows of my unhappy father, who has either perished far from Ithaca, or is wandering in some distant land, I throw no obstacles in the way of my mother's marriage; on the contrary I urge her to choose whomsoever she will, and I will give her numberless gifts into the bargain, but I dare not insist that she shall leave the house against her own wishes. Heaven forbid that I should do this."

Athena now made the suitors fall to laughing immoderately, and set their wits wandering; but they were laughing with a forced laughter. Their meat became smeared with blood; their eyes filled with tears, and their hearts were heavy with forebodings. Theoclymenus saw this and said, "Unhappy men, what is it that ails you? There is a shroud of darkness drawn over you from head to foot, your cheeks are wet with tears; the air is alive with wailing voices; the walls and roof-beams drip blood; the gate of the cloisters and the court beyond them are full of ghosts trooping down into the night of hell; the sun is blotted out of heaven, and a blighting gloom is over all the land."†

Thus did he speak, and they all of them laughed heartily. Eurymachus then said, "This stranger who has lately come here has lost his senses. Servants, turn him out into the streets, since he finds it so dark here."

But Theoclymenus said, "Eurymachus, you need not send anyone with me. I have eyes, ears, and a pair of feet of my own, to say nothing of an understanding mind. I will take these out of the house with me, for I see mischief overhanging you, from which not one of you men who are insulting people and plotting ill deeds in the house of Odysseus will be able to escape."

He left the house as he spoke, and went back to Piraeus who gave him welcome, but the suitors kept looking at one another and provoking Telemachus by laughing at the strangers. One insolent fellow said to him, "Telemachus, you are not happy in your guests; first you have this importunate tramp, who comes begging bread and wine and has no skill for work or for hard fighting, but is perfectly useless, and now here is another fellow who is setting himself up as a prophet. Let me persuade you, for it will be much better to put them on board ship and send them off to the Sicels to sell for what they will bring."

Telemachus gave him no heed, but sate silently watching his father, expecting every moment that he would begin his attack upon the suitors.

Meanwhile the daughter of Icarius, wise Penelope, had had a rich seat placed for her facing the court and cloisters, so that she could hear what everyone was saying. The dinner indeed had been prepared amid much merriment; it had been both good and abundant, for they had sacrificed many victims; but the supper was yet to come, and nothing can be conceived more gruesome than the meal which a goddess and a brave man were soon to lay before them—for they had brought their doom upon themselves.

B O O K *21* X X I

The trial of the Axes, during which Odysseus
reveals himself to Eumaeus and Philoetius

ATHENA NOW PUT it in Penelope's mind to make the suitors try their skill with the bow and with the iron axes, in contest among themselves, as a means of bringing about their destruction. She went upstairs and got the store-room key, which was made of bronze and had a handle of ivory; she then went with her maidens into the store-room at the end of the house, where her husband's treasures of gold, bronze, and wrought iron were kept, and where was also his bow, and the quiver full of deadly arrows that had been given him by a friend whom he had met in Lacedaemon—Iphitus the son of Eurytus. The two fell in with one another in Messene at the house of Ortilochus, where Odysseus was staying in order to recover a debt that was owing from the whole people; for the Messenians had carried off three hundred sheep from Ithaca, and had sailed away with them and with their shepherds. In quest of these Odysseus took a long journey while still quite young, for his father and the other chieftains sent him on a mission to recover them. Iphitus had gone there also to try and get back twelve brood mares that he had lost, and the mule foals that were running with them. These mares were the death of him in the end, for when he went to the house of Zeus' son, mighty Heracles, who performed such prodigies of valor, Heracles to his shame killed him, though he was his guest, for he feared not heaven's vengeance, nor yet respected his own table which he had set before Iphitus, but killed him in spite of everything, and kept the mares himself. It was when claiming these that Iphitus met Odysseus, and gave him the bow which mighty Eurytus had been used to carry, and which on his death had been left by him to his son. Odysseus gave him in return a sword and a spear, and this was the beginning of a fast friendship, although they never visited at one another's houses, for Zeus' son Heracles killed Iphitus ere they could do so. This bow, then, given him by Iphitus, had not been taken with him by Odysseus when he sailed for Troy; he had used it so long as he had been at home, but had left it behind as having been a keepsake from a valued friend.

Penelope presently reached the oak threshold of the store-room; the carpenter had planed this duly, and had drawn a line on it so as to get it quite straight; he had then set the door posts into it and hung the doors. She loosed the strap from the handle of the door, put in the key, and drove it straight home to shoot back the bolts that held the doors; these flew open with a noise like a bull bellowing in a meadow, and Penelope stepped upon the raised platform, where the chests stood in which the fair linen and clothes were laid by along with fragrant herbs: reaching thence, she took down the bow with its bow case from the peg on which it hung. She sat down with it on her knees, weeping bitterly as she took the bow out of its case, and when her tears had relieved her, she went to the cloister where the suitors were, carrying the bow and the quiver, with the many deadly arrows that were inside it. Along with her came her maidens, bearing a chest that contained much iron and bronze which her husband had won as prizes. When she reached the suitors, she stood by one of the bearing-posts supporting the roof of the cloister, holding a veil before her face, and with a maid on either side of her. Then she said:

"Listen to me you suitors, who persist in abusing the hospitality of this house because its owner has been long absent, and without other pretext than that you want to marry me; this, then, being the prize that you are contending for, I will bring out the mighty bow of Odysseus, and whomsoever of you shall string it most easily and send his arrow through each one of twelve axes, him will I follow and quit this house of my lawful husband, so goodly, and so abounding in wealth. But even so I doubt not that I shall remember it in my dreams."

As she spoke, she told Eumaeus to set the bow and the pieces of iron before the suitors, and Eumaeus wept as he took them to do as she had bidden him. Hard by, the stockman wept also when he saw his master's bow, but Antinous scolded them. "You country louts," said he, "silly simpletons; why should you add to the sorrows of your mistress by crying in this way? She has enough to grieve her in the loss of her husband; sit still, therefore, and eat your dinners in silence, or go outside if you want to cry, and leave the bow behind you. We suitors shall have to contend for it with might and main, for we shall find it no light matter to string such a bow as this is. There is not a man of us all who is such another as Odysseus; for I have seen him and remember him, though I was then only a child."

This was what he said, but all the time he was expecting to be able to string the bow and shoot through the iron, whereas in fact he was to be the first that should taste of the arrows from the hands of Odysseus, whom he was dishonoring in his own house—egging the others on to do so also.

Then Telemachus spoke. "Great heavens!" he exclaimed, "Zeus must have robbed me of my senses. Here is my dear and excellent mother saying she will quit this house and marry again, yet I am laughing and enjoying myself as though there were nothing happening. But, suitors, as the contest has been agreed upon, let it go forward. It is for a woman whose peer is not to be found in Pylos, Argos, or Mycene, nor yet in Ithaca nor on the mainland. You know this as well as I do; what need have I to speak in praise of my mother? Come on, then, make no excuses for delay, but let us see whether you can string the bow or no. I too will make trial of it, for if I can string it and shoot through the iron, I shall not suffer my mother to quit this house with a stranger, not if I can win the prizes which my father won before me."

As he spoke he sprang from his seat, threw his crimson cloak from him, and took his sword from his shoulder. First he set the axes in a row, in a long groove which he had dug for them, and had made straight by line. Then he stamped the earth tight round them, and everyone was surprised when they saw him set them up so orderly, though he had never seen anything of the kind before. This done, he went on to the pavement to make trial of the bow; thrice did he tug at it, trying with all his might to draw the string, and thrice he had to leave off, though he had hoped to string the bow and shoot through the iron. He was trying for the fourth time, and would have strung it had not Odysseus made a sign to check him in spite of all his eagerness. So he said:

"Alas! I shall either be always feeble and of no prowess, or I am too young, and have not yet reached my full strength so as to be able to hold my own if anyone attacks me. You others, therefore, who are stronger than I, make trial of the bow and get this contest settled."

On this he put the bow down, letting it lean against the door that led into the house with the arrow standing against the top of the bow. Then he sat down on the seat from which he had risen, and Antinous said:

"Come on each of you in his turn, going towards the right from the place at which the cupbearer begins when he is handing round the wine."

The rest agreed, and Leiodes son of Oenops was the first to rise. He was sacrificial priest to the suitors, and sat in the corner near the mixing-bowl. He was the only man who hated their evil deeds and was indignant with the others. He was now the first to take the bow and arrow, so he went on to the pavement to make his trial, but he could not string the bow, for his hands were weak and unused to hard work, they therefore soon grew tired, and he said to the suitors, "My friends, I cannot string it; let another have it, this bow shall take the life and soul out of many a chief among us, for it is better to die than to live after having missed the prize that we have so long striven for, and which has brought us so long together. Some one of us is even now hoping and praying that he may marry Penelope, but when he has seen this bow and tried it, let him woo and make bridal offerings to some other woman, and let Penelope marry whoever makes her the best offer and whose lot it is to win her."

On this he put the bow down, letting it lean against the door, with the arrow standing against the tip of the bow. Then he took his seat again on the seat from which he had risen; and Antinous rebuked him saying:

"Leiodes, what are you talking about? Your words are monstrous and intolerable; it makes me angry to listen to you. Shall, then, this bow take the life of many a chief among us, merely because you cannot bend it yourself? True, you were not born to be an archer, but there are others who will soon string it."

Then he said to Melanthius the goatherd, "Look sharp, light a fire in the court, and set a seat hard by with a sheep skin on it; bring us also a large ball of lard, from what they have in the house. Let us warm the bow and grease it—we will then make trial of it again, and bring the contest to an end."

Melanthius lit the fire, and set a seat covered with sheep skins beside it. He also brought a great ball of lard from what they had in the house, and the suitors warmed the bow and again made trial of it, but they were none of them nearly strong enough to string it. Nevertheless there still remained Antinous and Eurymachus, who were the ringleaders among the suitors and much the foremost among them all.

Then the swineherd and the stockman left the cloisters together, and Odysseus followed them. When they had got outside the gates and the outer yard, Odysseus said to them quietly:

"Stockman, and you swineherd, I have something in my mind which I am in doubt whether to say or no; but I think I will say it. What manner of men would you be to stand by Odysseus, if some god should bring him back here all of a sudden? Say which you are disposed to do—to side with the suitors, or with Odysseus?"

"Father Zeus," answered the stockman, "would indeed that you might so ordain it. If some god were but to bring Odysseus back, you should see with what might and main I would fight for him."

In like words Eumaeus prayed to all the gods that Odysseus might return; when, therefore, he saw for certain what mind they were of, Odysseus said, "It is I, Odysseus, who am here. I have suffered much, but at last, in the twentieth year, I am come back to my own country. I find that you two alone of all my servants are glad that I should do so, for I have not heard any of the others praying for my return. To you two, therefore, will I unfold the truth as it shall be. If heaven shall deliver the suitors into my hands, I will find wives for both of you, will give you house and holding close to my own, and you shall be to me as though you were brothers and friends of Telemachus. I will now give you convincing proofs that you may know me and be assured. See, here is the scar from the boar's tooth that ripped me when I was out hunting on Mt. Parnassus with the sons of Autolycus."

As he spoke he drew his rags aside from the great scar, and when they had examined it thoroughly, they both of them wept about Odysseus, threw their arms round him, and kissed his head and shoulders, while Odysseus kissed their hands and faces in return. The sun would have gone down upon their mourning if Odysseus had not checked them and said:

"Cease your weeping, lest someone should come outside and see us, and tell those who are within. When you go in, do so separately, not both together; I will go first, and do you follow afterwards; let this moreover be the token between us; the suitors will all of them try to prevent me from getting hold of the bow and quiver; do you, therefore, Eumaeus, place it in my hands when you are carrying it about, and tell the women to close the doors of their apartment. If they hear any groaning or uproar as of men fighting about the house, they must not come out; they must keep quiet, and stay where they are at their work. And I charge you, Philoetius, to make fast the doors of the outer court, and to bind them securely at once."

When he had thus spoken, he went back to the house and took the seat that he had left. Presently, his two servants followed him inside.

At this moment the bow was in the hands of Eurymachus, who was warming it by the fire,[†] but even so he could not string it, and he was greatly grieved. He heaved a deep sigh and said, "I grieve for myself and for us all; I grieve that I shall have to forgo the marriage, but I do not care nearly so much about this, for there are many other women in Ithaca and elsewhere; what I feel most is the fact of our being so inferior to Odysseus in strength that we cannot string his bow. This will disgrace us in the eyes of those who are yet unborn."

"It shall not be so, Eurymachus," said Antinous, "and you know it yourself. Today is the feast of Apollo throughout all the land; who can string a bow on such a day as this? Put it on one side—as for the axes they can stay where they are, for no one is likely to come to the house and take them away: let the cupbearer go round with his cups, that we may make our drink-offerings and drop this matter of the bow; we will tell Melanthius to bring us in some goats tomorrow—the best he has; we can then offer thigh bones to Apollo the mighty archer, and again make trial of the bow, so as to bring the contest to an end."

The rest approved his words, and thereon men servants poured water over the hands of the guests, while pages filled the mixing-bowls with wine and water and handed it round after giving every man his drink-offering.

Then, when they had made their offerings and had drunk each as much as he desired, Odysseus craftily said:—

"Suitors of the illustrious queen, listen that I may speak even as I am minded. I appeal more especially to Eurymachus, and to Antinous who has just spoken with so much reason. Cease shooting for the present and leave the matter to the gods, but in the morning let heaven give victory to whom it will. For the moment, however, give me the bow that I may prove the power of my hands among you all, and see whether I still have as much strength as I used to have, or whether travel and neglect have made an end of it."

This made them all very angry, for they feared he might string the bow, Antinous therefore rebuked him fiercely saying, "Wretched creature, you have not so much as a grain of sense in your whole body; you ought to think yourself lucky in being allowed to dine unharmed among your betters, without having any smaller portion served you than we others have had, and in being allowed to hear our conversation. No other beggar or stranger has been allowed to hear what we say among ourselves; the wine must have been doing you a mischief, as it does with all those who drink immoderately. It was wine that inflamed the Centaur Eurytion when he was staying with Peirithous among the Lapithae. When the wine had got into his head, he went mad and did ill deeds about the house of Peirithous; this angered the heroes who were there assembled, so they rushed at him and cut off his ears and nostrils; then they dragged him through the doorway out of the house, so he went away crazed, and bore the burden of his crime, bereft of understanding. Henceforth, therefore, there was war between mankind and the centaurs, but he brought it upon himself through his own drunkenness. In like manner I can tell you that it will go hardly with you if you string the bow: you will find no mercy from anyone here, for we shall at once ship you off to king Echetus, who kills everyone that comes near him: you will never get away alive, so drink and keep quiet without getting into a quarrel with men younger than yourself."

Penelope then spoke to him. "Antinous," said she, "it is not right that you should ill-treat any guest of Telemachus who comes to this house. If the stranger should prove strong enough to string the mighty bow of Odysseus, can you suppose that he would take me home with him and make me his wife? Even the man himself can have no such idea in his mind: none of you need let that disturb his feasting; it would be out of all reason."

"Queen Penelope," answered Eurymachus, "we do not suppose that this man will take you away with him; it is impossible; but we are afraid lest some of the baser sort, men or women among the Achaeans, should go gossiping about and say, 'These suitors are a feeble folk; they are paying court to the wife of a brave man whose bow not one of them was able to string, and yet a beggarly tramp who came to the house strung it at once and sent an arrow through the iron.' This is what will be said, and it will be a scandal against us."

"Eurymachus," Penelope answered, "people who persist in eating up the estate of a great chieftain and dishonoring his house must not expect others to think well of them. Why then should you mind if men talk as you think they will? This stranger is strong and well-built, he says moreover that he is of noble birth. Give him the bow, and let us see whether he can string it or no. I say—and it shall surely be—that if Apollo vouchsafes him the glory of string-ing it, I will give him a cloak and shirt of good wear, with a javelin to keep off dogs and robbers, and a sharp sword. I will also give him sandals, and will see him sent safely wherever he wants to go."

Then Telemachus said, "Mother, I am the only man either in Ithaca or in the islands that are over against Elis who has the right to let any one have the bow or to refuse it. No one shall force me one way or the other, not even though I choose to make the stranger a present of the bow outright, and let him take it away with him. Go, then, within the house and busy yourself with your daily duties, your loom, your distaff, and the ordering of your servants. This bow is a man's matter, and mine above all others, for it is I who am master here."

She went wondering back into the house, and laid her son's saying in her heart. Then going upstairs with her handmaids into her room, she mourned her dear husband till Athena sent sweet sleep over her eyelids.

The swineherd now took up the bow and was for taking it to Odysseus, but the suitors clamored at him from all parts of the cloisters, and one of them said, "You idiot, where are you taking the bow to? Are you out of your wits? If Apollo and the other gods will grant our prayer, your own boarhounds shall get you into some quiet little place, and worry you to death."

Eumaeus was frightened at the outcry they all raised, so he put the bow down then and there, but Telemachus shouted out at him from the other side of the cloisters, and threatened him saying, "Father Eumaeus, bring the bow on in spite of them, or young as I am I will pelt you with stones back to the country, for I am the better man of the two. I wish I was as much stronger than all the other suitors in the house as I am than you, I would soon send some of them off sick and sorry, for they mean mischief."

Thus did he speak, and they all of them laughed heartily, which put them in a better humor with Telemachus; so Eumaeus brought the bow on and placed it in the hands of Odysseus. When he had done this, he called Euryclea apart and said to her, "Euryclea, Telemachus says you are to close the doors of the women's apartments. If they hear any groaning or uproar as of men fight-ing about the house, they are not to come out, but are to keep quiet and stay where they are at their work."

Euryclea did as she was told and closed the doors of the women's apartments.

Meanwhile Philoetius slipped quietly out and made fast the gates of the outer court. There was a ship's cable of byblus fiber lying in the gatehouse, so he made the gates fast with it and then came in again, resuming the seat that he had left, and keeping an eye on Odysseus, who had now got the bow in his hands, and was turning it every way about, and proving it all over to see whether the worms had been eating into its two horns during his absence. Then would one turn towards his neighbor saying, "This is some tricky old bow-fancier; either he has got one like it at home, or he wants to make one, in such workmanlike style does the old vagabond handle it."

Another said, "I hope he may be no more successful in other things than he is likely to be in stringing this bow."

But Odysseus, when he had taken it up and examined it all over, strung it as easily as a skilled bard strings a new peg of his lyre and makes the twisted gut fast at both ends. Then he took it in his right hand to prove the string, and it sang sweetly under his touch like the twittering of a swallow. The suitors were dismayed, and turned color as they heard it; at that moment, moreover, Zeus thundered loudly as a sign, and the heart of Odysseus rejoiced as he heard the omen that the son of scheming Cronus had sent him.

He took an arrow that was lying upon the table—for those which the Achaeans were so shortly about to taste were all inside the quiver—he laid it on the center-piece of the bow, and drew the notch of the arrow and the string toward him, still seated on his seat. When he had taken aim he let fly, and his arrow pierced every one of the handle-holes of the axes from the first onwards till it had gone right through them, and into the outer courtyard. Then he said to Telemachus:

"Your guest has not disgraced you, Telemachus. I did not miss what I aimed at, and I was not long in stringing my bow. I am still strong, and not as the suitors twit me with being. Now, however, it is time for the Achaeans to prepare supper while there is still daylight, and then otherwise to disport themselves with song and dance which are the crowning ornaments of a banquet."

As he spoke he made a sign with his eyebrows, and Telemachus girded on his sword, grasped his spear, and stood armed beside his father's seat.

B O O K X X I I

The killing of the suitors
The maids who have misconducted themselves are
made to cleanse the cloisters and are then hanged.

THEN ODYSSEUS TORE off his rags, and sprang on to the broad pavement with his bow and his quiver full of arrows. He shed the arrows on to the ground at his feet and said, "The mighty contest is at an end. I will now see whether Apollo will vouchsafe it to me to hit another mark which no man has yet hit."

On this he aimed a deadly arrow at Antinous, who was about to take up a two-handled gold cup to drink his wine and already had it in his hands. He had no thought of death—who amongst all the revellers would think that one man, however brave, would stand alone among so many and kill him? The arrow struck Antinous in the throat, and the point went clean through his neck, so that he fell over and the cup dropped from his hand, while a thick stream of blood gushed from his nostrils. He kicked the table from him and upset the things on it, so that the bread and roasted meats were all soiled as they fell over on to the ground. The suitors were in an uproar when they saw that a man had been hit; they sprang in dismay one and all of them from their seats and looked everywhere towards the walls, but there was neither shield nor spear, and they rebuked Odysseus very angrily. "Stranger," said they, "you shall pay for shooting people in this way: you shall see no other contest; you are a doomed man; he whom you have slain was the foremost youth in Ithaca, and the vultures shall devour you for having killed him."

Thus they spoke, for they thought that he had killed Antinous by mistake, and did not perceive that death was hanging over the head of everyone of them. But Odysseus glared at them and said:

"Dogs, did you think that I should not come back from Troy? You have wasted my substance, have forced my women servants to lie with you, and have wooed my wife while I was still living. You have feared neither God nor man, and now you shall die."

They turned pale with fear as he spoke, and every man looked round about to see whither he might fly for safety, but Eurymachus alone spoke.

"If you are Odysseus," said he, "then what you have said is just. We have done much wrong on your lands and in your house. But Antinous who was the head and front of the offending lies low already.† It was all his doing. It was not that he wanted to marry Penelope; he did not so much care about that; what he wanted was something quite different, and Zeus has not vouchsafed it to him; he wanted to kill your son and to be chief man in Ithaca. Now, therefore, that he has met the death which was his due, spare the lives of your people. We will make everything good among ourselves, and pay you in full for all that we have eaten and drunk. Each one of us shall pay you a fine worth twenty oxen, and we will keep on giving you gold and bronze till your heart is softened. Until we have done this no one can complain of your being enraged against us."

Odysseus again glared at him and said, "Though you should give me all that you have in the world both now and all that you ever shall have, I will not stay my hand till I have paid all of you in full. You must fight, or fly for your lives; and fly, not a man of you shall."

Their hearts sank as they heard him, but Eurymachus again spoke saying:

"My friends, this man will give us no quarter. He will stand where he is and shoot us down till he has killed every man among us. Let us then show fight; draw your swords, and hold up the tables to shield you from his arrows. Let us have at him with a rush, to drive him from the pavement and doorway: we can then get through into the town, and raise such an alarm as shall soon stay his shooting."

As he spoke he drew his keen blade of bronze, sharpened on both sides, and with a loud cry sprang towards Odysseus, but Odysseus instantly shot an arrow into his breast that caught him by the nipple and fixed itself in his liver. He dropped his sword and fell doubled up over his table. The cup and all the meats went over on to the ground as he smote the earth with his forehead in the agonies of death, and he kicked the stool with his feet until his eyes were closed in darkness.

Then Amphinomus drew his sword and made straight at Odysseus to try and get him away from the door; but Telemachus was too quick for him, and struck him from behind; the spear caught him between the shoulders and went right through his chest, so that he fell heavily to the ground and struck the earth with his forehead. Then Telemachus sprang away from him, leaving his spear still in the body, for he feared that if he stayed to draw it out, some one of the Achaeans might come up and hack at him with his sword, or knock him down, so he set off at a run, and immediately was at his father's side. Then he said:

"Father, let me bring you a shield, two spears, and a brass helmet for your temples. I will arm myself as well, and will bring other armor for the swineherd and the stockman, for we had better be armed."

"Run and fetch them," answered Odysseus, "while my arrows hold out, or when I am alone they may get me away from the door."

Telemachus did as his father said, and went off to the store room where the armor was kept. He chose four shields, eight spears, and four brass helmets with horse-hair plumes. He brought them with all speed to his father, and armed himself first, while the stockman and the swineherd also put on their armor, and took their places near Odysseus. Meanwhile Odysseus, as long as his arrows lasted, had been shooting the suitors one by one, and they fell thick on one another: when his arrows gave out, he set the bow to stand against the end wall of the house by the door post, and hung a shield four hides thick about his shoulders; on his comely head he set his helmet, well wrought with a crest of horse-hair that nodded menacingly above it, and he grasped two redoubtable bronze-shod spears.

Now there was a trap door on the wall, while at one end of the pavement there was an exit leading to a narrow passage, and this exit was closed by a well-made door. Odysseus told Philoetius to stand by this door and guard it, for only one person could attack it at a time. But Agelaus shouted out, "Cannot someone go up to the trap door and tell the people what is going on? Help would come at once, and we should soon make an end of this man and his shooting."

"This may not be, Agelaus," answered Melanthius, "the mouth of the narrow passage is dangerously near the entrance to the outer court. One brave man could prevent any number from getting in. But I know what I will do, I will bring you arms from the store-room, for I am sure it is there that Odysseus and his son have put them."

On this the goatherd Melanthius went by back passages to the store-room of Odysseus' house. There he chose twelve shields, with as many helmets and spears, and brought them back as fast as he could to give them to the suitors. Odysseus' heart began to fail him when he saw the suitors putting on their armor and brandishing their spears. He saw the greatness of the danger, and said to Telemachus, "Some one of the women inside is helping the suitors against us, or it may be Melanthius."

Telemachus answered, "The fault, father, is mine, and mine only; I left the store room door open, and they have kept a sharper look out than I have. Go, Eumaeus, put the door to, and see whether it is one of the women who is doing this, or whether, as I suspect, it is Melanthius the son of Dolius."

Thus did they converse. Meanwhile Melanthius was again going to the store room to fetch more armor, but the swineherd saw him and said to Odysseus who was beside him, "Odysseus, noble son of Laertes, it is that scoundrel Melanthius, just as we suspected, who is going to the store room. Say, shall I kill him, if I can get the better of him, or shall I bring him here that you may take your own revenge for all the many wrongs that he has done in your house?"

Odysseus answered, "Telemachus and I will hold these suitors in check, no matter what they do; go back both of you and bind Melanthius' hands and feet behind him. Throw him into the store room and make the door fast behind you; then fasten a noose about his body, and string him close up to the rafters from a high bearing-post, that he may linger on in an agony."

Thus did he speak, and they did even as he had said; they went to the store room, which they entered before Melanthius saw them, for he was busy searching for arms in the innermost part of the room, so the two took their stand on either side of the door and waited. By and by Melanthius came out with a helmet in one hand, and an old dry-rotted shield in the other, which had been borne by Laertes when he was young, but which had been long since thrown aside, and the straps had become unsewn; on this the two seized him, dragged him back by the hair, and threw him struggling to the ground. They bent his hands and feet well behind his back, and bound them tight with a painful bond as Odysseus had told them; then they fastened a noose about his body and strung him up from a high pillar till he was close up to the rafters, and over him did you then vaunt, O swineherd Eumaeus saying, "Melanthius, you will pass the night on a soft bed as you deserve. You will know very well when morning comes from the streams of Oceanus, and it is time for you to be driving in your goats for the suitors to feast on."

There, then, they left him in very cruel bondage, and having put on their armor they closed the door behind them and went back to take their places by the side of Odysseus; whereon the four men stood in the cloister, fierce and full of fury; nevertheless, those who were in the body of the court were still both brave and many. Then Zeus' daughter Athena came up to them, having assumed the voice and form of Mentor. Odysseus was glad when he saw her and said, "Mentor, lend me your help, and forget not your old comrade, nor the many good turns he has done you. Besides, you are my age-mate."

But all the time he felt sure it was Athena, and the suitors from the other side raised an uproar when they saw her. Agelaus was the first to reproach her. "Mentor," he cried, "do not let Odysseus beguile you into siding with him and fighting the suitors. This is what we will do: when we have killed these people, father and son, we will kill you too. You shall pay for it with your head, and when we have killed you, we will take all you have, indoors or out, and bring it into hotch-pot with Odysseus' property; we will not let your sons live in your house, nor your daughters, nor shall your widow continue to live in the city of Ithaca."

This made Athena still more furious, so she scolded Odysseus very angrily. "Odysseus," said she, "your strength and prowess are no longer what they were when you fought for nine long years among the Trojans about the noble lady Helen. You killed many a man in those days, and it was through your stratagem that Priam's city was taken. How comes it that you are so lamentably less valiant now that you are on your own ground, face to face with the suitors in your own house? Come on, my good fellow, stand by my side and see how Mentor, son of Alcimus shall fight your foes and requite your kindnesses conferred upon him."

But she would not give him full victory as yet, for she wished still further to prove his own prowess and that of his brave son, so she flew up to one of the rafters in the roof of the cloister and sat upon it in the form of a swallow.†

Meanwhile Agelaus son of Damastor, Eurynomus, Amphimedon, Demoptolemus, Pisander, and Polybus son of Polyctor bore the brunt of the fight upon the suitors' side; of all those who were still fighting for their lives they were by far the most valiant, for the others had already fallen under the arrows of Odysseus. Agelaus shouted to them and said, "My friends, he will soon have to leave off, for Mentor has gone away after having done nothing for him but brag. They are standing at the doors unsupported. Do not aim at him all at once, but six of you throw your spears first, and see if you cannot cover yourselves with glory by killing him. When he has fallen we need not be uneasy about the others."

They threw their spears as he bade them, but Athena made them all of no effect. One hit the door post; another went against the door; the pointed shaft of another struck the wall; and as soon as they had avoided all the spears of the suitors Odysseus said to his own men, "My friends, I should say we too had better let drive into the middle of them, or they will crown all the harm they have done us by killing us outright."

They therefore aimed straight in front of them and threw their spears. Odysseus killed Demoptolemus, Telemachus Euryades, Eumaeus Elatus, while the stockman killed Pisander. These all bit the dust, and as the others drew back into a corner Odysseus and his men rushed forward and regained their spears by drawing them from the bodies of the dead.

The suitors now aimed a second time, but again Athena made their weapons for the most part without effect. One hit a bearing-post of the cloister; another went against the door; while the pointed shaft of another struck the wall. Still, Amphimedon just took a piece of the top skin from off Telemachus' wrist, and Ctesippus managed to graze Eumaeus' shoulder above his shield; but the spear went on and fell to the ground. Then Odysseus and his men let drive into the crowd of suitors. Odysseus hit Eurydamas, Telemachus Amphimedon, and Eumaeus Polybus. After this the stockman hit Ctesippus in the breast, and taunted him saying, "Foul-mouthed son of Polytherses, do not be so foolish as to talk wickedly another time, but let heaven direct your speech, for the gods are far stronger than men. I make you a present of this advice to repay you for the foot which you gave Odysseus when he was begging about in his own house."

Thus spoke the stockman, and Odysseus struck the son of Damastor with a spear in close fight, while Telemachus hit Leocritus son of Evenor in the belly, and the dart went clean through him, so that he fell forward full on his face upon the ground. Then Athena from her seat on the rafter held up her deadly aegis, and the hearts of the suitors quailed. They fled to the other end of the court like a herd of cattle maddened by the gadfly in early summer when the days are at their longest. As eagle-beaked, crook-taloned vultures from the mountains swoop down on the smaller birds that cower in flocks upon the ground, and kill them, for they cannot either fight or fly, and lookers on enjoy the sport—even so did Odysseus and his men fall upon the suitors and smite them on every side. They made a horrible groaning as their brains were being battered in, and the ground seethed with their blood.

Leiodes then caught the knees of Odysseus and said, "Odysseus, I beseech you! Have mercy upon me and spare me. I never wronged any of the women in your house either in word or deed, and I tried to stop the others. I saw them, but they would not listen, and now they are paying for their folly. I was their sacrificing priest; if you kill me, I shall die without having done anything to deserve it, and shall have got no thanks for all the good that I did."

Odysseus looked sternly at him and answered, "If you were their sacrificing priest, you must have prayed many a time that it might be long before I got home again, and that you might marry my wife and have children by her. Therefore you shall die."

With these words he picked up the sword that Agelaus had dropped when he was being killed, and which was lying upon the ground. Then he struck Leiodes on the back of his neck, so that his head fell rolling in the dust while he was yet speaking.

The minstrel Phemius son of Terpes—he who had been forced by the suitors to sing to them—now tried to save his life. He was standing near towards the trap door, and held his lyre in his hand. He did not know whether to fly out of the cloister and sit down by the altar of Zeus that was in the outer court, and on which both Laertes and Odysseus had offered up the thigh bones of many an ox, or whether to go straight up to Odysseus and embrace his knees, but in the end he deemed it best to embrace Odysseus' knees. So he laid his lyre on the ground between the mixing bowl and the silver-studded seat; then going up to Odysseus he caught hold of his knees and said, "Odysseus, I beseech you have mercy on me and spare me. You will be sorry for it afterwards if you kill a bard who can sing both for gods and men as I can. I make all my lays myself, and heaven visits me with every kind of inspiration. I would sing to you as though you were a god, do not therefore be in such a hurry to cut my head off. Your own son Telemachus will tell you that I did not want to frequent your house and sing to the suitors after their meals, but they were too many and too strong for me, so they made me."†

Telemachus heard him, and at once went up to his father. "Hold!" he cried, "the man is guiltless, do him no hurt; and we will spare Medon too, who was always good to me when I was a boy, unless Philoetius or Eumaeus has already killed him, or he has fallen in your way when you were raging about the court."

Medon caught these words of Telemachus, for he was crouching under a seat beneath which he had hidden by covering himself up with a freshly flayed heifer's hide, so he threw off the hide, went up to Telemachus, and laid hold of his knees.

"Here I am, my dear sir," said he, "stay your hand therefore, and tell your father, or he will kill me in his rage against the suitors for having wasted his substance and been so foolishly disrespectful to yourself."

Odysseus smiled at him and answered, "Fear not; Telemachus has saved your life, that you may know in future, and tell other people, how greatly better good deeds prosper than evil ones. Go, therefore, outside the cloisters into the outer court, and be out of the way of the slaughter—you and the bard—while I finish my work here inside."

The pair went into the outer court as fast as they could, and sat down by Zeus' great altar, looking fearfully round, and still expecting that they would be killed. Then Odysseus searched the whole court carefully over, to see if anyone had managed to hide himself and was still living, but he found them all lying in the dust and weltering in their blood. They were like fishes which fishermen have netted out of the sea, and thrown upon the beach to lie gasping for water till the heat of the sun makes an end of them. Even so were the suitors lying all huddled up one against the other.

Then Odysseus said to Telemachus, "Call nurse Euryclea; I have something to say to her."

Telemachus went and knocked at the door of the women's room. "Make haste," said he, "you old woman who have been set over all the other women in the house. Come outside; my father wishes to speak to you."

When Euryclea heard this she unfastened the door of the women's room and came out, following Telemachus. She found Odysseus among the corpses bespattered with blood and filth like a lion that has just been devouring an ox, and his breast and both his cheeks are all bloody, so that he is a fearful sight; even so was Odysseus besmirched from head to foot with gore. When she saw all the corpses and such a quantity of blood, she was beginning to cry out for joy, for she saw that a great deed had been done; but Odysseus checked her, "Old woman," said he, "rejoice in silence;† restrain yourself, and do not make any noise about it; it is an unholy thing to vaunt over dead men. Heaven's doom and their own evil deeds have brought these men to destruction, for they respected no man in the whole world, neither rich nor poor, who came near them, and they have come to a bad end as a punishment for their wickedness and folly. Now, however, tell me which of the women in the house have misconducted themselves, and who are innocent."

"I will tell you the truth, my son," answered Euryclea. "There are fifty women in the house whom we teach to do things, such as carding wool, and all kinds of household work. Of these, twelve in all have misbehaved, and have been wanting in respect to me, and also to Penelope. They showed no disrespect to Telemachus, for he has only lately grown and his mother never permitted him to give orders to the female servants; but let me go upstairs and tell your wife all that has happened, for some god has been sending her to sleep."

"Do not wake her yet," answered Odysseus, "but tell the women who have misconducted themselves to come to me."

Euryclea left the cloister to tell the women, and make them come to Odysseus; in the meantime he called Telemachus, the stockman, and the swineherd. "Begin," said he, "to remove the dead, and make the women help you. Then, get sponges and clean water to swill down the tables and seats. When you have thoroughly cleansed the whole cloisters, take the women into the space between the domed room and the wall of the outer court, and run them through with your swords till they are quite dead, and have forgotten all about love and the way in which they used to lie in secret with the suitors."

On this the women came down in a body, weeping and wailing bitterly. First they carried the dead bodies out, and propped them up against one another in the gatehouse. Odysseus ordered them about and made them do their work quickly, so they had to carry the bodies out. When they had done this, they cleaned all the tables and seats with sponges and water, while Telemachus and the two others shovelled up the blood and dirt from the ground, and the women carried it all away and put it out of doors. Then when they had made the whole place quite clean and orderly, they took the women out and hemmed them in the narrow space between the wall of the domed room and that of the yard, so that they could not get away: and Telemachus said to the other two, "I shall not let these women die a clean death, for they were insolent to me and my mother, and used to sleep with the suitors."

So saying he made a ship's cable fast to one of the bearing-posts that supported the roof of the domed room, and secured it all around the building, at a good height, lest any of the women's feet should touch the ground; and as thrushes or doves beat against a net that has been set for them in a thicket just as they were getting to their nest, and a terrible fate awaits them, even so did the women have to put their heads in nooses one after the other and die most miserably.[†] Their feet moved convulsively for a while, but not for very long.

As for Melanthius, they took him through the cloister into the inner court. There they cut off his nose and his ears; they drew out his vitals and gave them to the dogs raw, and then in their fury they cut off his hands and his feet.

When they had done this they washed their hands and feet and went back into the house, for all was now over; and Odysseus said to the dear old nurse Euryclea, "Bring me sulphur, which cleanses all pollution, and fetch fire also that I may burn it, and purify the cloisters. Go, moreover, and tell Penelope to come here with her attendants, and also all the maidservants that are in the house."

"All that you have said is true," answered Euryclea, "but let me bring you some clean clothes—a shirt and cloak. Do not keep these rags on your back any longer. It is not right."

"First light me a fire," replied Odysseus.

She brought the fire and sulphur, as he had bidden her, and Odysseus thoroughly purified the cloisters and both the inner and outer courts. Then she went inside to call the women and tell them what had happened; whereon they came from their apartment with torches in their hands, and pressed round Odysseus to embrace him, kissing his head and shoulders and taking hold of his hands. It made him feel as if he should like to weep, for he remembered every one of them.

B O O K X X I I I

Penelope eventually recognizes her husband
Early in the morning Odysseus, Telemachus,
Eumaeus, and Philoetius leave the town

EURYCLEA NOW WENT upstairs laughing to tell her mistress that her dear husband had come home. Her aged knees became young again and her feet were nimble for joy as she went up to her mistress and bent over her head to speak to her. "Wake up Penelope, my dear child," she exclaimed, "and see with your own eyes something that you have been wanting this long time past. Odysseus has at last indeed come home again, and has killed the suitors who were giving so much trouble in his house, eating up his estate and ill treating his son."

"My good nurse," answered Penelope, "you must be mad. The gods sometimes send some very sensible people out of their minds, and make foolish people become sensible. This is what they must have been doing to you; for you always used to be a reasonable person. Why should you thus mock me when I have trouble enough already—talking such nonsense, and waking me up out of a sweet sleep that had taken possession of my eyes and closed them? I have never slept so soundly from the day my poor husband went to that city with the ill-omened name. Go back again into the women's room; if it had been anyone else who had woke me up to bring me such absurd news I should have sent her away with a severe scolding. As it is your age shall protect you."

"My dear child," answered Euryclea, "I am not mocking you. It is quite true as I tell you that Odysseus is come home again. He was the stranger whom they all kept on treating so badly in the cloister. Telemachus knew all the time that he was come back, but kept his father's secret that he might have his revenge on all these wicked people."

Then Penelope sprang up from her couch, threw her arms round Euryclea, and wept for joy. "But my dear nurse," said she, "explain this to me; if he has really come home as you say, how did he manage to overcome the wicked suitors single handed, seeing what a number of them there always were?"

"I was not there," answered Euryclea, "and do not know; I only heard them groaning while they were being killed. We sat crouching and huddled up in a corner of the women's room with the doors closed, till your son came to fetch me because his father sent him. Then I found Odysseus standing over the corpses that were lying on the ground all round him, one on top of the other. You would have enjoyed it if you could have seen him standing there all bespattered with blood and filth, and looking just like a lion. But the corpses are now all piled up in the gatehouse that is in the outer court, and Odysseus has lit a great fire to purify the house with sulphur. He has sent me to call you, so come with me that you may both be happy together after all; for now at last the desire of your heart has been fulfilled; your husband is come home to find both wife and son alive and well, and to take his revenge in his own house on the suitors who behaved so badly to him."

"My dear nurse," said Penelope, "do not exult too confidently over all this. You know how delighted everyone would be to see Odysseus come home—more particularly myself, and the son who has been born to both of us; but what you tell me cannot be really true. It is some god who is angry with the suitors for their great wickedness, and has made an end of them; for they respected no man in the whole world, neither rich nor poor, who came near them, and they have come to a bad end in consequence of their iniquity; Odysseus is dead far away from the Achaean land; he will never return home again."

Then nurse Euryclea said, "My child, what are you talking about? but you were all hard of belief and have made up your mind that your husband is never coming, although he is in the house and by his own fire side at this very moment. Besides I can give you another proof; when I was washing him I perceived the scar which the wild boar gave him, and I wanted to tell you about it, but in his wisdom he would not let me, and clapped his hands over my mouth; so come with me and I will make this bargain with you—if I am deceiving you, you may have me killed by the most cruel death you can think of."

"My dear nurse," said Penelope, "however wise you may be you can hardly fathom the counsels of the gods. Nevertheless, we will go in search of my son, that I may see the corpses of the suitors, and the man who has killed them."

On this she came down from her upper room, and while doing so she considered whether she should keep at a distance from her husband and question him, or whether she should at once go up to him and embrace him. When, however, she had crossed the stone floor of the cloister, she sat down opposite Odysseus by the fire, against the wall at right angles to that by which she had entered, while Odysseus sat near one of the bearing-posts, looking upon the ground, and waiting to see what his brave wife would say to him when she saw him. For a long time she sat silent and as one lost in amazement. At one moment she looked him full in the face, but then again directly, she was misled by his shabby clothes and failed to recognize him, till Telemachus began to reproach her and said:

"Mother—but you are so hard that I cannot call you by such a name—why do you keep away from my father in this way? Why do you not sit by his side and begin talking to him and asking him questions? No other woman could bear to keep away from her husband when he had come back to her after twenty years of absence, and after having gone through so much; but your heart always was as hard as a stone."

Penelope answered, "My son, I am so lost in astonishment that I can find no words in which either to ask questions or to answer them. I cannot even look him straight in the face. Still, if he really is Odysseus come back to his own home again, we shall get to understand one another better by and by, for there are tokens with which we two are alone acquainted, and which are hidden from all others."

Odysseus smiled at this, and said to Telemachus, "Let your mother put me to any proof she likes; she will make up her mind about it presently. She rejects me for the moment and believes me to be somebody else, because I am covered with dirt and have such bad clothes on; let us, however, consider what we had better do next. When one man has killed another—even though he was not one who would leave many friends to take up his quarrel—the man who has killed him must still say good bye to his friends and fly the country; whereas we have been killing the stay of a whole town, and all the picked youth of Ithaca. I would have you consider this matter."

"Look to it yourself, father," answered Telemachus, "for they say you are the wisest counsellor in the world, and that there is no other mortal man who can compare with you. We will follow you with right good will, nor shall you find us fail you in so far as our strength holds out."

"I will say what I think will be best," answered Odysseus. "First wash and put your shirts on; tell the maids also to go to their own room and dress; Phemius shall then strike up a dance tune on his lyre, so that if people outside hear, or any of the neighbors, or someone going along the street happens to notice it, they may think there is a wedding in the house, and no rumours about the death of the suitors will get about in the town, before we can escape to the woods upon my own land. Once there, we will settle which of the courses heaven vouchsafes us shall seem wisest."

Thus did he speak, and they did even as he had said. First they washed and put their shirts on, while the women got ready. Then Phemius took his lyre and set them all longing for sweet song and stately dance. The house re-echoed with the sound of men and women dancing, and the people outside said, "I suppose the queen has been getting married at last. She ought to be ashamed of herself for not continuing to protect her husband's property until he comes home."

This was what they said, but they did not know what it was that had been happening. The upper servant Eurynome washed and anointed Odysseus in his own house and gave him a shirt and cloak, while Athena made him look taller and stronger than before; she also made the hair grow thick on the top of his head, and flow down in curls like hyacinth blossoms; she glorified him about the head and shoulders just as a skilful workman who has studied art of all kinds under Hephaestus or Athena—and his work is full of beauty— enriches a piece of silver plate by gilding it. He came from the bath looking like one of the immortals, and sat down opposite his wife on the seat he had left. "My dear," said he, "heaven has endowed you with a heart more unyielding than woman ever yet had. No other woman could bear to keep away from her husband when he had come back to her after twenty years of absence, and after having gone through so much. But come, nurse, get a bed ready for me; I will sleep alone, for this woman has a heart as hard as iron."

"My dear," answered Penelope, "I have no wish to set myself up, nor to depreciate you; but I am not struck by your appearance, for I very well remember what kind of a man you were when you set sail from Ithaca.[†] Nevertheless, Euryclea, take his bed outside the bed chamber that he himself built. Bring the bed outside this room, and put bedding upon it with fleeces, good coverlets, and blankets."

She said this to try him, but Odysseus was very angry and said, "Wife, I am much displeased at what you have just been saying. Who has been taking my bed from the place in which I left it? He must have found it a hard task, no matter how skilled a workman he was, unless some god came and helped him to shift it. There is no man living, however strong and in his prime, who could move it from its place, for it is a marvelous curiosity which I made with my very own hands. There was a young olive growing within the precincts of the house, in full vigor, and about as thick as a bearing-post. I built my room round this with strong walls of stone and a roof to cover them, and I made the doors strong and well-fitting. Then I cut off the top boughs of the olive tree and left the stump standing. This I dressed roughly from the root upwards and then worked with carpenter's tools well and skillfully, straightening my work by drawing a line on the wood, and making it into a bed-prop. I then bored a hole down the middle, and made it the center-post of my bed, at which I worked till I had finished it, inlaying it with gold and silver; after this I stretched a hide of crimson leather from one side of it to the other. So you see I know all about it, and I desire to learn whether it is still there, or whether anyone has been removing it by cutting down the olive tree at its roots."

When she heard the sure proofs Odysseus now gave her, she fairly broke down.[†] She flew weeping to his side, flung her arms about his neck, and kissed him. "Do not be angry with me Odysseus," she cried, "you, who are the wisest of mankind. We have suffered, both of us. Heaven has denied us the happiness of spending our youth, and of growing old, together; do not then be aggrieved or take it amiss that I did not embrace you thus as soon as I saw you. I have been shuddering all the time through fear that someone might come here and deceive me with a lying story; for there are many very wicked people going about. Zeus' daughter Helen would never have yielded herself to a man from a foreign country, if she had known that the sons of Achaeans would come after her and bring her back. Heaven put it in her heart to do wrong, and she gave no thought to that sin, which has been the source of all our sorrows. Now, however, that you have convinced me by showing that you know all about our bed (which no human being has ever seen but you and I and a single maidservant, the daughter of Actor, who was given me by my father on my marriage, and who keeps the doors of our room) hard of belief though I have been I can mistrust no longer."

Then Odysseus in his turn melted, and wept as he clasped his dear and faithful wife to his bosom. As the sight of land is welcome to men who are swimming towards the shore, when Poseidon has wrecked their ship with the fury of his winds and waves; a few alone reach the land, and these, covered with brine, are thankful when they find themselves on firm ground and out of danger—even so was her husband welcome to her as she looked upon him, and she could not tear her two fair arms from about his neck. Indeed they would have gone on indulging their sorrow till rosy-fingered morn appeared, had not Athena determined otherwise, and held night back in the far west, while she would not suffer Dawn to leave Oceanus, nor to yoke the two steeds Lampus and Phaethon that bear her onward to break the day upon mankind.

At last, however, Odysseus said, "Wife, we have not yet reached the end of our troubles. I have an unknown amount of toil still to undergo. It is long and difficult, but I must go through with it, for thus the shade of Teiresias prophesied concerning me, on the day when I went down into Hades to ask about my return and that of my companions. But now let us go to bed, that we may lie down and enjoy the blessed boon of sleep."

"You shall go to bed as soon as you please," replied Penelope, "now that the gods have sent you home to your own good house and to your country. But as heaven has put it in your mind to speak of it, tell me about the task that

lies before you. I shall have to hear about it later, so it is better that I should
be told at once."

"My dear," answered Odysseus, "why should you press me to tell you?
Still, I will not conceal it from you, though you will not like it. I do not like
it myself, for Teiresias bade me travel far and wide, carrying an oar, till I came
to a country where the people have never heard of the sea, and do not even
mix salt with their food. They know nothing about ships, nor oars that are as
the wings of a ship. He gave me this certain token which I will not hide from
you. He said that a wayfarer should meet me and ask me whether it was a
winnowing shovel that I had on my shoulder. On this, I was to fix my oar in
the ground and sacrifice a ram, a bull, and a boar to Poseidon;† after which I
was to go home and offer hecatombs to all the gods in heaven, one after the
other. As for myself, he said that death should come to me from the sea, and
that my life should ebb away very gently when I was full of years and peace
of mind, and my people should bless me. All this, he said, should surely come
to pass."

And Penelope said, "If the gods are going to vouchsafe you a happier time
in your old age, you may hope then to have some respite from misfortune."

Thus did they converse. Meanwhile Eurynome and the nurse took torches
and made the bed ready with soft coverlets; as soon as they had laid them,
the nurse went back into the house to go to her rest, leaving the bed chamber woman Eurynome to show Odysseus and Penelope to bed by torch light.
When she had conducted them to their room she went back, and they then
came joyfully to the rites of their own old bed. Telemachus, Philoetius, and
the swineherd now left off dancing, and made the women leave off also. They
then laid themselves down to sleep in the cloisters.

When Odysseus and Penelope had had their fill of love they fell talking
with one another. She told him how much she had had to bear in seeing the
house filled with a crowd of wicked suitors who had killed so many sheep
and oxen on her account, and had drunk so many casks of wine. Odysseus in
his turn told her what he had suffered, and how much trouble he had himself
given to other people. He told her everything, and she was so delighted to
listen that she never went to sleep till he had ended his whole story.

He began with his victory over the Cicons, and how he thence reached
the fertile land of the Lotus-eaters. He told her all about the Cyclops and
how he had punished him for having so ruthlessly eaten his brave comrades;
how he then went on to Aeolus, who received him hospitably and furthered
him on his way, but even so he was not to reach home, for to his great grief a
hurricane carried him out to sea again; how he went on to the Laestrygonian
city Telepylos, where the people destroyed all his ships with their crews, save
himself and his own ship only. Then he told of cunning Circe and her craft,
and how he sailed to the chill house of Hades, to consult the ghost of the

Theban prophet Teiresias, and how he saw his old comrades in arms, and his mother who bore him and brought him up when he was a child; how he then heard the wondrous singing of the Sirens, and went on to the wandering rocks and terrible Charybdis and to Scylla, whom no man had ever yet passed in safety; how his men then ate the cattle of the sun-god, and how Zeus therefore struck the ship with his thunderbolts, so that all his men perished together, himself alone being left alive; how at last he reached the Ogygian island and the nymph Calypso, who kept him there in a cave, and fed him, and wanted him to marry her, in which case she intended making him immortal so that he should never grow old, but she could not persuade him to let her do so; and how after much suffering he had found his way to the Phaeacians, who had treated him as though he had been a god, and sent him back in a ship to his own country after having given him gold, bronze, and raiment in great abundance. This was the last thing about which he told her, for here a deep sleep took hold upon him and eased the burden of his sorrows.

Then Athena bethought her of another matter. When she deemed that Odysseus had had both of his wife and of repose, she bade gold-enthroned Dawn rise out of Oceanus that she might shed light upon mankind. On this, Odysseus rose from his comfortable bed and said to Penelope, "Wife, we have both of us had our full share of troubles, you, here, in lamenting my absence, and I in being prevented from getting home though I was longing all the time to do so. Now, however, that we have at last come together, take care of the property that is in the house. As for the sheep and goats which the wicked suitors have eaten, I will take many myself by force from other people, and will compel the Achaeans to make good the rest till they have filled all my yards.† I am now going to the wooded lands out in the country to see my father who has so long been grieved on my account, and to yourself I will give these instructions, though you have little need of them. At sunrise it will at once get abroad that I have been killing the suitors; go upstairs, therefore, and stay there with your women. See nobody and ask no questions."†

As he spoke he girded on his armor. Then he roused Telemachus, Philoetius, and Eumaeus, and told them all to put on their armor also. This they did, and armed themselves. When they had done so, they opened the gates and sallied forth, Odysseus leading the way. It was now daylight, but Athena nevertheless concealed them in darkness and led them quickly out of the town.

BOOK XXIV

The ghosts of the suitors in Hades
Odysseus and his men go to the house of Laertes
The people of Ithaca come out to attack Odysseus, but Athena concludes a peace

THEN HERMES OF Cyllene summoned the ghosts of the suitors, and in his hand he held the fair golden wand with which he seals men's eyes in sleep or wakes them just as he pleases; with this he roused the ghosts and led them, while they followed whining and gibbering behind him. As bats fly squealing in the hollow of some great cave, when one of them has fallen out of the cluster in which they hang, even so did the ghosts whine and squeal as Hermes the healer of sorrow led them down into the dark abode of death. When they had passed the waters of Oceanus and the rock Leucas, they came to the gates of the sun and the land of dreams, whereon they reached the meadow of asphodel where dwell the souls and shadows of them that can labor no more.

Here they found the ghost of Achilles son of Peleus, with those of Patroclus, Antilochus, and Ajax, who was the finest and handsomest man of all the Danaans after the son of Peleus himself.

They gathered round the ghost of the son of Peleus, and the ghost of Agamemnon joined them, sorrowing bitterly. Round him were gathered also the ghosts of those who had perished with him in the house of Aegisthus; and the ghost of Achilles spoke first.

"Son of Atreus," it said, "we used to say that Zeus had loved you better from first to last than any other hero, for you were captain over many and brave men, when we were all fighting together before Troy; yet the hand of death, which no mortal can escape, was laid upon you all too early. Better for you had you fallen at Troy in the hey-day of your renown, for the Achaeans would have built a mound over your ashes, and your son would have been heir to your good name, whereas it has now been your lot to come to a most miserable end."

"Happy son of Peleus," answered the ghost of Agamemnon, "for having died at Troy far from Argos, while the bravest of the Trojans and the Achaeans fell round you fighting for your body. There you lay in the whirling clouds of dust, all huge and hugely, heedless now of your chivalry. We fought the whole of the livelong day, nor should we ever have left off if Zeus had not sent a hurricane to stay us. Then, when we had borne you to the ships out of the fray, we laid you on your bed and cleansed your fair skin with warm water and with ointments. The Danaans tore their hair and wept bitterly round about you. Your mother, when she heard, came with her immortal nymphs from out of the sea, and the sound of a great wailing went forth over the waters so that the Achaeans quaked for fear. They would have fled panic-stricken to their ships had not wise old Nestor whose counsel was ever truest checked them saying, 'Hold, Argives, fly not sons of the Achaeans, this is his mother coming from the sea with her immortal nymphs to view the body of her son.'

"Thus he spoke, and the Achaeans feared no more. The daughters of the old man of the sea stood round you weeping bitterly, and clothed you in immortal raiment. The nine muses also came and lifted up their sweet voices in lament—calling and answering one another; there was not an Argive but wept for pity of the dirge they chanted. Days and nights seven and ten we mourned you, mortals and immortals, but on the eighteenth day we gave you to the flames, and many a fat sheep with many an ox did we slay in sacrifice around you. You were burnt in raiment of the gods, with rich resins and with honey, while heroes, horse and foot, clashed their armor round the pile as you were burning, with the tramp as of a great multitude. But when the flames of heaven had done their work, we gathered your white bones at daybreak and laid them in ointments and in pure wine. Your mother brought us a golden vase to hold them—gift of Dionysus, and work of Hephaestus himself; in this we mingled your bleached bones with those of Patroclus who had gone before you, and separate we enclosed also those of Antilochus, who had been closer to you than any other of your comrades now that Patroclus was no more.

"Over these the host of the Argives built a noble tomb, on a point jutting out over the open Hellespont, that it might be seen from far out upon the sea by those now living and by them that shall be born hereafter. Your mother begged prizes from the gods, and offered them to be contended for by the noblest of the Achaeans. You must have been present at the funeral of many a hero, when the young men gird themselves and make ready to contend for prizes on the death of some great chieftain, but you never saw such prizes as silver-footed Thetis offered in your honor; for the gods loved you well. Thus even in death your fame, Achilles, has not been lost, and your name lives evermore among all mankind. But as for me, what solace had I when the days of my fighting were done? For Zeus willed my destruction on my return, by the hands of Aegisthus and those of my wicked wife."

Thus did they converse, and presently Hermes came up to them with the ghosts of the suitors who had been killed by Odysseus. The ghosts of Agamemnon and Achilles were astonished at seeing them, and went up to them at once. The ghost of Agamemnon recognized Amphimedon son of Melaneus, who lived in Ithaca and had been his host, so it began to talk to him.

"Amphimedon," it said, "what has happened to all you fine young men—all of an age too—that you are come down here under the ground? One could pick no finer body of men from any city. Did Poseidon raise his winds and waves against you when you were at sea, or did your enemies make an end of you on the mainland when you were cattle-lifting or sheep-stealing, or while fighting in defense of their wives and city? Answer my question, for I have been your guest. Do you not remember how I came to your house with Menelaus, to persuade Odysseus to join us with his ships against Troy? It was a whole month ere we could resume our voyage, for we had hard work to persuade Odysseus to come with us."

And the ghost of Amphimedon answered, "Agamemnon, son of Atreus, king of men, I remember everything that you have said, and will tell you fully and accurately about the way in which our end was brought about. Odysseus had been long gone, and we were courting his wife, who did not directly say that she would not marry, nor yet bring matters to an end, for she meant to compass our destruction: this, then, was the trick she played us. She set up a great tambour frame in her room and began to work on an enormous piece of fine needlework. 'Sweethearts,' said she, 'Odysseus is indeed dead, still, do not press me to marry again immediately; wait—for I would not have my skill in needlework perish unrecorded—till I have completed a pall for the hero Laertes, against the time when death shall take him. He is very rich, and the women of the place will talk if he is laid out without a pall.' This is what she said, and we assented; whereupon we could see her working upon her great web all day long, but at night she would unpick the stitches again by torchlight. She fooled us in this way for three years without our finding it out, but as time wore on and she was now in her fourth year, in the waning of moons and many days had been accomplished, one of her maids who knew what she was doing told us, and we caught her in the act of undoing her work, so she had to finish it whether she would or no; and when she showed us the robe she had made, after she had had it washed, its splendor was as that of the sun or moon.

"Then some malicious god conveyed Odysseus to the upland farm where his swineherd lives. Thither presently came also his son, returning from a voyage to Pylos, and the two came to the town when they had hatched their plot for our destruction. Telemachus came first, and then after him, accompanied by the swineherd, came Odysseus, clad in rags and leaning on a staff as though he were some miserable old beggar. He came so unexpectedly that none of us knew him, not even the older ones among us, and we reviled him and threw things at him. He endured both being struck and insulted without a word, though he was in his own house; but when the will of Aegis-bearing Zeus inspired him, he and Telemachus took the armor and hid it in an inner chamber, bolting the doors behind them. Then he cunningly made his wife offer his bow and a quantity of iron to be contended for by us ill-fated suitors; and this was the beginning of our end, for not one of us could string the bow—nor nearly do so. When it was about to reach the hands of Odysseus, we all of us shouted out that it should not be given him, no matter what he might say, but Telemachus insisted on his having it. When he had got it in his hands he strung it with ease and sent his arrow through the iron. Then he stood on the floor of the cloister and poured his arrows on the ground, glaring fiercely about him. First he killed Antinous, and then, aiming straight before him, he let fly his deadly darts and they fell thick on one another. It was plain that one of the gods was helping them, for they fell upon us with might and main throughout the cloisters, and there was a hideous sound of groaning as our brains were being battered in, and the ground seethed with our blood. This, Agamemnon, is how we came by our end, and our bodies are lying still uncared for in the house of Odysseus, for our friends at home do not yet know what has happened, so that they cannot lay us out and wash the black blood from our wounds, making moan over us according to the offices due to the departed."

"Happy Odysseus, son of Laertes," replied the ghost of Agamemnon, "you are indeed blessed in the possession of a wife endowed with such rare excellence of understanding, and so faithful to her wedded lord as Penelope the daughter of Icarius. The fame, therefore, of her virtue shall never die, and the immortals shall compose a song that shall be welcome to all mankind in honor of the constancy of Penelope. How far otherwise was the wickedness of the daughter of Tyndareus who killed her lawful husband; her song shall be hateful among men, for she has brought disgrace on all womankind even on the good ones."

Thus did they converse in the house of Hades deep down within the bowels of the earth. Meanwhile Odysseus and the others passed out of the town and soon reached the fair and well-tilled farm of Laertes, which he had reclaimed with infinite labor. Here was his house, with a lean-to running all round it, where the slaves who worked for him slept and sat and ate, while inside the house there was an old Sicel woman, who looked after him in this his country-farm. When Odysseus got there, he said to his son and to the other two:

"Go to the house, and kill the best pig that you can find for dinner. Meanwhile I want to see whether my father will know me, or fail to recognize me after so long an absence."

He then took off his armor and gave it to Eumaeus and Philoetius, who went straight on to the house, while he turned off into the vineyard to make trial of his father. As he went down into the great orchard, he did not see Dolius, nor any of his sons nor of the other bondsmen, for they were all gathering thorns to make a fence for the vineyard, at the place where the old man had told them; he therefore found his father alone, hoeing a vine. He had on a dirty old shirt, patched and very shabby; his legs were bound round with thongs of oxhide to save him from the brambles, and he also wore sleeves of leather; he had a goat skin cap on his head, and was looking very woe-begone. When Odysseus saw him so worn, so old and full of sorrow, he stood still under a tall pear tree and began to weep. He doubted whether to embrace him, kiss him, and tell him all about his having come home, or whether he should first question him and see what he would say. In the end he deemed it best to be crafty with him, so in this mind he went up to his father, who was bending down and digging about a plant.

"I see, sir," said Odysseus, "that you are an excellent gardener—what pains you take with it, to be sure. There is not a single plant, not a fig tree, vine, olive, pear, nor flower bed, but bears the trace of your attention. I trust, however, that you will not be offended if I say that you take better care of your garden than of yourself. You are old, unsavory, and very meanly clad. It cannot be because you are idle that your master takes such poor care of you, indeed your face and figure have nothing of the slave about them, and proclaim you of noble birth. I should have said that you were one of those who should wash well, eat well, and lie soft at night as old men have a right to do; but tell me, and tell me true, whose bondman are you, and in whose garden are you working? Tell me also about another matter. Is this place that I have come to really Ithaca? I met a man just now who said so, but he was a dull fellow, and had not the patience to hear my story out when I was asking him about an old friend of mine, whether he was still living, or was already dead and in the house of Hades. Believe me when I tell you that this man came to my house once when I was in my own country and never yet did any stranger come to me whom I liked better. He said that his family came from Ithaca and that his father was Laertes, son of Arceisius. I received him hospitably, making him welcome to all the abundance of my house, and when he went away I gave him all customary presents. I gave him seven talents of fine gold, and a cup of solid silver with flowers chased upon it. I gave him twelve light cloaks, and as many pieces of tapestry; I also gave him twelve cloaks of single fold, twelve rugs, twelve fair mantles, and an equal number of shirts. To all this I added four good looking women skilled in all useful arts, and I let him take his choice."

His father shed tears and answered, "Sir, you have indeed come to the country that you have named, but it is fallen into the hands of wicked people. All this wealth of presents has been given to no purpose. If you could have found your friend here alive in Ithaca, he would have entertained you hospitably and would have requited your presents amply when you left him—as would have been only right considering what you had already given him. But tell me, and tell me true, how many years is it since you entertained this guest—my unhappy son, as ever was? Alas! He has perished far from his own country; the fishes of the sea have eaten him, or he has fallen a prey to the birds and wild beasts of some continent. Neither his mother, nor I his father, who were his parents, could throw our arms about him and wrap him in his shroud, nor could his excellent and richly dowered wife Penelope bewail her husband as was natural upon his death bed, and close his eyes according to the offices due to the departed. But now, tell me truly for I want to know. Who and where are you from—tell me of your town and parents? Where is the ship lying that has brought you and your men to Ithaca? Or were you a passenger on some other man's ship, and those who brought you here have gone on their way and left you?"

"I will tell you everything," answered Odysseus, "quite truly. I come from Alybas, where I have a fine house. I am son of king Apheidas, who is the son of Polypemon. My own name is Eperitus; heaven drove me off my course as I was leaving Sicania, and I have been carried here against my will. As for my ship it is lying over yonder, off the open country outside the town, and this is the fifth year since Odysseus left my country. Poor fellow, yet the omens were good for him when he left me. The birds all flew on our right hands, and both he and I rejoiced to see them as we parted, for we had every hope that we should have another friendly meeting and exchange presents."

A dark cloud of sorrow fell upon Laertes as he listened. He filled both hands with the dust from off the ground and poured it over his grey head, groaning heavily as he did so.[†] The heart of Odysseus was touched, and his nostrils quivered as he looked upon his father; then he sprang towards him, flung his arms about him and kissed him, saying, "I am he, father, about whom you are asking—I have returned after having been away for twenty years. But cease your sighing and lamentation—we have no time to lose, for I should tell you that I have been killing the suitors in my house, to punish them for their insolence and crimes."

"If you really are my son Odysseus," replied Laertes, "and have come back again, you must give me such manifest proof of your identity as shall convince me."

"First observe this scar," answered Odysseus, "which I got from a boar's tusk when I was hunting on Mt. Parnassus. You and my mother had sent me to Autolycus, my mother's father, to receive the presents which when he was over here he had promised to give me. Furthermore I will point out to you the trees in the vineyard which you gave me, and I asked you all about them as I followed you round the garden. We went over them all, and you told me their names and what they all were. You gave me thirteen pear trees, ten apple trees, and forty fig trees; you also said you would give me fifty rows of vines; there was corn planted between each row, and they yield grapes of every kind when the heat of heaven has been laid heavy upon them."

Laertes' strength failed him when he heard the convincing proofs which his son had given him. He threw his arms about him, and Odysseus had to support him, or he would have gone off into a swoon; but as soon as he came to, and was beginning to recover his senses, he said, "O father Zeus, then you gods are still in Olympus after all, if the suitors have really been punished for their insolence and folly. Nevertheless, I am much afraid that I shall have all the townspeople of Ithaca up here directly, and they will be sending messengers everywhere throughout the cities of the Cephallenians."

Odysseus answered, "Take heart and do not trouble yourself about that, but let us go into the house hard by your garden. I have already told Telemachus, Philoetius, and Eumaeus to go on there and get dinner ready as soon as possible."

Thus conversing the two made their way towards the house. When they got there they found Telemachus with the stockman and the swineherd cutting up meat and mixing wine with water. Then the old Sicel woman took Laertes inside and washed him and anointed him with oil. She put him on a good cloak, and Athena came up to him and gave him a more imposing presence, making him taller and stouter than before. When he came back his son was surprised to see him looking so like an immortal, and said to him, "My dear father, some one of the gods has been making you much taller and better-looking."

Laertes answered, "Would, by Father Zeus, Athena, and Apollo, that I were the man I was when I ruled among the Cephallenians, and took Nericum, that strong fortress on the foreland. If I were still what I then was and had been in our house yesterday with my armor on, I should have been able to stand by you and help you against the suitors. I should have killed a great many of them, and you would have rejoiced to see it."

Thus did they converse; but the others, when they had finished their work and the feast was ready, left off working, and took each his proper place on the benches and seats. Then they began eating; by and by old Dolius and his sons left their work and came up, for their mother, the Sicel woman who looked after Laertes now that he was growing old, had been to fetch them. When they saw Odysseus and were certain it was he, they stood there lost in astonishment; but Odysseus scolded them good naturedly and said, "Sit down to your dinner, old man, and never mind about your surprise; we have been wanting to begin for some time and have been waiting for you."

Then Dolius put out both his hands and went up to Odysseus. "Sir," said he, seizing his master's hand and kissing it at the wrist, "we have long been wishing you home: and now heaven has restored you to us after we had given up hoping. All hail, therefore, and may the gods prosper you. But tell me, does Penelope already know of your return, or shall we send someone to tell her?"

"Old man," answered Odysseus, "she knows already, so you need not trouble about that." On this he took his seat, and the sons of Dolius gathered round Odysseus to give him greeting and embrace him one after the other; then they took their seats in due order near Dolius their father.

While they were thus busy getting their dinner ready, Rumour went round the town, and noised abroad the terrible fate that had befallen the suitors; as soon, therefore, as the people heard of it they gathered from every quarter, groaning and hooting before the house of Odysseus. They took the dead away, buried every man his own, and put the bodies of those who came from elsewhere on board the fishing vessels, for the fishermen to take each of them to his own place. They then met angrily in the place of assembly, and when they were got together Eupeithes rose to speak. He was overwhelmed with grief for the death of his son Antinous, who had been the first man killed by Odysseus, so he said, weeping bitterly, "My friends, this man has done the Achaeans great wrong. He took many of our best men away with him in his fleet, and he has lost both ships and men; now, moreover, on his return he has been killing all the foremost men among the Cephallenians. Let us be up and doing before he can get away to Pylos or to Elis where the Epeans rule, or we shall be ashamed of ourselves for ever afterwards. It will be an everlasting disgrace to us if we do not avenge the murder of our sons and brothers. For my own part I should have no more pleasure in life, but had rather die at once. Let us be up, then, and after them, before they can cross over to the main land."

He wept as he spoke and everyone pitied him. But Medon and the bard Phemius had now woke up, and came to them from the house of Odysseus. Everyone was astonished at seeing them, but they stood in the middle of the assembly, and Medon said, "Hear me, men of Ithaca. Odysseus did not do these things against the will of heaven. I myself saw an immortal god take the form of Mentor and stand beside him. This god appeared, now in front of him encouraging him, and now going furiously about the court and attacking the suitors whereon they fell thick on one another."

On this pale fear laid hold of them, and old Halitherses, son of Mastor, rose to speak, for he was the only man among them who knew both past and future; so he spoke to them plainly and in all honesty, saying,

"Men of Ithaca, it is all your own fault that things have turned out as they have; you would not listen to me, nor yet to Mentor, when we bade you check the folly of your sons who were doing much wrong in the wantonness of their hearts—wasting the substance and dishonoring the wife of a chieftain who they thought would not return. Now, however, let it be as I say, and do as I tell you. Do not go out against Odysseus, or you may find that you have been drawing down evil on your own heads."

This was what he said, and more than half raised a loud shout, and at once left the assembly. But the rest stayed where they were, for the speech of Halitherses displeased them, and they sided with Eupeithes; they therefore hurried off for their armor, and when they had armed themselves, they met together in front of the city, and Eupeithes led them on in their folly. He thought he was going to avenge the murder of his son, whereas in truth he was never to return, but was himself to perish in his attempt.

Then Athena said to Zeus, "Father, son of Cronus, king of kings, answer me this question—What do you propose to do? Will you set them fighting still further, or will you make peace between them?"

And Zeus answered, "My child, why should you ask me? Was it not by your own arrangement that Odysseus came home and took his revenge upon the suitors? Do whatever you like, but I will tell you what I think will be most reasonable arrangement. Now that Odysseus is revenged, let them swear to a solemn covenant, in virtue of which he shall continue to rule, while we cause the others to forgive and forget the massacre of their sons and brothers. Let them then all become friends as heretofore, and let peace and plenty reign."†

This was what Athena was already eager to bring about, so down she darted from off the topmost summits of Olympus.

Now when Laertes and the others had done dinner, Odysseus began by saying, "Some of you go out and see if they are not getting close up to us." So one of Dolius' sons went as he was bid. Standing on the threshold he could see them all quite near, and said to Odysseus, "Here they are, let us put on our armor at once."

They put on their armor as fast as they could—that is to say Odysseus, his three men, and the six sons of Dolius. Laertes also and Dolius did the same— warriors by necessity in spite of their grey hair. When they had all put on their armor, they opened the gate and sallied forth, Odysseus leading the way.

Then Zeus' daughter Athena came up to them, having assumed the form and voice of Mentor. Odysseus was glad when he saw her, and said to his son Telemachus, "Telemachus, now that you are about to fight in an engagement, which will show every man's mettle, be sure not to disgrace your ancestors, who were eminent for their strength and courage all the world over."

"You say truly, my dear father," answered Telemachus, "and you shall see, if you will, that I am in no mind to disgrace your family."

Laertes was delighted when he heard this. "Good heavens," he exclaimed, "what a day I am enjoying: I do indeed rejoice at it. My son and grandson are vying with one another in the matter of valor."

On this Athena came close up to him and said, "Son of Arceisius—-best friend I have in the world—pray to the blue-eyed damsel, and to Zeus her father; then poise your spear and hurl it."

As she spoke she infused fresh vigor into him, and when he had prayed to her he poised his spear and hurled it. He hit Eupeithes' helmet, and the spear went right through it, for the helmet stayed it not, and his armor rang rattling round him as he fell heavily to the ground.† Meantime Odysseus and his son fell upon the front line of the foe and smote them with their swords and spears; indeed, they would have killed every one of them, and prevented them from ever getting home again, only Athena raised her voice aloud, and made everyone pause. "Men of Ithaca," she cried, "cease this dreadful war, and settle the matter at once without further bloodshed."

On this pale fear seized everyone; they were so frightened that their arms dropped from their hands and fell upon the ground at the sound of the goddess' voice, and they fled back to the city for their lives. But Odysseus gave a great cry, and gathering himself together swooped down like a soaring eagle. Then the son of Cronus sent a thunderbolt of fire that fell just in front of Athena, so she said to Odysseus, "Odysseus, noble son of Laertes, stop this warful strife, or Zeus will be angry with you."

Thus spoke Athena, and Odysseus obeyed her gladly. Then Athena assumed the form and voice of Mentor, and presently made a covenant of peace between the two contending parties.

Glossary

Book I

O Muse – Muses were given credit for inspiring all artistic genres of Greek and Roman culture. According to mythology, the muses were the daughters of Zeus and Mnemosyne (Memory). There were nine all together, and each was responsible for a specific area of art. Calliope is the muse alluded to here, as she was the muse of epic poetry. The other eight Muses and their domains are: Clio (history), Erato (love poetry), Euterpe (music), Melpomene (tragedy), Polyhymnia (sacred poetry), Terpsichore (dance), Thalia (comedy), and Urania (astronomy).

"...but do what...ever reaching home." – Time and time again, Odysseus and his men are delayed, injured, killed, or enchanted by yielding to desire. Even though the gods behave similarly, Odysseus is ultimately rewarded for heeding his mind, rather than following his base desires. Even at the end of their long journey, Odysseus' men could not overcome their sensual instincts.

Ethiopians – The precarious nature of travel in those days made the world much larger for the Greeks. India, Ethiopia, and the end of the Mediterranean Sea surrounded the known world.

"...Aegisthus...Orestes..." – Aegisthus was the lover that Clytemnestra took after Agamemnon left for the Trojan War, and who murdered Agamemnon upon his return. In Aegisthus' defense, Agamemnon *did* sacrifice his own daughter to the gods to gain favorable winds for returning to Troy.

"...I sent Hermes to warn him..." – Hermes, the gods' messenger, will carry several warnings throughout this epic.

"...Athena said...from all his friends." – Athena's favorite is Odysseus—his cunning is compelling to the goddess of wisdom.

"Sparta and to Pylos" – Sparta and Pylos are ruled by Menelaus (whose wife, Helen, was the cause of the Trojan War) and Nestor, two of the kings who went with Odysseus to fight Troy.

"stout and sturdy and strong" – Note the alliteration (the repetition of sounds at the beginning of words). This is not the work of Homer, but of the translator, who has worked diligently to preserve the poetic nature of this epic.

"...he was vexed...for admittance." – Here, Telemachus is roused from his anger by thoughts of hospitality, which is a crucial Greek virtue that will appear throughout the *Odyssey*.

"I am Mentes...Taphians." – Athena disguises herself here (as she will throughout the epic) to appear as a respected Ithacan.

Temesa – a city on Italy's western coast, famous for its copper mines.

Argives – Argives, Achaeans, and Danaans are virtually interchangeable here— all refer to Greeks. Greece was not a country during the time of the Trojan

War, but a loose network of affiliated kingdoms.

"...**he who they...father.**" – Telemachus has come to doubt even the possibility of his father's return.

"...**have built a mound over his ashes...**" – It was tradition to build a pyre of wood on which to burn a dead hero's body, and then cover the ashes with a mound of dirt.

"...**all the principal men...she will not marry...**" – Telemachus is referring to Penelope, but it is never logically explained why she cannot do this, and from the second book, it is clear that she continues to encourage the suitors deliberately, yet readers are asked to believe that she is only fooling them.

"**It rests with...is to return...**" – Here the Greek idea of fate appears. In a world where so much of a person's fate seemed out of his or her control, it was a Greek reflex to leave the large matter of fate to the gods.

"**With these words...into the air...**" – Many times the gods would appear as animals.

"...**knew that...a god...**" – Telemachus was unaware that "Mentes" was really a deity until the old man suddenly became a bird.

Hellas and middle Argos – a reference to different regions of the Greek peninsula

"**My father...been the goddess.**" – Telemachus is taking on much of the suspicious nature of his father, Odysseus.

Book II

"...**the child of...Dawn...**" – This is the first of many appearances of "rosy-fingered Dawn"—one of the mnemonic formulas that were useful to the oral performers of the epic.

"**Athena endowed...comeliness...**" – Physical attractiveness was a virtue highly prized in Greece—as it has been throughout history. The Greek word *pur* had a much more abrasive, more powerful connotation than the English word *beauty*. *Pur* carried with it the license to be powerful, to be cruel, and to be admired all the more for it.

Ilius – *[Ilion]* another word for Troy; it is where *Iliad* gets its name.

"...**they keep hanging...turn upon you.**" – Even the gods were said to enforce the virtue of hospitality. The suitor's lengthy violations of this virtue carry a heavy price at the story's close.

"**With this Telemachus...into tears.**" – Telemachus has not yet reached the masculine maturity of his father, or even of the suitors, and here he loses any advantage he may have had with the Ithacans.

"**We never...any one of them.**" – While women had a servile role in Greek society, powerful women were honored and almost feared.

"**It will be hard...back to him.**" – Interestingly, Telemachus will have to repay the dowry that Penelope's father had given to Odysseus if she is sent back to her father.

Erinyes – The Erinyes are also known as the Furies—a group of vulture-like divinities who would appear any time they were called upon to punish those who committed crimes against their family, especially matricide. Once the Erinyes were called upon, they would take off after the criminals attacking and tormenting until death. This would often start a cycle of escalating revenge, until great tragedy occurred.

two eagles – Eagles often appear in Greek literature carrying omens from the gods.

"…everything has…coming true." – Halitherses is the first voice foreshadowing Odysseus' return.

"As for Telemachus…such rare perfection." – Eurymachus' brash condescension toward Halitherses' warning is a clear example of *hubris*. The Greek word for "pride" is *hubris*, which indicates the sort of pride that leads to foolish acts. Throughout *The Odyssey*, the prideful acts of mortals bring them to destruction (*nemesis*).

"…speed this boy…tells him something." – Most of the suitors are aware that Telemachus has yet to develop the courage his father has.

the buildings – probably referring to the outer court, and the uncovered parts of the inner house

"'Antinous,' answered…as they did so." – Telemachus is in the awkward position of being a young head of a household, whose home is full of men who would not mind seeing him dead.

" 'Or will he…kill us?'" – Ephyra was known as a source of poisons.

unblended – "Blended" wine was watered down to reduce the alcoholic effect; therefore, "unblended" wine was often prized.

"She caused…full of drowsiness." – As the goddess of wisdom, Athena often would alter the minds of mortals to carry out her plans.

grey-eyed daughter of Zeus – sometimes translated as "bright-eyed"

Book III

"…they were eating…thigh bones…" – The thigh bone was a part of the offerings sacrificed to the gods throughout the ancient world. The thigh was seen as a place of power, and so was often cooked first.

"Offer a prayer…joining…" – It is ironic that Telemachus would sacrifice to Poseidon, considering he is the source of his father's troubles.

"…hence many…daughter Athena…" – While Odysseus was Athena's favorite, she was not fond of all the Achaean kings.

"…who brought…sons of Atreus." – Agamemnon and Menelaus fought over whether or not to give offerings to Athena. This struggle would separate the Greeks, leading to trouble for many of them on the way home.

"Who knows…behind him?" – This is another instance of foreshadowing, a frequent literary technique in the *Odyssey*.

"Heaven has a long…they are of him." – Note here the ambivalence of what aid even the gods can give, when they choose to. Or is it *if* they choose to?

"...he had done...wickedness..." – It would not have been difficult for Aegisthus to seduce Clytemnestra, whose last memory of Agamemnon was his sacrifice of their daughter, Iphigenia, to get a favorable wind toward Troy.

"People should...religious festival." – Moderation was a virtue honored (but not often practiced) in much of Greek society.

"...it will be much...to my crew..." – Athena skillfully avoids offending Nestor's offer of hospitality.

"When they had...screamed with delight." – The "delight" here may seem morbid, but this was part of the custom of sacrifice.

Book IV

"Menelaus was...henceforward." – Menelaus also subscribes to the Greek ideal of hospitality.

"Polybus lived in...upon the top of it." – At least in public, Menelaus and Helen have restored the relationship that was sundered when Helen ran off to Troy with Paris.

"Then Pisistratus...as your own." – Telemachus is still very reserved in his dealings with others. Pisistratus covers up what might be seen as weakness by calling it "modesty."

"In this disguise...was too cunning for me." – Odysseus may well be cunning, but Helen is even more so.

"...you came up to us;...took you away again." – There is ambiguity in Menelaus' statement: Did Helen mean to betray the Greeks waiting inside the horse? Or is Menelaus' interpretation of a god's intervention incorrect?

"He bound his sandals...immortal god." – Those whom the gods favor will often enter a room looking "like an immortal god"—often taller and younger-looking as well.

"I was trying...having their dues." – The Greek gods were not above acting like mortals in their fickleness, but they insisted on being recognized as immortal anyway.

" 'First he will look...over the seas.'" – Courage and tenacity were prized virtues in Greek society—and they are required to get information from Proteus.

"We were among...done counting." – Cunning is another virtue prized by the Greeks, and it pays off for more people than Odysseus.

"Ajax was wrecked...Athena's hatred..." – Some gods are more powerful than others, as Poseidon's rescue of Ajax shows.

"...he would have escaped...by boasting." – Pride was Ajax's downfall—*hubris* creating *nemesis*.

"As for your own end...Zeus' son-in-law.'" – Most mortals ended up in Hades after death, but a lucky few ended up in the Elysian Fields—an Eden-like setting of immortal happiness. To get there, one had to be highly regarded by the gods—or related to them in some way.

"I will also...to the immortal gods." – This chalice is one of the many presents in this story given to honor the virtue of hospitality.

"As for those...exactly like him." – The idea of gods disguising themselves as mortals was obviously a common one.

"And the vision...idle conversation." – Even this vision has limits—another sign of the limited assistance that the gods could (or would) provide.

Book V

"Father Zeus...news of his father." – Here, Athena treats her father, Zeus, much like a mortal daughter might treat her father: she uses guilt to get what she wants. Athena's actions are an example of *anthropomorphism*. Anthropomorphism is where other beings, such as animals, or, in this case, gods, are made to seem like humans. Greek gods are said to be *anthropomorphic*—even though they are not human, they behave and look much like humans do.

"Forthwith he bound...nymph Calypso lived." – Note the vivid imagery here. This descriptive technique is part of the flowery language that is part of the epic genre.

" 'You gods,' she...I have a man here.'" – Jealousy and selfishness are just as much a part of a god's makeup in the Greek world as they are part of a human's, which is another example of anthropomorphism.

"...they laid their hands...before them." – one of the many mnemonic formulas used throughout the *Odyssey*. This epic was presented orally, often by memory. There are many phrases in this epic that are repeated word for word—no doubt to help stimulate the memory of the performer.

" 'Good luck go...beauty with an immortal.'" – Calypso appeals to Odysseus' sensual side to tempt him to stay with her. One sign of Odysseus' maturity is his ability to refuse.

"Thereon he gathered...is all coming true.'" – It seems ironic that Odysseus would have survived the ten-year Trojan War and the following years of turmoil with his men, only to drown in the sea.

" 'Alas,' he said...quit my raft.'" – The trickster, Odysseus, sees trickery everywhere—Odysseus' paranoia makes him suspect the innocent advice of Ino.

" 'At any rate...better than this.'" – Even after all the years of experiencing the gods' superiority firsthand, Odysseus still refuses to follow Ino's advice, until he is brought to the point where his own effort is completely worthless.

"While he was thus...what to do." – Ambivalence can be deadly, as Odysseus discovers here.

"Here poor Odysseus...wits about him." – Even the decisions of the gods can pale in comparison to one's own mental strength. Or is it the other way around?

"Here at last...from sheer exhaustion..." – Poseidon's revenge is not Odysseus' death—Zeus will not permit that. Poseidon has, however, completely broken and humbled Odysseus.

"There he crept...had been grafted." – Even ancient farmers knew how to produce hybrid plants.

"Then, as one who lives...get a light elsewhere..." – This powerful simile shows how far Odysseus has to fall in order to find maturity and humility.

Book VI

"Athena took the form...hovered over her head and said..." – Here, Athena again assumes a disguise to pave the way for Odysseus to find hospitality.

"Here no wind...for ever and ever." – The description of Mount Olympus sounds much like the description of the new Garden of Eden in the Book of Revelations.

"He looked like...for he was in great want." – This powerful simile expresses the raw masculinity that Odysseus represents in the eyes of Nausicaa—this virility is one of the prized Greek virtues.

"to clasp her knees" – Clasping one's knees was the customary way to beg—placing oneself in a posture of absolute vulnerability.

" 'There is no accounting...best of it.'" – Once again, it is shown that the Greek's believe there is no luck—the human part is taken out of equations of the unknown, and replaced by the inscrutable will of Zeus.

" 'This is only some...under Zeus' protection.'" – Nausicaa restates the importance of hospitality.

"Athena then made him...quite young and handsome..." – Notice, once again, the flowery language used to describe the appearance of the hero—this language is part of the conventions of the epic.

" 'I am afraid...against me later on...'" – Nausicaa is also cunning—even under the spell of Odysseus, she thinks about her reputation in the city.

"...for you gave no...wrecking me." – The irony here is that Zeus did hear and did answer Odysseus' prayer—even though Odysseus thinks otherwise.

Book VII

"Athena shed...carrying a pitcher." – Here, Athena uses a double disguise—she makes Odysseus invisible, and then appears to him as a little girl to guide him.

"...do not be afraid;..." – Odysseus is clearly broken and humiliated from his experience in the sea—he needs the encouragement of a stranger to enter

Alcinous' castle and ask for help.

Alcinous – Polyphemus was also Poseidon's son and was, therefore, Nausithous' half brother, King Alcinous' half uncle, and Nausicaa's half great uncle.

"…'it is not creditable…may be in the house.'" – By sitting by the hearth, Odysseus makes it imperative for Alcinous to offer some form of hospitality—even the use of a chair. This opens the door for Odysseus to ask for help on a much larger level—for a ship.

Book VIII

"Athena took…Alcinous' servants…" – Note again Athena's use of disguise to assist Odysseus.

"…Athena had…taller and stouter…" – Every time Odysseus emerges from a bath here in Phaeacia, he is taller and stronger.

"…leave the ship…in the cloisters." – There were two distinctive classes—members of the lower class were forced to find their own provisions which they had to cook for themselves and eat in the yards and outer limits. The upper class, however, would eat in the gazeboes or tents located in the inner court, and their meals were prepared for them.

"A servant presently…his eyesight." – The ambivalent nature of fate is attributed also to the gods—here, a famous bard has the gift of song but has been robbed of his sight.

"…Agamemnon…one another…" – Agamemnon, who enjoyed the quarrels of others, was brought down by a tragic dispute in his own home.

"I suppose…homeward cargoes." – Euryalus' reaction shows the dislike that the nobles had for the working class.

"…I excel in…stung me to the quick." – Some of Odysseus' pride has returned, as his retort to Euryalus shows.

"Athena, in the form…it had fallen." – Here, Athena's disguise helps Odysseus avoid a tense situation that could have earned him the enmity of Alcinous—and cost him his escort.

" '…I will box…foreign country.'" – The stress of competition can cool the warmth of even the best host.

"…they went to the couch…were in a trap." – This is another example of anthropomorphism (see note: *"Father Zeus…news of his father"* in Book V). Here, Aphrodite and Ares are caught just as any adulterous mortal couple might have been.

"As for Euryalus…great deal to him." – Euryalus' gift to Odysseus is not a voluntary one—Alcinous' tone suggests the depth of Euryalus' inhospitable attitude.

"I shall myself…or to any of the gods." – This is virtually the same gift that Menelaus offers Telemachus—a goblet to use during drink-offerings, and so a daily reminder of the giver.

Circe – an enchantress

"Then Odysseus cut off…tell him to eat it;…" – The first layers of fat would fall while the offering was burning on the fire. What remained was left for the supplicants to eat.

"…change your song…sacked the city." – Odysseus is weary of the sad parts of his story and wants to hear a good memory.

"…nevertheless…victorious." – The song attributes the Greek victory to Athena. It was Greek arrogance at the end of the war that led to her wrath—and the effects of *hubris* run throughout this story.

"…Odysseus was overcome…sighs that he was heaving." – Note the detailed imagery in the description of Odysseus' sorrow—one of the conventions of the epic.

"Still I do remember…under a high mountain." – This mention of Poseidon is another example of foreshadowing—Poseidon does not respond well to Odysseus' easy journey home.

Book IX

"I then said that we…were hard pressed." – The *hubris* of the Achaeans almost gets them slaughtered by the Cicones, just after winning a ten-year war against Troy.

"…the Lotus-eaters,…of their return;…" – Evidently, the lotus plant produced a fruit that, when eaten, induced pleasure and laziness. Because of its effects, the drug-like fruit was highly addictive. The Lotus-eaters ate nothing but the lotus fruit and refused to leave their island. Some of Odysseus' men who ate some of the lotus fruit, had to be physically removed from the island.

"…the lawless and inhuman Cyclopes." – The Cyclopes have none of the forms of civilization (laws, assemblies, etc.) that the Greeks prided themselves on and that the gods also followed.

"He was a horrid creature…a high mountain." – This metaphor expresses how uncivilized the Cyclopes were considered by Greek standards.

"…I wanted to see…with his sheep." – Odysseus cannot stifle his desire for adventure—this desire will cost his men dearly.

"He gobbled…anything uneaten." – Note the contrast between this lion and Odysseus' appearance as a lion in the eyes of Nausicaa (see note: *"He looked like…for he was in great want"* in Book V). The imagery here is more animalistic, and thus more barbaric.

"…covering myself with glory." – Despite the death of several of his men, Odysseus is still plotting his own glory. He has much maturing to do before the gods will send him home.

" 'Cyclops, you ask…have always called me.'" – Odysseus' trick foreshadows his anonymous return to Ithaca. He will have to accept great humility before he can return.

"**I kept turning it round…with an auger,…**" – This dehumanizing simile makes the Cyclops seem like a thing that the men are dismantling, rather than a living being. Farther down in this description, another simile is used in the same manner and gives the same impression: "As a blacksmith plunges an axe or hatchet…"

"**boiling blood bubbled**" – Note the use of alliteration here, which lends a rhythm to the imagery of this hissing eye.

"**smote the grey with their oars**" – This phrase is one of many phrases that appears repeatedly throughout the *Odyssey*—another mnemonic formula.

"**…I was jeering…hold my tongue.**" – Odysseus still has not learned to control his *hubris*—and this time the price will be Poseidon's grudge, and the lives of Odysseus' men.

"**I have been all along…insignificant weakling…**" – The irony here is that the Cyclops expected a much larger nemesis—and so his own *hubris* brings him to his destruction.

" **'I wish I could…eye of yours.'**" – Here, Odysseus adds to his own *hubris* by taunting Poseidon's powers as well as Poseidon's son (the Cyclops).

Book X

"**All day long…yard and all…**" – The personification of a table or a house "groaning" with plenty is commonplace in Greek literature.

"**…but it all came…our own folly.**" – It is Odysseus' hindsight that permits him to see the folly of his, and his men's past actions.

" **'Odysseus, what brings you…abhorred of heaven.'**" – Aeolus' willingness to help clearly has limits—here, he comes to realize that more powerful gods are arrayed against Odysseus, and Aeolus does not want to risk their anger. This is another example of anthropomorphism.

"**glad to have escaped death, though we had lost our comrades**" – another mnemonic aid throughout the *Odyssey*

" **'Stay where you are…bound to do so.'**" – As the leader of his men, Odysseus is bound to go after those whom he sent into danger, if he wants to keep the allegiance of those left behind.

" **'And I will tell you…to charm you…'**" – In this example of anthropomorphism, Circe is at least as cunning as Odysseus, but more treacherous.

"**…surely you can be…home from Troy…**" – This is the second time a prophecy about Odysseus is fulfilled (the first was the blinding of the Cyclops).

"**When they saw me…round their mothers…**" – After the Cyclops, the Laestrygonians, and the enchantment of Circe, Odysseus' men certainly have reason to celebrate in such an unrestrained fashion.

"**You must go to…prophet Teiresias…**" – Part of Odysseus' quest is to learn humility, which he will learn from his conversation with Teirsias and from the others he meets in Hades.

"...**many dead men's ghosts... answered your questions.**" – According to Greek tradition, the souls in Hades were only the "shades" of their former physical selves, as their bodies had been either buried or burned. They craved their own physical substance, so the taste of blood would be tantalizing.

"**The men were...groaning and tearing their hair...**" – Groaning, tearing one's hair, and even tearing one's clothes were common customs of mourning during ancient times.

Book XI

"**We had left...Circe's house...**" – It was considered a great dishonor to leave a corpse unmourned, and especially unburied. The Greek tragedy *Antigone*, written by Sophocles, centers around a quarrel over whether or not to bury the corpse of a rebel.

"**If you leave...hardship reach Ithaca...**" – Moderation in indulging one's tastes is one of the primary Greek virtues. If Odysseus' men can withstand hunger, they will make it home safely.

"...**but tell me and tell me and tell me...**" – Polysyndeton is a literary device where more conjunctions are used than are necessary. The purpose is to slow the rhythm of the reading and emphasize each word or phrase. Odysseus wants the truth after his long, frightening journey to the land of the dead.

" '**Your wife still...night and day.**'" – In Greek thought, the dead would still be able to see the doings of the living.

"...**Antiope, daughter...Zeus himself...**" – This anecdote is the first in a series that shows the interactions between deities and mortals.

" '**Be sure, therefore,...no trusting women.**" – Agamemnon's justified suspicions will later contribute to Odysseus' caution when he returns to Ithaca.

" '...**in death's favor...among the dead.**" – In Greek culture, glory was to be gained during one's lifetime. The afterlife promised no further joy or glory, unless he or she were fortunate enough to be taken to the Elysian Fields, the place where people who were deemed as "good" by the gods went after death (see: "*As for your own end...Zeus' son-in-law.*" in Book IV).

"...**for the rage...great chance'**" – The chaotic nature of war is reflected in the Greek view of Ares, whose anger makes his dealings with fate inconsistent.

"**bring your...subjection...**" – Ajax is struggling with the same lesson that bedevils Odysseus—how to control his pride and find moderation.

Book XII

Jason – The *Argo* was the ship carrying Jason and the Argonauts on his legendary quest for the Golden Fleece.

You will find…your whole crew." – To successfully avoid Charybdis, the crew is forced to stay on the side of the pass where the six-headed Scylla waits to snatch up six men to eat them. At the same time, the crew must move quickly so Scylla can only make one pass at them.

"I said nothing…if I did…" – Odysseus has to make a difficult decision—he will lose at least six of his men going between Scylla and Charybdis; if he is honest with them, though, he will probably lose them all. He makes the decision to lie and avoid the greater danger, so the losses will be minimal and will not include him.

"I was looking at once…throughout all my voyages." – Odysseus' reaction, that this was the worst thing he had encountered, could be the result of the guilt he feels.

"As long as corn…for they were starving." – The gods are testing Odysseus' men, driving them to the brink of starvation to see if they will eat the sun-god's cattle.

Book XIII

"Our guest has…handsome present." – This is basically a tax that Alcinous is levying on all the Phaeacians to pay for the gifts given to Odysseus.

" 'Father Zeus…without misadventure.'" – Poseidon approaches Zeus with an almost childish envy, which is another example of the anthropomorphism with which the gods are depicted.

"Athena had made it…his having come…" – This is the second time Athena has made Odysseus less visible in order to protect him—the first time was during his walk to Alcinous' cloister.

Athena came up to him…straight up to her." – Just as Odysseus was gladdened by Athena's appearance as a young girl, her appearance as the young shepherd also increases his confidence.

"…he began to answer…wiliness of his heart." – Even after all this time, Odysseus' instincts and cleverness work together so he can lie.

"I will begin by…son whom you left behind you." – Note that Odysseus is hiding within the disguise Athena provides for him; this is somewhat similar to his idea for the Trojan Horse. Both deceptions conceal what is underneath the skin, and both lead directly to many deaths.

Book XIV

"There were fifty pigs…always with them." – The suitors have been constantly draining Odysseus' resources for some time. From this description, it is easy to imagine the size of Odysseus' original fortune.

"…come inside…your misfortunes." – The Greek demand for hospitality was not only heeded by the nobility, but by all social classes. Eumaeus is also expecting an interesting story in return for his hospitality.

"...I wish that...many a good man." – Some ancient cultures believed that ethics were genetically transmitted and that people would behave much like their ancestors.

" 'Old man, no...lost their husbands." – Apparently, fraud is an ancient tradition—tramps would impose on Penelope's hospitality by telling her fictitious tales of Odysseus' whereabouts.

"To this...Eumaeus..." – At times, the narrator turns to address various characters in the story.

the house of Arcesius – Odysseus' paternal grandfather was named Arcesius. He was a wily thief, and it is from him that Odysseus supposedly inherited cleverness and wisdom.

"But the men...labor for them." – One similarity between Odysseus' real story and the one he makes up for Eumaeus concerns the ways in which Odysseus' men betrayed him through their foolishness.

Book XV

"Telemachus, you should...dead and done with." – Athena uses cunning here to motivate Telemachus into returning home; she goads him by insinuating that his mother may not remain true to him and by telling him things that have not yet happened.

"...he will be very angry." – Nestor does not have the calm temperament that Menelaus has—it is likely that Nestor will take Telemachus' haste as a snub of the hospitality that has been shown.

"Servants want sometimes...good humor." – Notice the uneasy balance that holds kings in power—if they gave their servants enough material happiness and respect, the servants supposedly would not do them harm.

"...a bird flew...royal than your own." – Theoclymenus appears at an opportune time—he will interpret signs for Telemachus and for the suitors, foreshadowing Odysseus' triumph.

Book XVI

"So be it,...with cobwebs." – Telemachus is now starting to show the same cunning his father has.

"How can I take...attacks me." – Telemachus is caught in a dilemma: Should he refuse hospitality and incur the gods' wrath, or should he welcome the suitors and risk losing all his wealth?

"I wish I were...never be accomplished." – Here Odysseus foreshadows his own triumph in an attempt to stir up his son's anger.

"I am sorry...way to tell Laertes." – Telemachus' delay before going to see Laertes is another sign that he is learning to be a shrewd leader.

" 'Stranger,...mercy upon me." – Telemachus fears fate and wants to maintain as much control of his life as possible.

"The suitors were...the main entrance." – The suitors were not expecting Telemachus to return, because of the ambush they had set for his return from Pylos and Sparta.

"...his conversation...natural disposition." – Amphinomus seems to be the most ethical suitor. However, he also fails to heed Odysseus' warning and dies with the rest of them.

"Therefore Telemachus...he cannot escape it." – Eurymachus is purposefully ambiguous here because he wants to murder Telemachus, but cannot appear obvious about his desire.

Book XVII

"...promise full...upon the suitors." – Telemachus' confidence is of that dual sort that is vital to the Greeks—faith in human effort as well as reliance on the gods.

"Meanwhile the suitors...all their old insolence." – The suitors' main form of entertainment was competition with each other, which sometimes was friendly, but sometimes was not.

Then Malanthius...come home again." – Melanthius demonstrates *hubris* here in his treatment of Eumaeus. Pay careful attention to Melanthius' fate (see note: *"As for Telemachus...such rare perfection."* in Book II).

"Athena went up to...single one of them." – Ethics do not help an individual's standing with the gods. Characteristics like audacity, cunning, and physical attractiveness are far more compelling to them.

"The other suitors...who righteously." – Here is another instance of foreshadowing leading to the suitors' demise.

"As she spoke...them shall escape." – Sneezing while someone else talked, which indicated that something evil would occur, was a well-known Greek omen.

Book XVIII

"to throw them off the scent" – Odysseus is still at great risk here—if his true identity were discovered, he would be overwhelmed by the suitors. He must devise a plan to overcome the numerical disadvantage he finds in dealing with the suitors. Once again, Odysseus' cleverness is emphasized.

"Nay, he will be...Telemachus." – Amphinomus does not escape Odysseus' wrath, even though he senses his own doom may be coming. Many critics believe that this foreshadowing is a matter of the gods' control of fate, rather than that of free will.

"They are excellent...than this." – Hand-to-hand combat was a difficult, dangerous, arduous, and violent form of war for the foot soldier, so any army possessing vehicles had a great advantage over the enemy.

"This was what...did not mean." – Odysseus is glad to see Penelope take as many presents from the suitors as possible before he exacts his revenge.

"a little world" – Ithaca; Eurymachus' ego comes from his superiority in Ithaca—a small area. Odysseus has prevailed over much larger enemies, and, therefore, has little respect for this braggart.

Book XIX

"Many a plausible...restrain his tears." – Odysseus is testing Penelope's loyalty through his stories. Note the long simile in this section.

" 'Now, stranger...with his companions.'" – Penelope is Odysseus' equal at questioning—she persists in testing the stranger's knowledge about Odysseus to see if the tales are true.

"Men live but for...call him blessed." – Fair dealing with others is another virtue that was prized in Greek society.

"I am certain...Zeus hates you." – Euryclea's understanding of the gods is limited. Zeus has promised Odysseus a safe passage home—it is Poseidon whose wrath is targeted at Odysseus.

"Autolycus...in the whole world." – It may be that Odysseus learned his cunning from Autolycus, his maternal grandfather, a well-known thief in Greek mythology.

"I have twenty...killed my geese." – If the geese in Penelope's dream represent the twenty suitors, as Odysseus claims, then her feelings in the dream seem to be saying that she would accept a suitor as Odysseus' successor. It is not surprising that after years of doubting whether Odysseus was even alive and after being pursued by this large group of men, Penelope would start to feel attracted to at least some of the men who want her hand.

Book XX

"Supposing...when it is all over." – Odysseus fears the revenge cycle, which is referenced in Book I regarding the Erinyes.

"Father Zeus...house of Odysseus." – The Greek gods often immediately granted a human's request for signs.

"Meanwhile the suitors...dinner instead." – Yet another omen appears before the men. Amphinomus recognizes it, yet they still fail to heed the warning.

"Telemachus...good earnest." – Telemachus is clearly gaining courage by the return of his father. What had been simply the empty words of a teenager is starting to have the potential to worry the suitors.

Sardinian fashion – a reference to the island of Sardinia, part of Italy and located in the Mediterranean Sea. This island was originally settled by the Phoenicians, Greeks, and Carthaginians prior to the sixth century B.C. The Romans conquered the island in 238 B.C. This reference to Sardinia is one of the factors that dates Odyssey later than 1200 B.C.

"Athena now made...over all the land." – As a seer, Theoclymenus can see the futures of the suitors and foretells their coming doom. The instances of foreshadowing come closer and closer as Odysseus' revenge nears.

Book XXI

"At this moment...by the fire..." – Eurymachus warms the bow to soften it and make it easier to bend.

Book XXII

"Antinous who...low already." – Eurymachus is a crafty speaker and attempts to place all the blame on Antinous. Odysseus, however, is beyond persuasion, despite all of Eurymachus' offers of repayment.

"But she would not...form of a swallow." – Here, Athena appears in complete control of the battle, but she wants Odysseus and Telemachus to savor their own courage, as a reward for their years of suffering.

"Odysseus, I beseech...so they made me." – Phemius not only has good intentions, but he also has value to Telmachus and Odysseus. It is crucial that he have both qualities in order to have his life spared.

"rejoice in silence" – It would be prideful to rejoice over the death of the suitors. Odysseus does not want the gods to have any excuse to bring vengeance back down upon him, so he quiets Euryclea.

"So saying he...die most miserably." – The women have behaved improperly, because they have started to act as the suitors' property, not as Odysseus'.

Book XXIII

" 'My dear,...from Ithaca." – Odysseus has clearly aged during his twenty years away, and so Penelope is not as taken by his looks as he would like her to be.

"When she heard...broke down." – No other man would know the unique construction of Odysseus and Penelope's bed. Penelope has no more doubts about the stranger's identity.

"...I was to fix...a boar to Poseidon..." – Odysseus has to repay his debt to Poseidon, as Teiresias had foretold.

"As for the sheep...filled all my yards." – Much like Alcinous, Odysseus taxes the public to rebuild his own personal wealth.

"At sunrise...ask no questions." – Odysseus is preparing for attacks from the suitors' relatives.

Book XXIV

"Your mother...among all mankind." – Greek men of action prized the idea of heroic death—this is one of the reasons why Agamemnon's ghost is so unhappy. Instead of dying in war, Clytemnestra, his wife, stabbed him to death in his bathtub.

"He filled both hands…as he did so." – Covering oneself with dust was a ritual of mourning in the ancient world.

"And Zeus answered…plenty reign." – Zeus is acting as a diplomat—he tells Athena how to bring peace, but gives her the illusion of autonomy to placate her strong will.

"He hit Eupeithes'…to the ground." – As with the suitors, Odysseus kills the ringleader first. Fortunately, this time Athena intervenes, averting more needless death.

Vocabulary

Book I

acquainted – familiar or knowledgeable

asunder – apart

atrociously – horribly, terribly

bard – a poet

barrow – a mound of dirt or stones placed over a burial site

bearing-post – a post that is vital to holding up the building

clamorous – loud, riotous

counsel – advice

embellishments – final touches

ewer – an oval pitcher with a base and wide spout, with decorations on the body

fleece – a soft, woolen blanket

havoc – chaos, ruin

hecatomb – a great sacrifice; in Greek times, involving 100 oxen

hied – hurried

insolence – rudeness, disrespect

lyre – a small harp with two curved arms, connected by a bar across the top

mettle – courage

nymph – a minor goddess who usually either lives in or personifies water, a tree, or a mountain

pacified – calmed, soothed

partaken – eaten

persecuted – harmed in an unfair way

pretext – an excuse

propitiate – to appease; to gain forgiveness

quells – subdues, silences

redoubtable – causing fear, awe

renown – fame, glory

sea-girt – surrounded by the sea

sheer – pure, absolute

short shrift – rude treatment

soothsayer – a fortune-teller

spunging – living at another person's expense

staid – dignified, serious

suitors – men seeking to marry a woman

tongue – language

torments – tortures

weal – well-being

Book II

abetting – assisting

aggrieved – offended, upset

artful – tricky

bade – asked someone to do something; requested

barren – without life

barrow – a burial mound

braggart – one who boasts

comeliness – attractiveness

convene – to call together

creditable – reputable, honorable

criers – people who would run through the town and shout announcements

discernment – perceptiveness; having keen judgment

drawing – pouring

ere – before

flaying – cutting open, skinning

forestays – braces on the front side of the mast to keep it vertical

hawsers – ropes used to tow a ship or secure it to a dock

henceforward – from here on out

hoisted – lifted

omen – a sign of things to come

pall – a burial cover

plaguing – harassing

prating – talking foolishly, instead of acting

remedy – a compensation

rigorously – harshly

tackle – fishing equipment

tambour frame – a circular frame, across which the work is stretched for sewing

victuals – food and drink

vying – competing

watches – the night was divided into different "watches"—duty shifts when certain sailors had to stay awake

Book III

bandying – trading

bane – undoing; nemesis

batten – to overfeed

befell – happened to

certify – to confirm, prove

citadel – a fortress city

embarked – departed, took off

embers – ashes
firmament – a firm surface thought to be in the heavens, where the stars sat
gilding – gold leaf, used as decoration
guilds – military units
helm – steering control
import – significance
incessant – without stopping
mettle – courage
precedence – a place of honor
propitiate – to agree, appease
spits – long metal sticks on which meat was roasted
stratagem – a strategy, tactic
suppliant – placing oneself at another's mercy

Book IV
affliction – a trial
ambrosia – food of the gods
ambuscade – a caravan
avail – to use
banishes – eliminates
baths – tubs for water
bereft of – robbed of
bondsmen – men bound to work for others
bustled – hurried
chalice – a drinking vessel made from precious metals
clamorous – unruly, loud
cloister – a fortified house
cunning – sly
dissipated – broken up
exterminate – to destroy completely
fall to – to eat
freemen – independent men (as opposed to slaves)
hemming – confining
hewn – carved
hussies – promiscuous women
intercourse – a relationship
lotus – an addictive plant
miscreants – criminals
perfidy – treachery
prevaricate – to lie
rue – to regret
shoals – land left exposed by low tides

singularly – unusually
transport – to fit
usurp – to wrongly fill a place
valiant – brave
vouchsafed – granted, gave
yearned – ached

Book V
adze – a tool used to cut wood
astride – sitting atop
augers – drills
bliss – joy
bounteous – generous, fruitful
calamities – disasters
cormorant – a predatory bird found near the sea
deemed – thought
dismay – sorrow
harbinger – an omen, sign
keel – the bottom of a boat
raiment – clothing
reek – odor
reeled – turned violently
squally – stormy, rainy
transgress – to disobey
trident – a long, three-pronged fork (symbol of Poseidon)

Book VI
begrimed – covered (usually associated with dirt, grime)
cruse – an ornamental jar, vessel
discomfits – irritates
disparaging – insulting
ravenously – with extreme hunger and thirst
scandalized – embarrassed
scion – a son
unkempt – messy
unweariable – incapable of being tired
want – having lack or need

Book VII
comely – beautiful
consummate – absolute
disposition – personality

endowed – blessed
importunate – insistent
precincts – confines, limits
shuttles – spinning devices
westering – sinking (in the west)

Book VIII
amiss – wrongly (to offend)
chieftains – lower-level leaders
cloisters – tents, gazeboes, porches
defiled – stained, violated, made impure
festooned – decorated
freighting – hauling
intrigue – a secret plot
loth – *[loath]* unwilling
piteously – very sadly
raiment – garments, dress
reviled – loathed, despised
vestibule – an outer chamber (a large foyer)

Book IX
array – a formation
besmirched – covered, smeared
entrails – intestines, inner organs
esconced – buried
gobbets – chunks
hoggets – sheep that are at least one year old
invoked – prayed for
livelong – entire
ramping – fussing
renown – fame
smote – struck

Book X
arrayed – set up, arranged
dumb – unable to speak
fathom – a unit of length equal to six feet
fawned – made a fuss over
flayed – skinned
flit – to fly about without a particular goal
forthwith – immediately
gambol – to frolic

gossamer – a sheer, translucent fabric
halloa-ballooing – loud weeping or moaning
lairs – hiding places
lamented – moaned, complained
prevailed – won
reconnoiter – to spy from a distance
savour – aroma

Book XI
aft – the rear of the ship (wind that blows in the same direction as a ship)
asphodel – the flowers of Hades
august – noble
charlatan – a trickster or scoundrel
ebb – to flow out
feckless – weak, timid
indomitable – invincible
prodigious – unusually large in size
rankle – to burn, irritate
winnowing – separating straw from wheat

Book XII
backstay – a brace holding the mast of a ship up from the back
behests – demands
coherent – logical, understandable
jutted – stuck out sharply
unwarily – without caution

Book XIII
blear – to fog up, or cloud
diadem – a crown
enthralled – captivated
mien – a facial expression

Book XIV
apace – rapidly
billet – a club
clouts – clothes
doughty – courageous
frugal – thrifty
stint – hesitation
strewed – spread out
styes – places for pigs to lie

Book XV
dearth – a shortage, lack
gewgaws – trinkets

Book XVI
boon – a blessing
compunction – having a guilty feeling
dissuade – to talk someone out of doing something
exploit – to test
heinous – outrageous; unspeakably evil
propitious – merciful
redoubtable – courageous
superintend – to oversee
wrought – made in a fire

Book XVII
abominable – worthy of hatred
gadding – flaunting, showing off
lavishly – richly

Book XVIII
braziers – torches
cudgel – to beat violently
drubbing – beating
gibes – insults
importunity – impudence, insolence
incorrigible – incapable of change for the better
infamy – notoriety, fame for a negative reason
propriety – social right and wrong
smithy – a blacksmith's forge
staid – courageous, solid
vixen – a treacherous woman

Book XIX
fatuous – insignificant
perjurer – one who lies under oath
plausible – believable
portended – prophesied, foretold
wanton – to strut

Book XX
public house – a pub, or bar

ribald – rowdy
stockman – a man who keeps his master's cattle
suffering – here, permitting

Book XXI
pretext – an excuse
louts – people with no manners
prowess – power
holding – a settled property
twit – to ridicule

Book XXII
weltering – soaking

Book XXIII
depreciate – to insult

Book XXIV
dirge – a song of mourning
infused – injected

Odysseus leaves Troy and sails to Ismarus.

He is driven from Ismarus by Circonians, and after a storm, arrives at the Land of Lotus-eaters. Those shipmates who eat the Lotus wish never to leave and have to be bound to the ships.

In the land of the Cyclopes, Odysseus outwits and blinds Polyphemus, son of Poseidon.

Aeolus, the steward of the winds, provides a west wind to send Odysseus home.

Foolish crew members open a sack containing all the winds, and the ships are driven back to Aeolia.

Aeolus sends the travellers away, and they arrive at Telopylus. There, Laestrygonians hurl boulders killing men and destroying ships.

On the Island of Aeaea, Odysseus, with the assistance of Hermes, frees his crew from the spell of Circe. Circe sends Odysseus on to the land of Hades.

In Hades, Odysseus consults the spirit of Teiresias of Thebes on how to get home; he then speaks with others who have died.

 Odysseus returns to the Island of Aeaea to bury his dead comrade, Elpenor.

His deafened crew binds Odysseus so that he may hear the Sirens' song.

Odysseus sails past the whirlpool Charybdis and the sea monster Scylla but loses crew members.

 While stranded on the Island of the Sun, the crew feasts upon the sacred flocks incurring the wrath of Zeus.

Upon leaving the Island of the Sun, a storm destroys Odysseus' ship, and he drifts to the Island of Ogygia, where Calypso imprisons him.

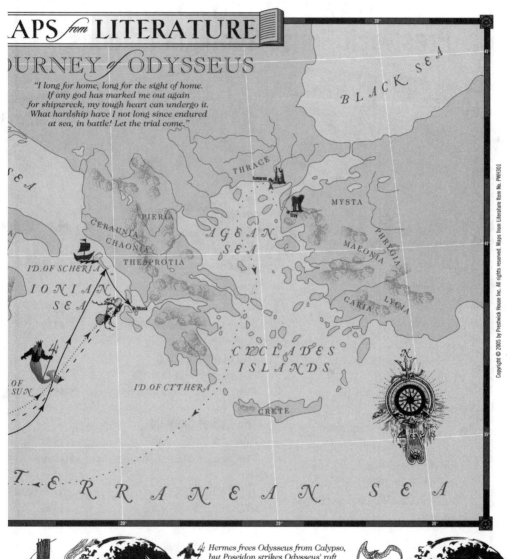

MAPS *from* LITERATURE

JOURNEY *of* ODYSSEUS

"I long for home, long for the sight of home.
If any god has marked me out again
for shipwreck, my tough heart can undergo it.
What hardship have I not long since endured
at sea, in battle! Let the trial come."

BLACK SEA

THRACE
Ismarus
Troy
MYSTA
PIERIA
CERAUNIA
CHAONIA
THESPROTIA
PHRYGIA
AEGEAN SEA
MAEONIA
I'D. OF SCHERIA
IONIAN SEA
Ithaca
CARIA
LYCIA
CYCLADES ISLANDS
I'D. OF CYTHERA
OF SUN
CRETE

MEDITERRANEAN SEA

Hermes frees Odysseus from Calypso,
but Poseidon strikes Odysseus' raft
in retribution for the blinding of
Polyphemus. The goddess Ino rescues
Odysseus, and he lands in Scheria.

After sharing his tale, the Phaeacians
provide him with passage home to
Ithaca.

Insightful and Reader-Friendly, Yet Affordable

Prestwick House Literary Touchstone Editions–
The Editions By Which All Others May Be Judged

Every Prestwick House Literary Touchstone Edition™ is enhanced with Reading Pointers for Sharper Insight to improve comprehension and provide insights that will help students recognize key themes, symbols, and plot complexities. In addition, each title includes a Glossary of the more difficult words and concepts.

For the Shakespeare titles, along with the Reading Pointers and Glossary, we include margin notes and eleven strategies to understanding the language of Shakespeare.

Special Introductory Educator's Discount – At Least 50% Off

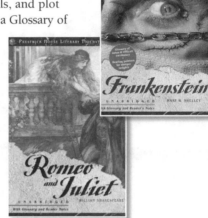

		Retail Price	Intro. Discount
IPWH5869	**Red Badge of Courage, The**	$3.99	$1.99
IPWH5788	**Romeo and Juliet**	$3.99	$1.99
IPWH5753	**Heart of Darkness**	$3.99	$1.99
IPWH5761	**Narrative of the Life of Frederick Douglass**	$3.99	$1.99
IPWH5893	**Macbeth**	$3.99	$1.99
IPWH5834	**Adventures of Huckleberry Finn, The**	$4.99	$2.49
IPWH5885	**Midsummer Night's Dream, A**	$3.99	$1.99
IPWH5796	**Christmas Carol, A**	$3.99	$1.99
IPWH5842	**Call of the Wild, The**	$3.99	$1.99
IPWH577X	**Dr. Jekyll and Mr. Hyde**	$3.99	$1.99
IPWH5826	**Awakening, The**	$3.99	$1.99
IPWH580X	**Importance of Being Earnest, The**	$3.99	$1.99
IPWH5850	**Ethan Frome**	$3.99	$1.99
IPWH5877	**Julius Caesar**	$3.99	$1.99
IPWH5907	**Othello**	$3.99	$1.99
IPWH5915	**Hamlet**	$3.99	$1.99
IPWH5923	**Taming of the Shrew, The**	$3.99	$1.99
IPWH5818	**Metamorphosis, The**	$3.99	$1.99

PRESTWICK HOUSE, INC.
"Everything for the English Classroom!"

Prestwick House, Inc. • P.O. Box 658, Clayton, DE 19938
Phone (800) 932-4593 • Fax (888) 718-9333 • www.prestwickhouse.com